What makes a song great?
Is it the melody, the lyrics?

Can a song's greatness be measured by its cultural impact or its influence on other musicians? Or can we just say a song is great because it makes us want to dance? Or, just because...

Choosing the 100 greatest songs was an overwhelming proposition so VH1 sent ballots to over 700 musicians, songwriters, disc jockeys and radio programmers and asked them to vote on the 100 greatest songs of rock and roll. The votes were calculated and the songs were ranked, producing the following list. While it's possible to debate the placement of some of these songs (too high or too low is an argument for you to enjoy), it's difficult to deny that each is an achievement on some level and deserving of the accolade "a great song," as these are truly great songs.

ISBN 0-634-07751-1

HAL•LEONARD®
CORPORATION
7777 W. BLUEMOUND RD. P.O. BOX 13819 MILWAUKEE, WI 53213

Visit Hal Leonard Online at
www.halleonard.com

CONTENTS

ALL ALONG THE WATCHTOWER

Words and Music by
BOB DYLAN

There must be some kind a way out-ta here,____

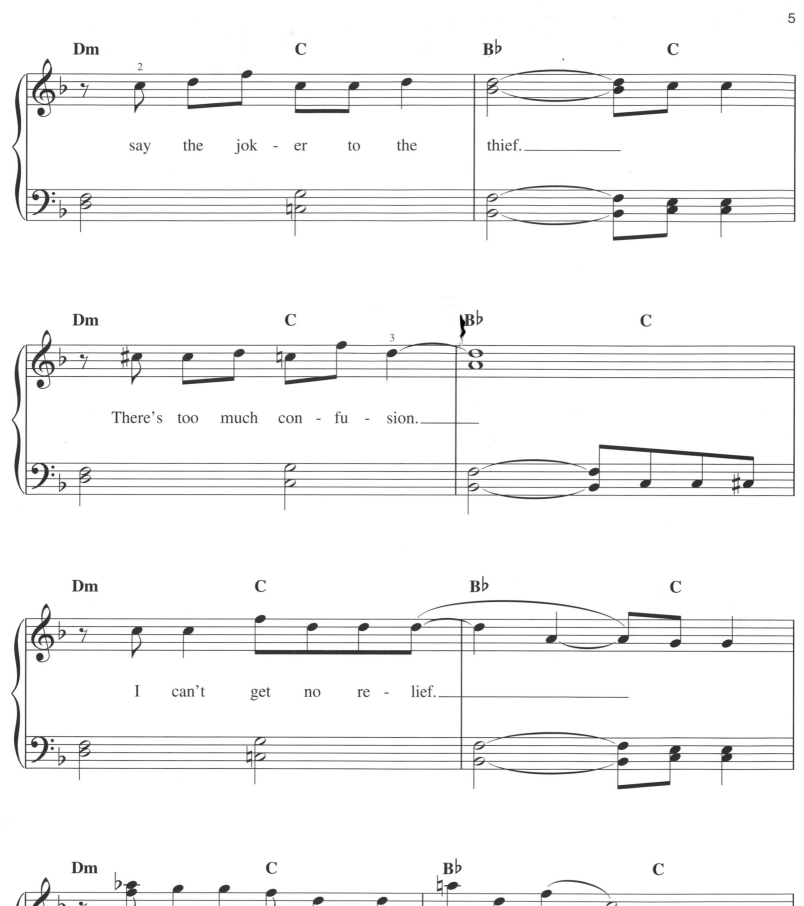

say the jok - er to the thief._____

There's too much con - fu - sion._____

I can't get no re - lief._____

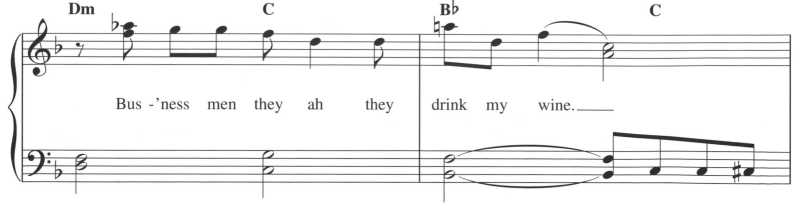

Bus -'ness men they ah they drink my wine._____

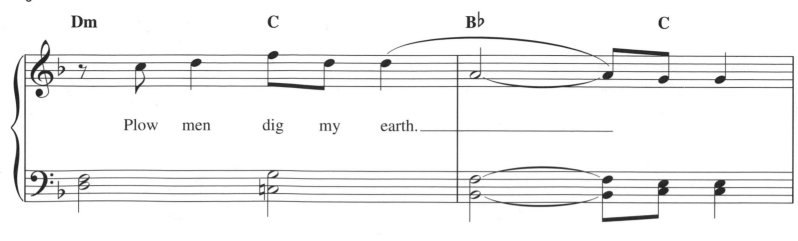

Plow men dig my earth.

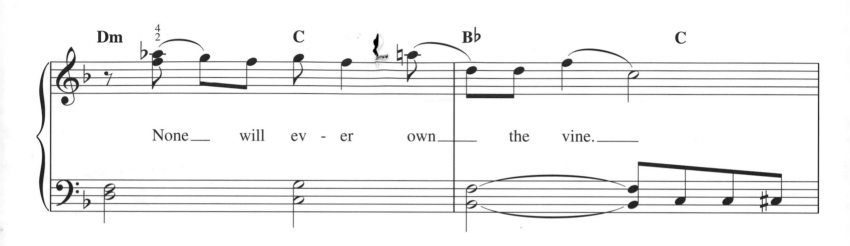

None will ev - er own the vine.

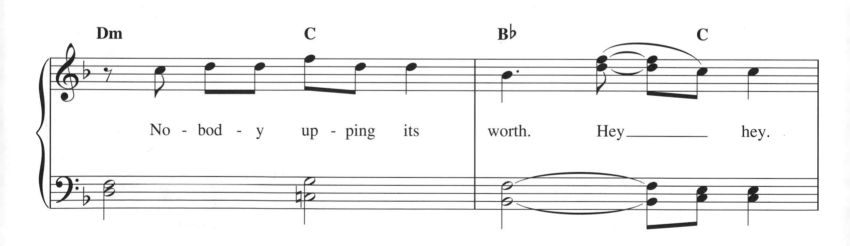

No - bod - y up - ping its worth. Hey hey.

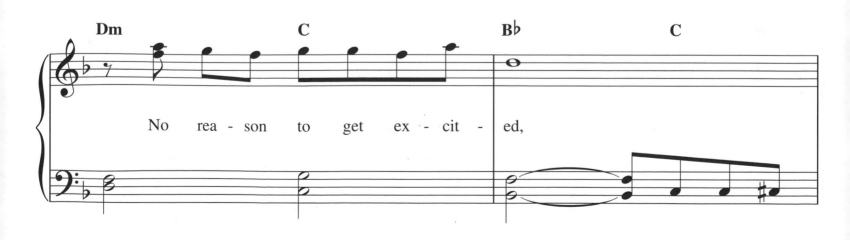

No rea - son to get ex - cit - ed,

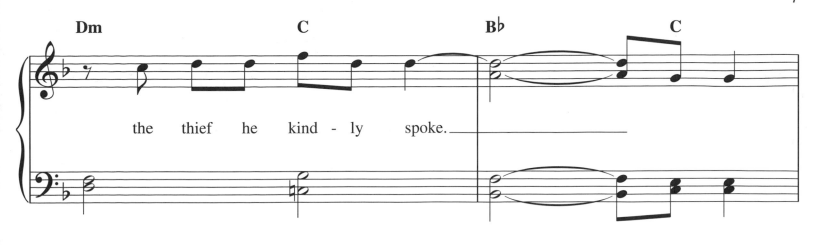

the thief he kind - ly spoke.

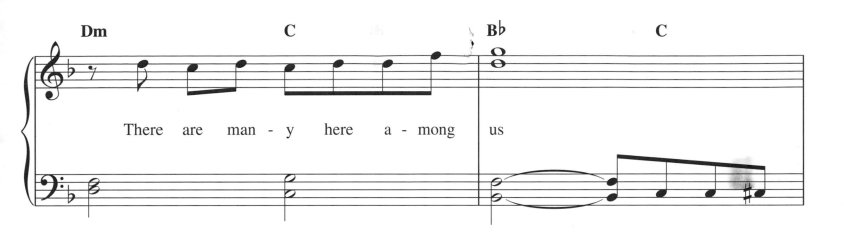

There are man - y here a - mong us

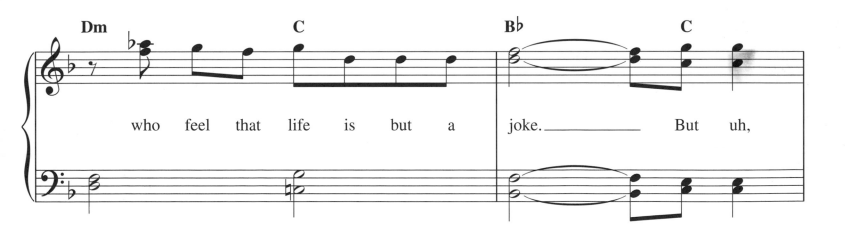

who feel that life is but a joke._____ But uh,

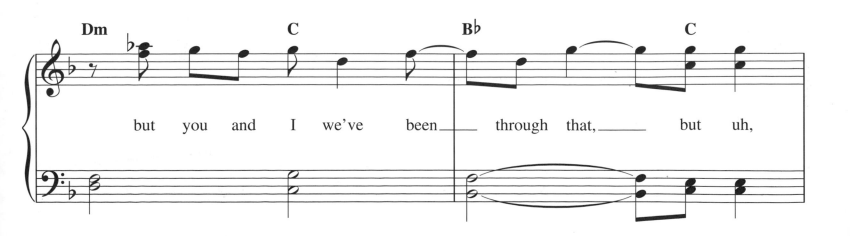

but you and I we've been____ through that,____ but uh,

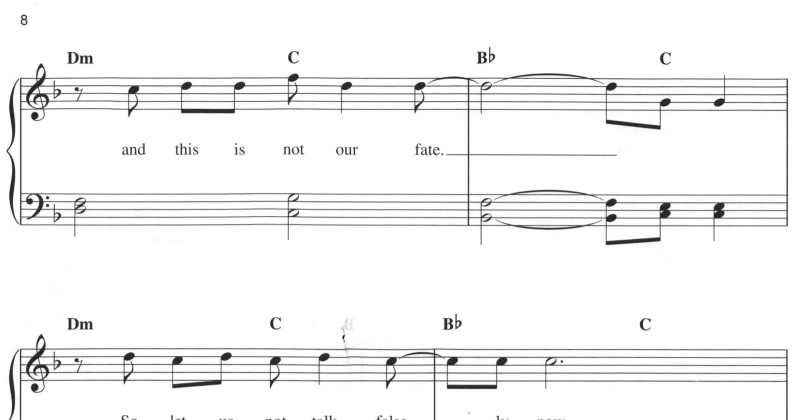

and this is not our fate.

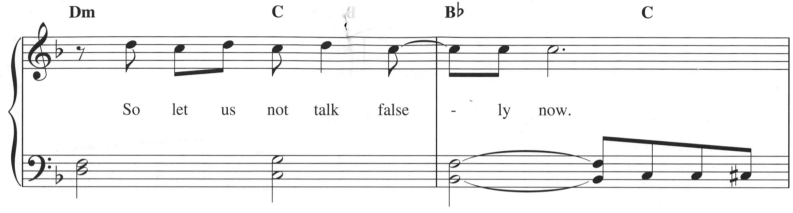

So let us not talk false - ly now.

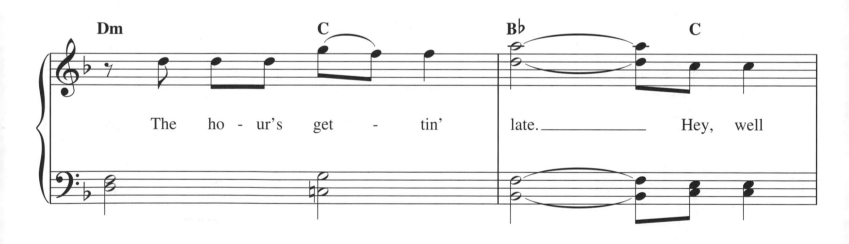

The ho - ur's get - tin' late._____ Hey, well

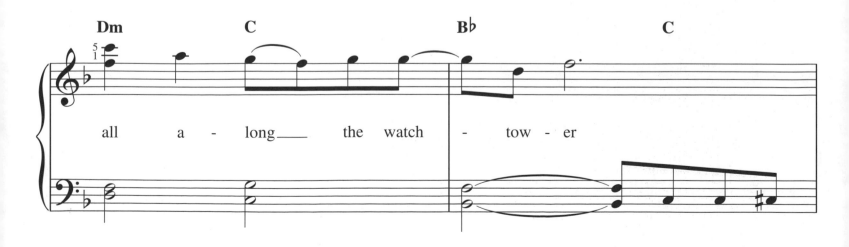

all a - long___ the watch - tow - er

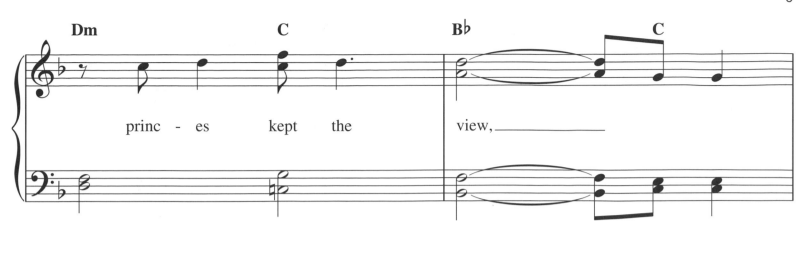

princ - es kept the view, _____

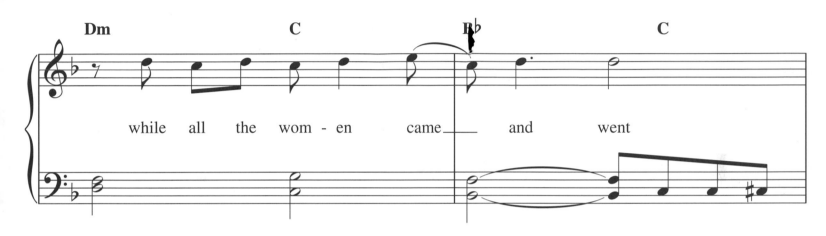

while all the wom - en came __ and went

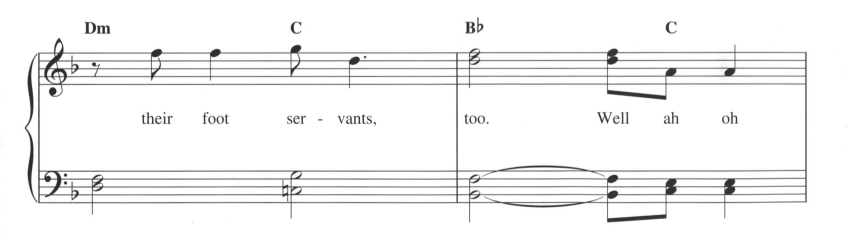

their foot ser - vants, too. Well ah oh

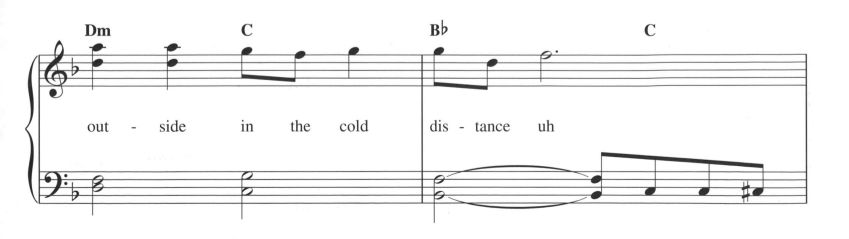

out - side in the cold dis - tance uh

ALL SHOOK UP

Words and Music by OTIS BLACKWELL
and ELVIS PRESLEY

13

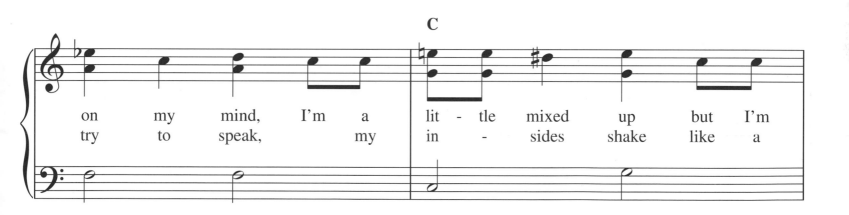

14

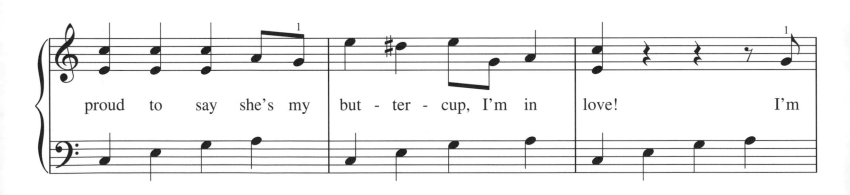

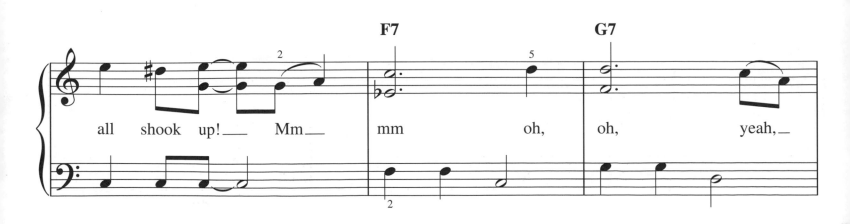

15

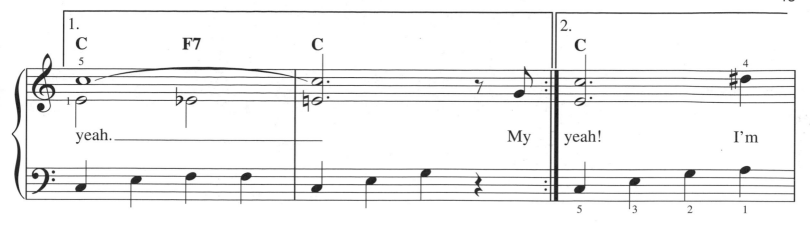

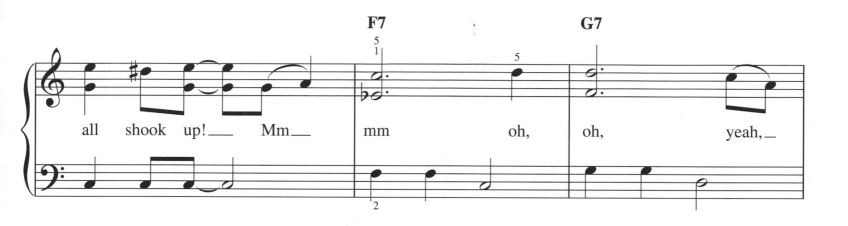

AMERICAN PIE

Words and Music by
DON McLEAN

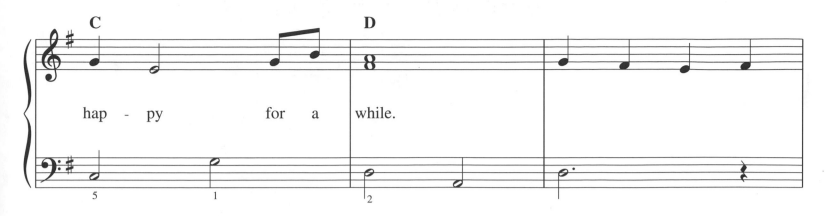

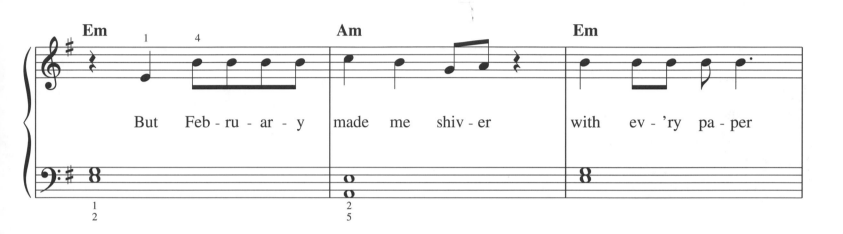

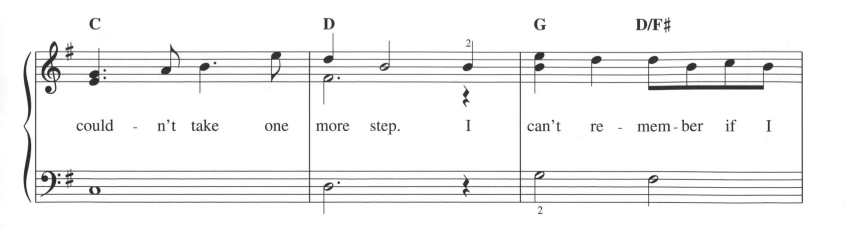

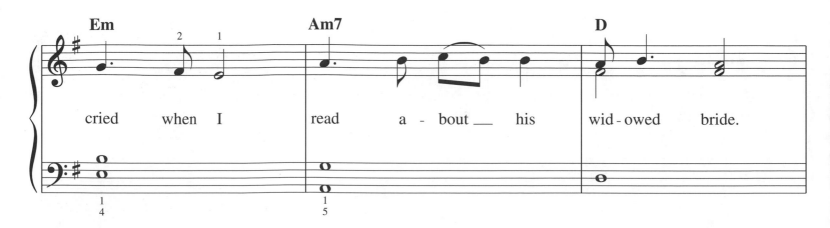

cried when I read a - bout __ his wid - owed bride.

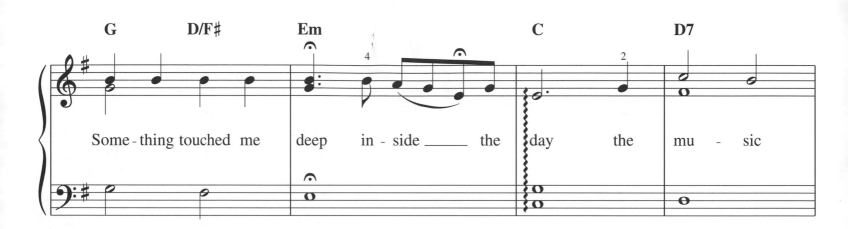

Some - thing touched me deep in - side __ the day the mu - sic

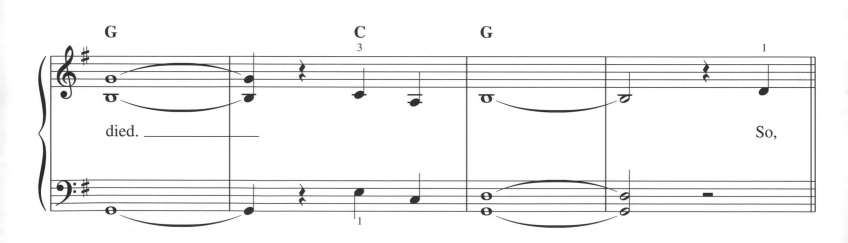

died. ____ So,

Moderately, with a beat

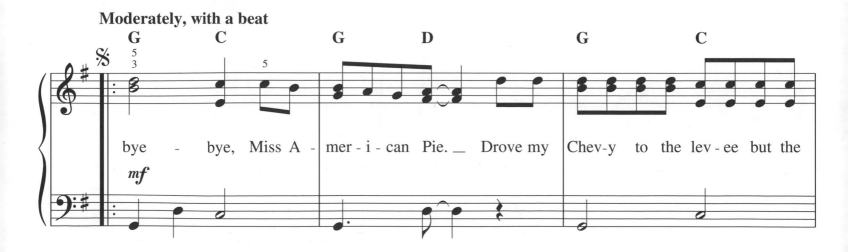

bye - bye, Miss A - mer - i - can Pie. __ Drove my Chev-y to the lev - ee but the

lev - ee was dry. __ Them good ole boys were drink-in' whis-key and rye, __ sing-in',

this - 'll be the day that I die, this - 'll be the day that I

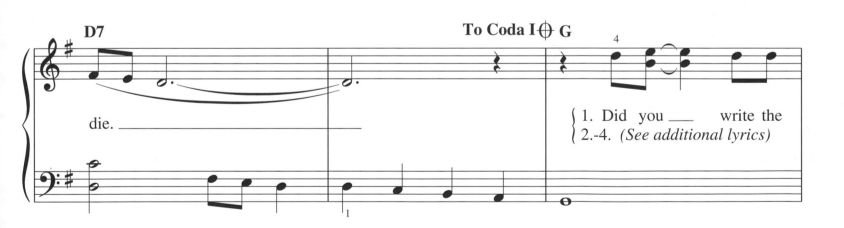

die. _____

1. Did you __ write the
2.-4. *(See additional lyrics)*

book of love, __ and do you have faith in God a - bove __

if the Bi - ble tells you so? ___ Now do

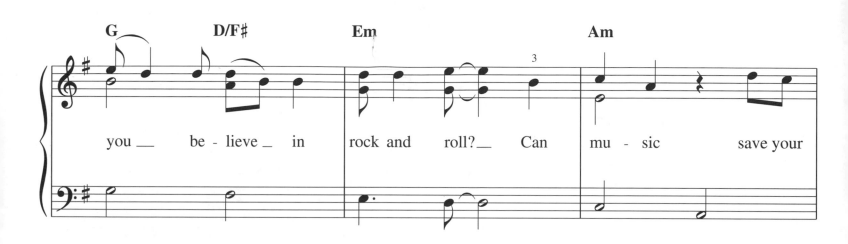

you ___ be - lieve ___ in rock and roll? ___ Can mu - sic save your

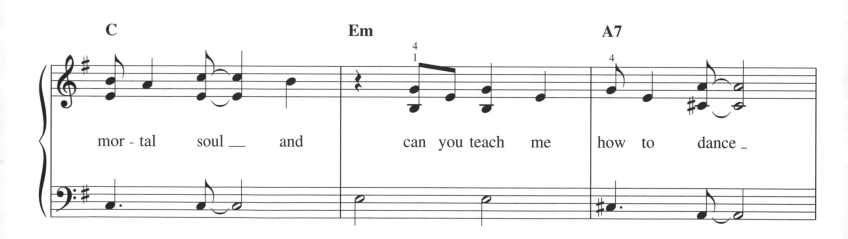

mor - tal soul ___ and can you teach me how to dance ___

real slow? _____ Well, I know that you're ___ in

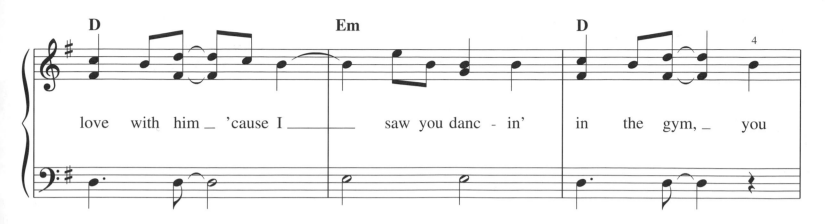

love   with   him __ 'cause I _____   saw you danc - in'   in   the   gym, _   you

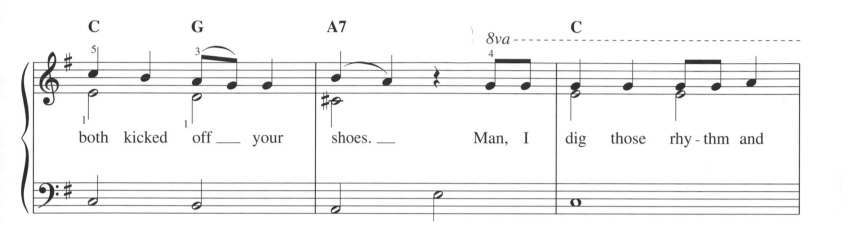

both   kicked   off ___ your   shoes. __   Man,   I   dig   those   rhy - thm and

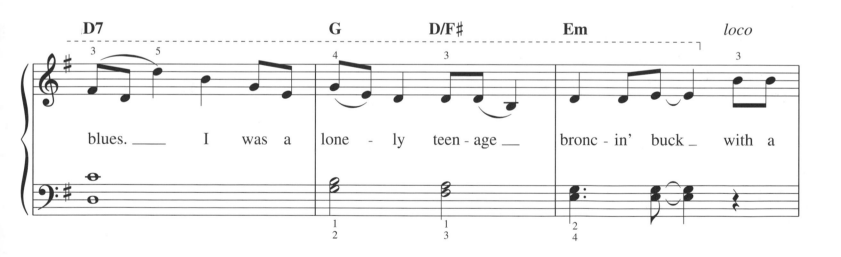

blues. ____   I   was   a   lone - ly   teen-age __   bronc - in'   buck _   with a

pink   car - na - tion and a   pick - up   truck. _   But   I   knew   I _____   was

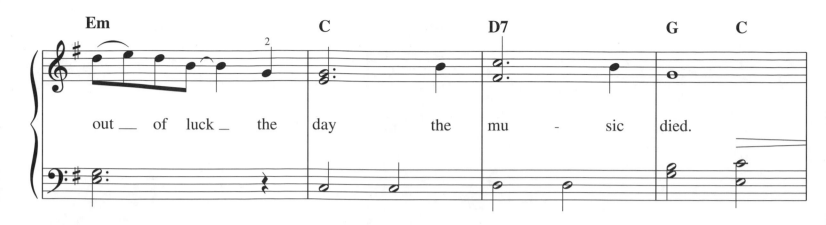

out — of luck — the day the mu - sic died.

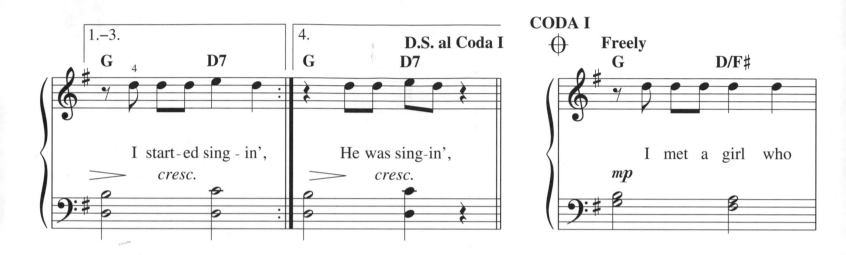

CODA I **Freely**

1.–3.
I start-ed sing - in', *cresc.*

4. **D.S. al Coda I**
He was sing-in', *cresc.*

I met a girl who *mp*

sang — the blues —— and I asked her for some hap - py news, —— but

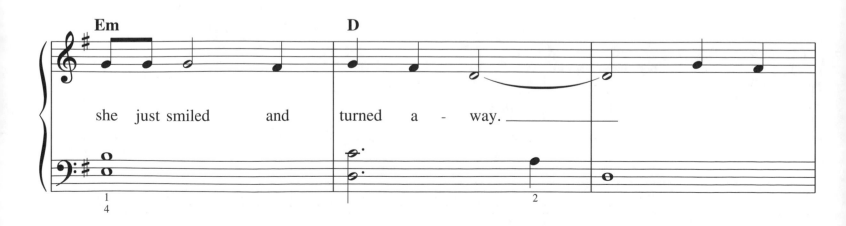

she just smiled and turned a - way. ——

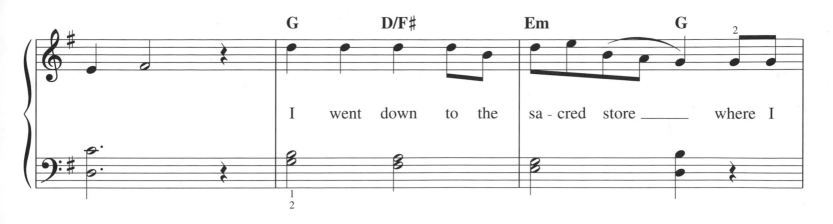

I went down to the sa - cred store _____ where I

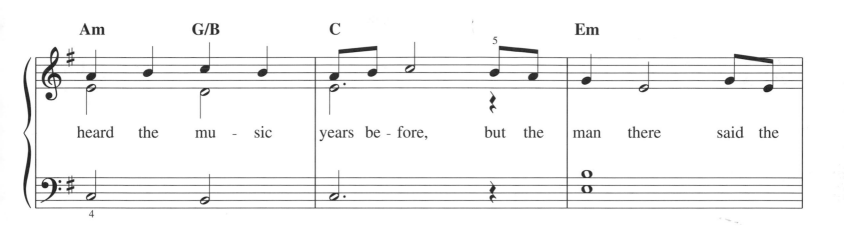

heard the mu - sic years be - fore, but the man there said the

mu - sic would-n't play. _____ And

in the streets the chil - dren screamed,_ the lov - ers cried and the

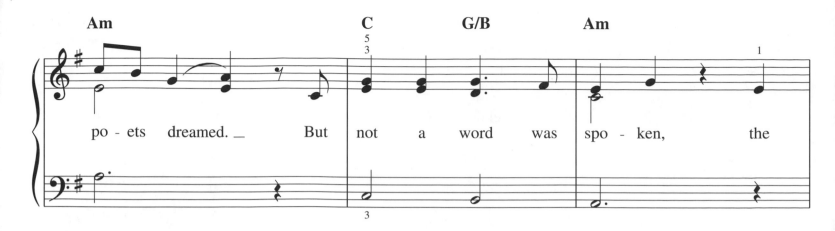

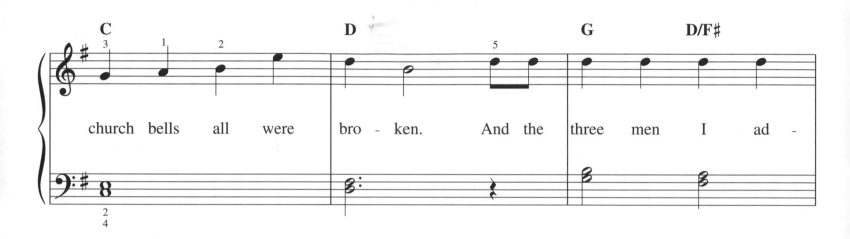

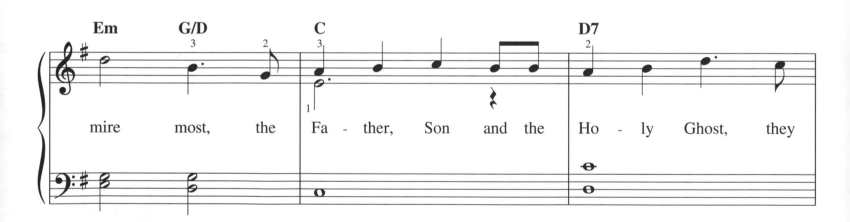

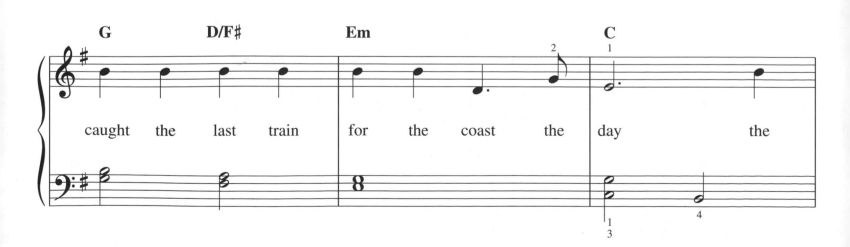

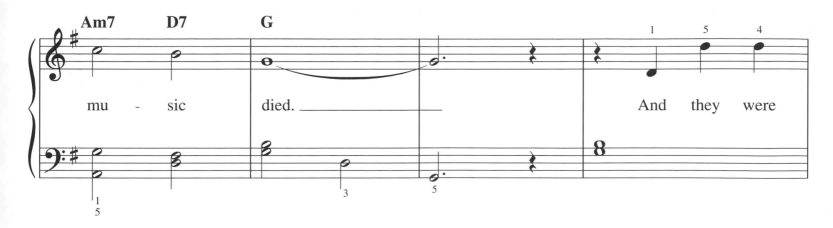

mu - sic   died. _____   And   they   were

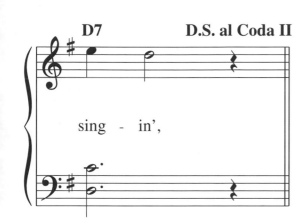

sing - in',

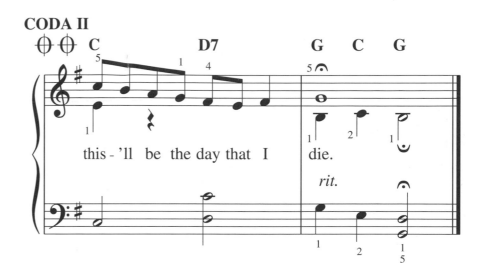

CODA II

this-'ll be the day that I   die.

rit.

Additional Lyrics

2. Now for ten years we've been on our own,
And moss grows fat on a rollin' stone
But that's not how it used to be
When the jester sang for the king and queen
In a coat he borrowed from James Dean
And a voice that came from you and me
Oh and while the king was looking down,
The jester stole his thorny crown
The courtroom was adjourned,
No verdict was returned
And while Lenin read a book on Marx
The quartet practiced in the park
And we sang dirges in the dark
The day the music died
We were singin'... bye-bye... etc.

3. Helter-skelter in the summer swelter
The birds flew off with a fallout shelter
Eight miles high and fallin' fast,
It landed foul on the grass
The players tried for a forward pass,
With the jester on the sidelines in a cast
Now the half-time air was sweet perfume
While the sergeants played a marching tune
We all got up to dance
But we never got the chance
'Cause the players tried to take the field,
The marching band refused to yield
Do you recall what was revealed
The day the music died
We started singin'... bye-bye... etc.

4. And there we were all in one place,
A generation lost in space
With no time left to start again
So come on, Jack be nimble, Jack be quick
Jack Flash sat on a candlestick
'Cause fire is the devil's only friend
And as I watched him on the stage
My hands were clenched in fists of rage
No angel born in hell
Could break that Satan's spell
And as the flames climbed high into the night
To light the sacrificial rite
I saw Satan laughing with delight
The day the music died
He was singin'... bye-bye... etc.

BEAT IT

Written and Composed by
MICHAEL JACKSON

Moderately fast

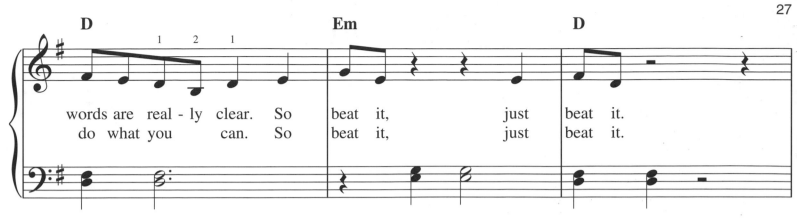

words are real - ly clear. So beat it, just beat it.
do what you can. So beat it, just beat it.

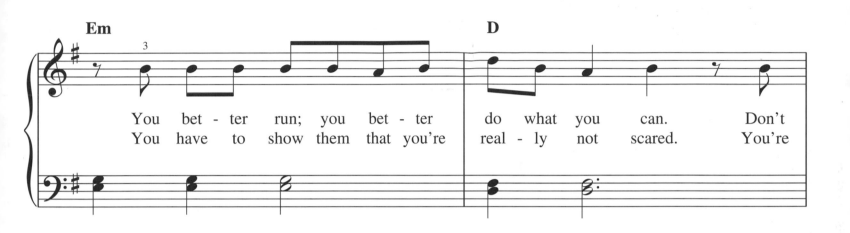

You bet - ter run; you bet - ter do what you can. Don't
You have to show them that you're real - ly not scared. You're

wan - na see no blood. Don't be a ma - cho man. You
play - in' with your life. This ain't no "truth or dare." They'll

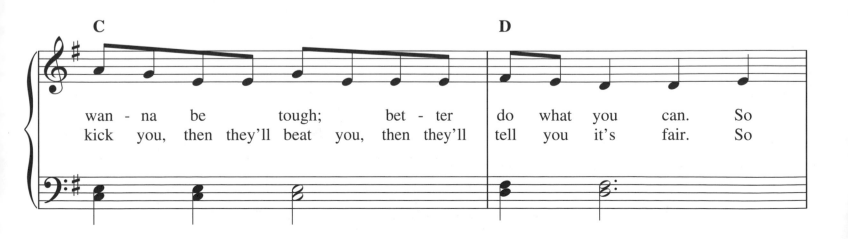

wan - na be tough; bet - ter do what you can. So
kick you, then they'll beat you, then they'll tell you it's fair. So

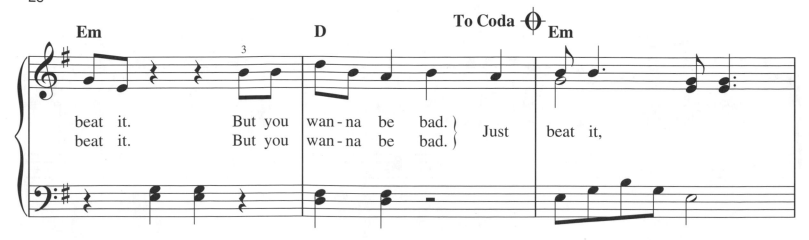

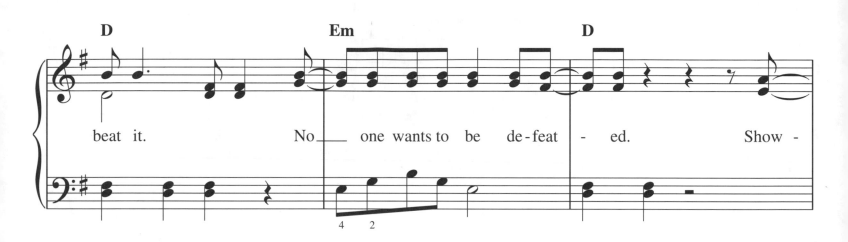

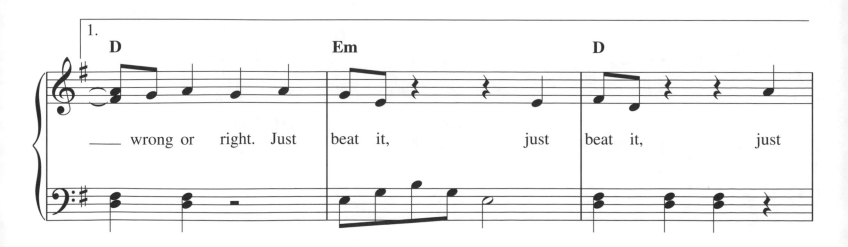

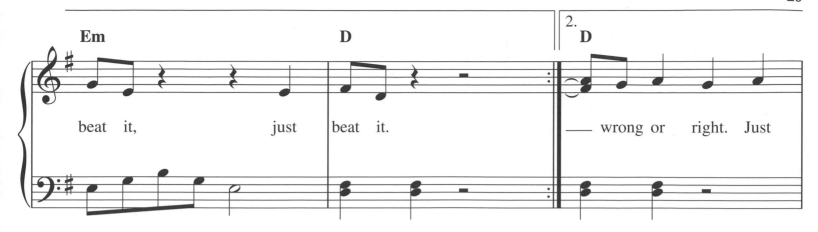

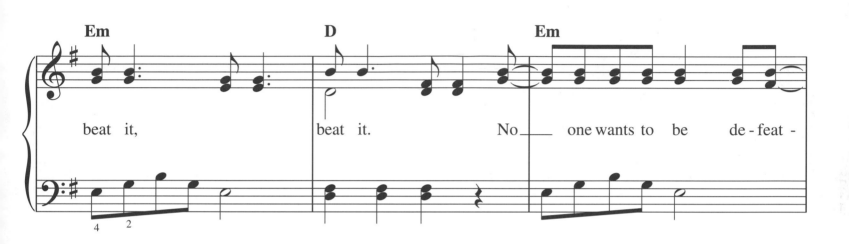

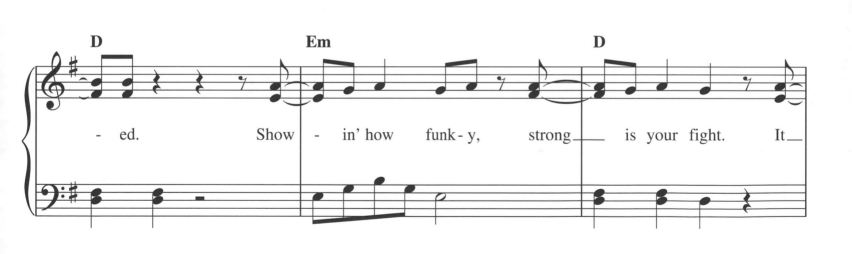

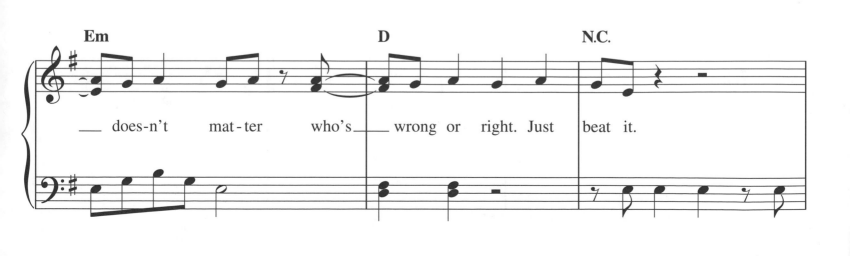

Beat it.

Beat it.

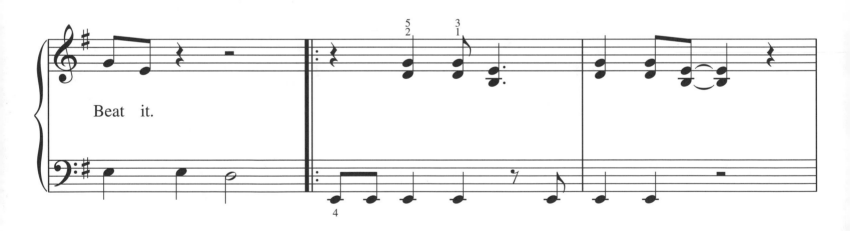

Beat it.

1.

2.

D.S. al Coda

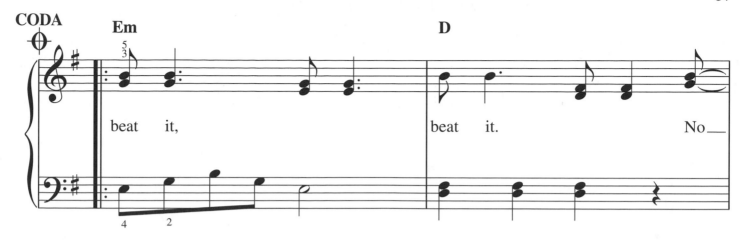

CODA

beat it, beat it. No___

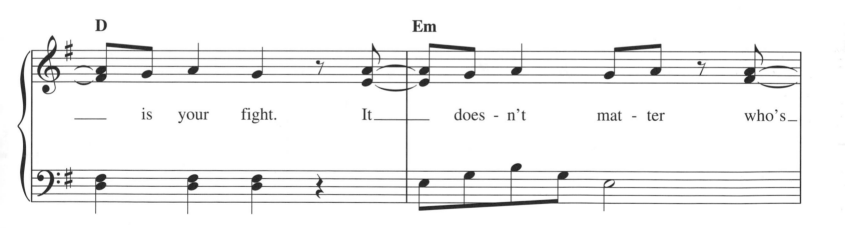

___ one wants to be de-feat - ed. Show - in' how funk-y, strong___

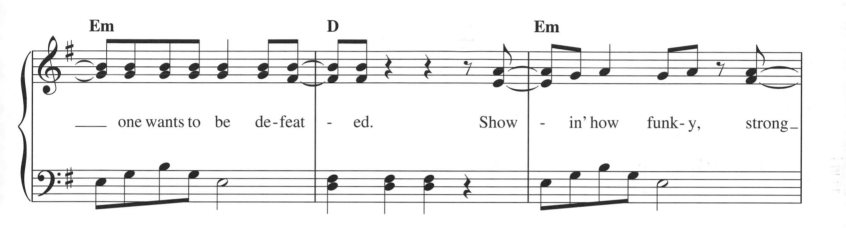

___ is your fight. It___ does - n't mat - ter who's___

___ wrong or right. Just beat it.

BLOWIN' IN THE WIND

Words and Music by
BOB DYLAN

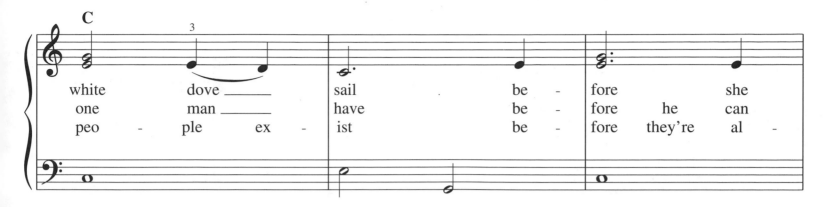

white dove _____ sail   be - fore   she
one man _____ have   be - fore   he can
peo - ple ex - ist   be - fore   they're al -

sleeps in the sand? _____ Yes, 'n' how man - y
hear peo - ple cry? _____ Yes, 'n' how man - y
lowed to be free? _____ Yes, 'n' how man - y

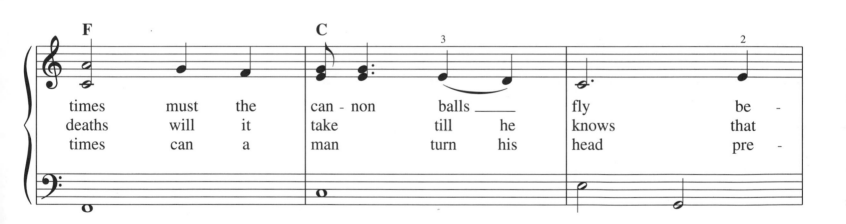

times must the can - non balls _____ fly be -
deaths will it take till he knows that
times can a man turn his head pre -

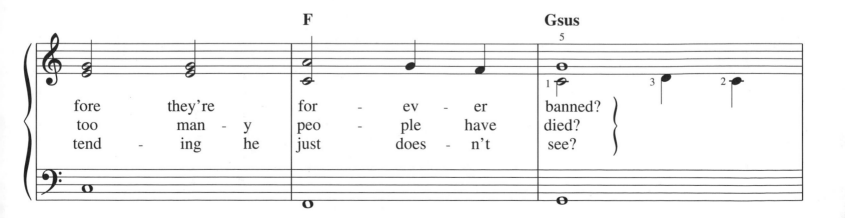

fore they're for - ev - er banned?
too man - y peo - ple have died?
tend - ing he just does - n't see?

The an - swer, my friend, is blow-in' in the

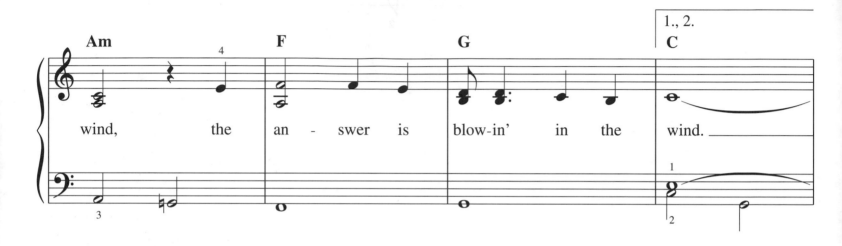

1., 2.

wind, the an - swer is blow-in' in the wind.

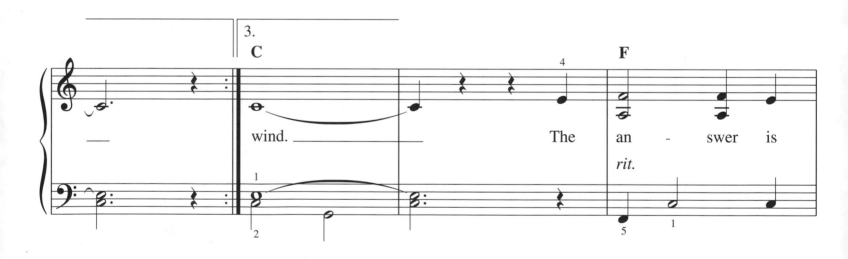

3.

wind. The an - swer is

rit.

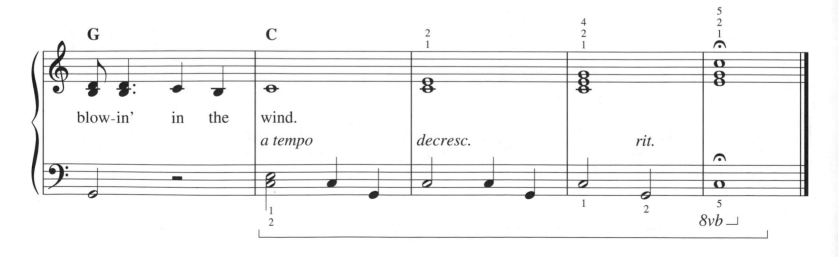

blow-in' in the wind.

a tempo   *decresc.*   *rit.*

8vb

BLUE SUEDE SHOES

Words and Music by
CARL LEE PERKINS

do an-y-thing but lay off of my blue suede shoes.

Well, you can knock me down, ___
burn my house, ___

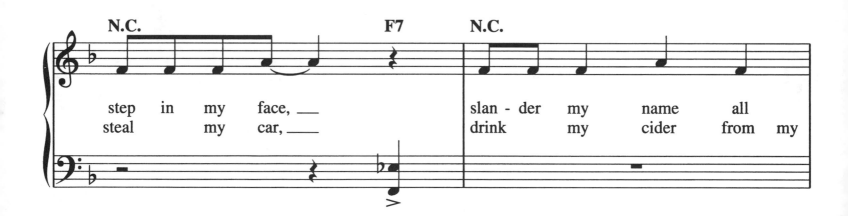

step in my face, ___
steal my car, ___

slan-der my name all
drink my cider all from my

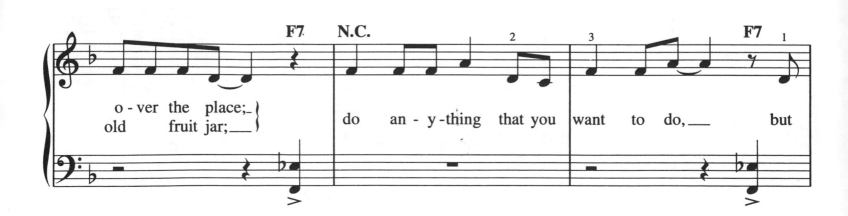

o-ver the place; ⎫
old fruit jar; ⎭

do an-y-thing that you want to do, ___ but

37

uh uh, hon-ey, lay off of my shoes. _ Don't you

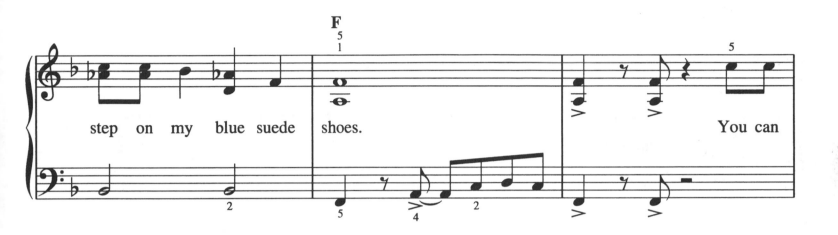

step on my blue suede shoes. You can

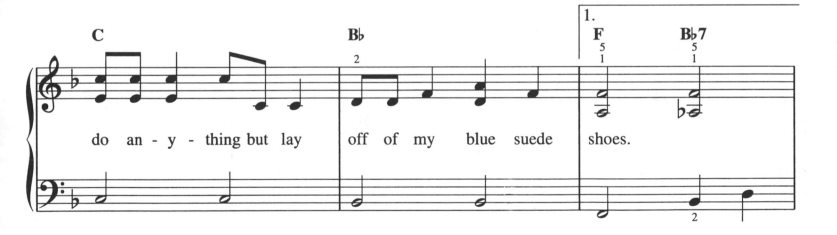

do an - y - thing but lay off of my blue suede shoes.

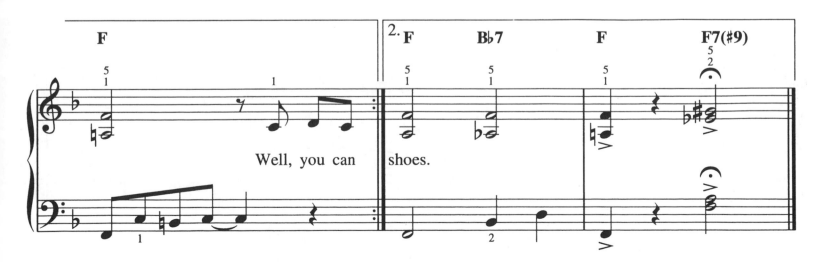

Well, you can shoes.

BOHEMIAN RHAPSODY

Words and Music by
FREDDIE MERCURY

Slowly, freely

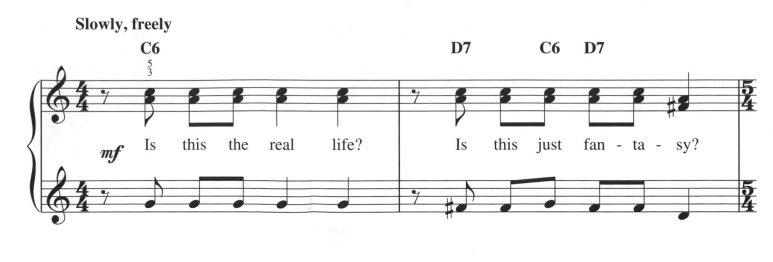

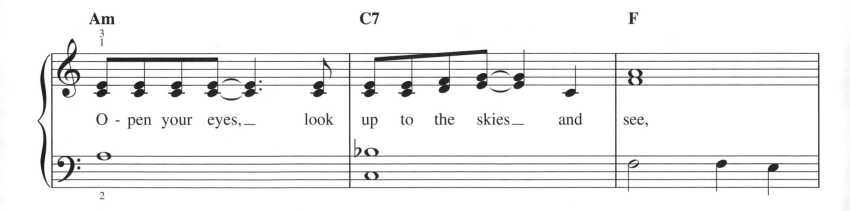

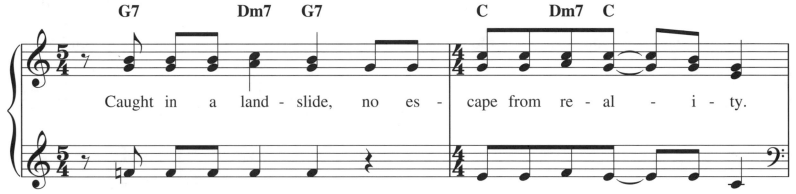

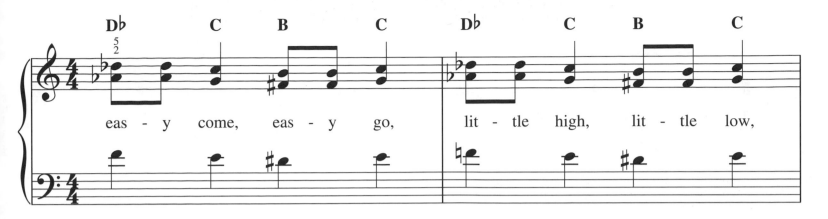

eas - y come, eas - y go, | lit - tle high, lit - tle low,

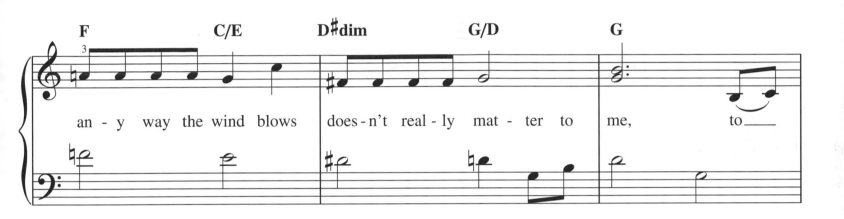

an - y way the wind blows | does - n't real - ly mat - ter to | me, to____

me. | | Ma - ma____ just
Too late,__ my

Slowly, steady tempo

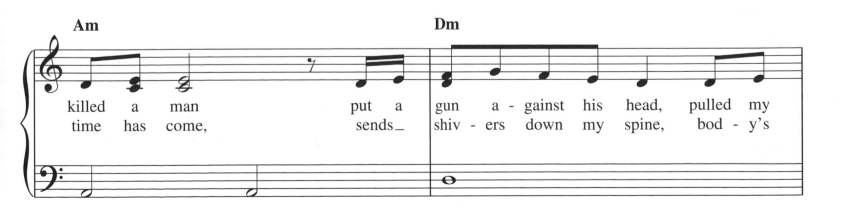

killed a man | put a | gun a - gainst his head, pulled my
time has come, | sends_ | shiv - ers down my spine, bod - y's

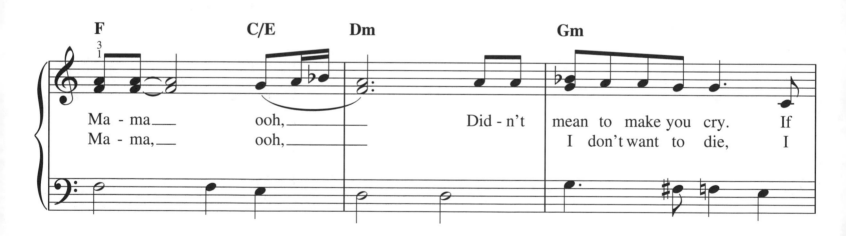

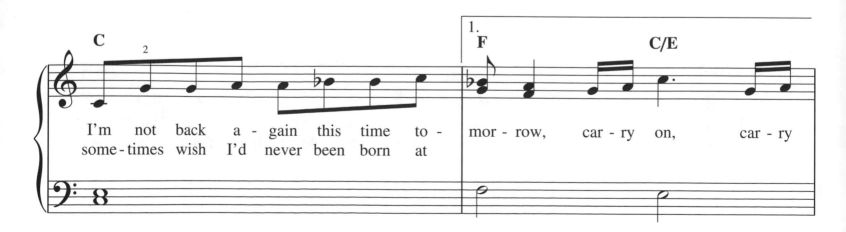

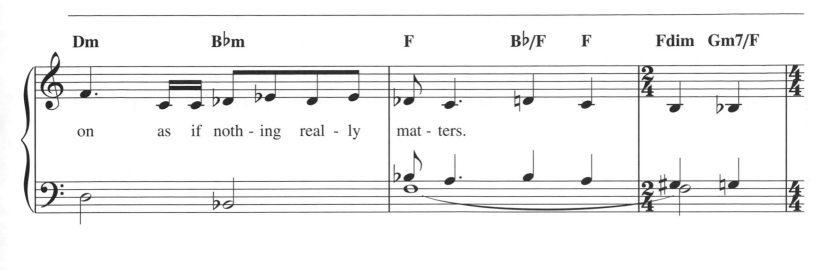

on   as   if   noth-ing real-ly   mat-ters.

all.

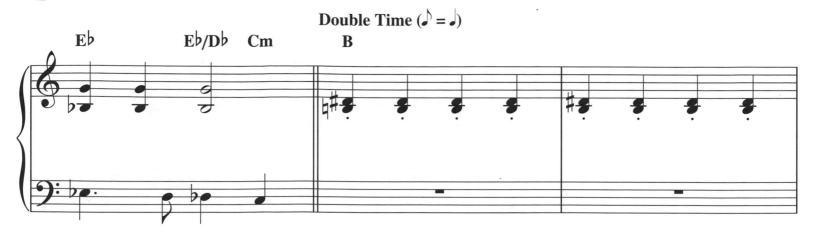

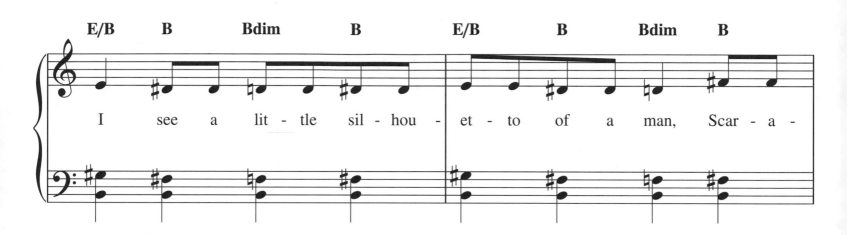

I see a lit - tle sil - hou - et - to of a man, Scar - a -

mouche, Scar - a - mouche, will you do the Fan - dan - go.

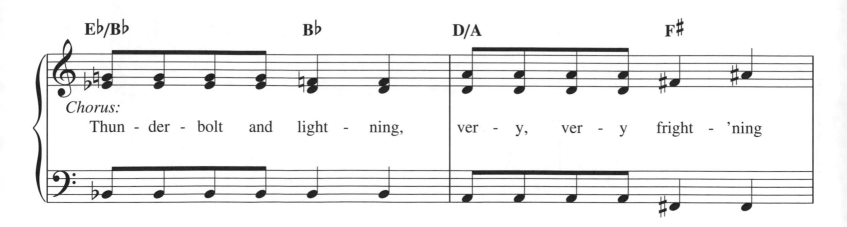

Chorus:
Thun - der - bolt and light - ning, ver - y, ver - y fright - 'ning

me. (Gal - li - le - o.) Gal - li - le - o. (Gal - li - le - o.) Gal - li -

le - o, Gal - li - le - o Fig - a - ro Mag - ni - fi - co._____

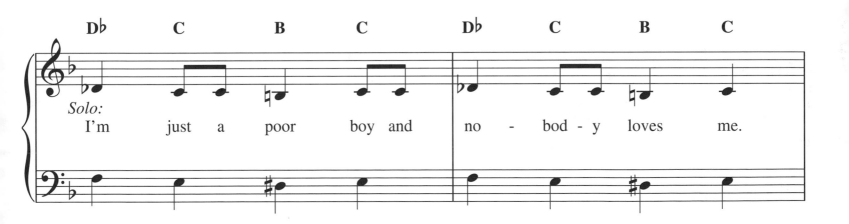

Solo:
I'm   just   a   poor   boy   and   no - bod - y   loves   me.

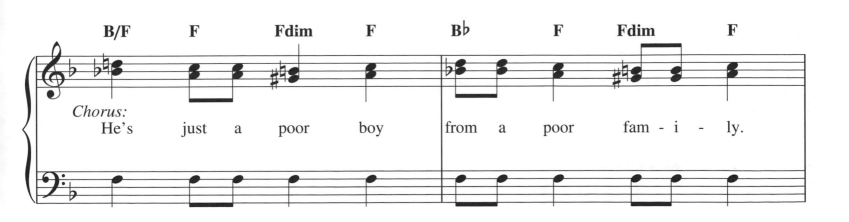

Chorus:
He's   just   a   poor   boy   from   a   poor   fam - i - ly.

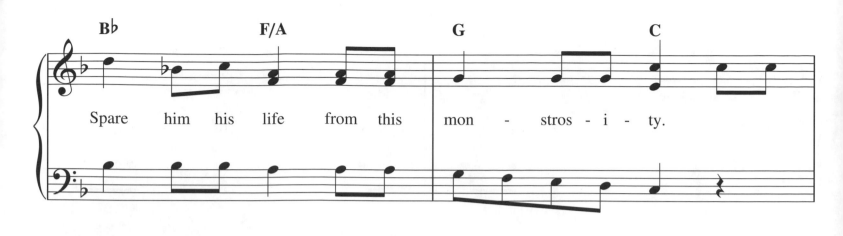

Spare him his life from this mon - stros - i - ty.

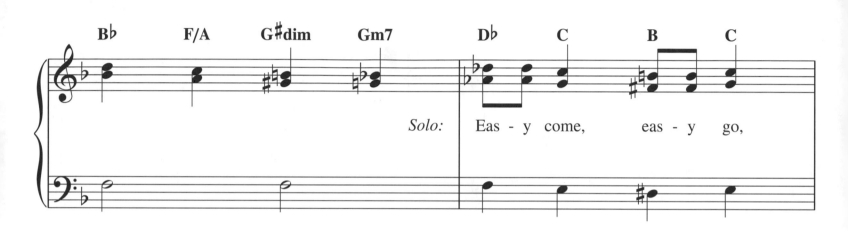

Solo: Eas - y come, eas - y go,

will you let me go, Bis - mil - lah! No, we

Chorus:

will not let you go. (Let him go!) Bis - mil - lah! We

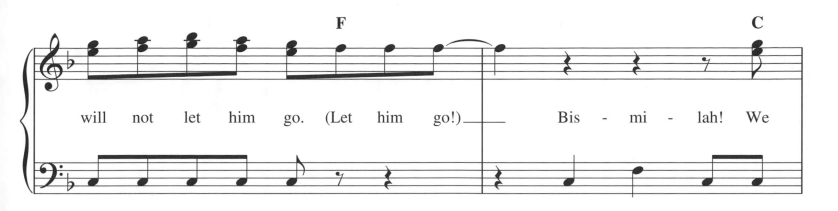

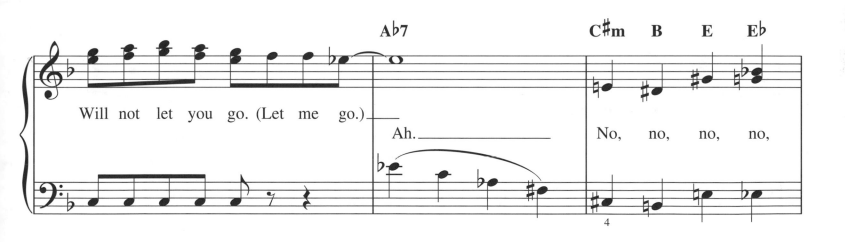

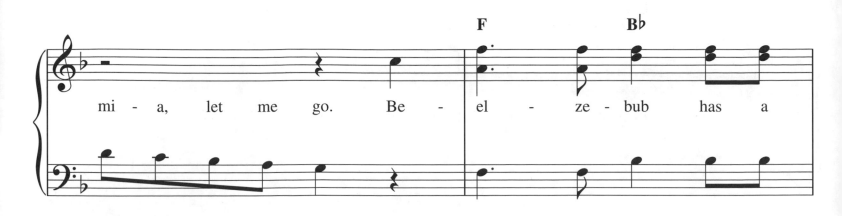

mi - a, let me go. Be - el - ze - bub has a

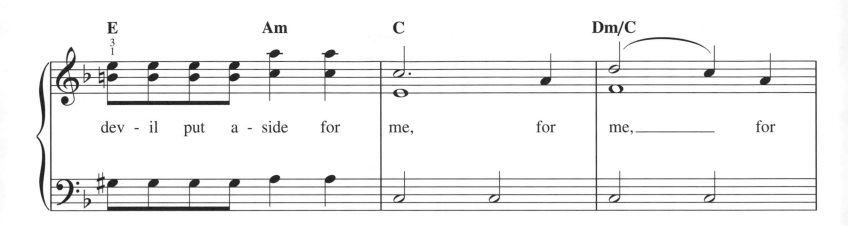

dev - il put a - side for me, for me, _____ for

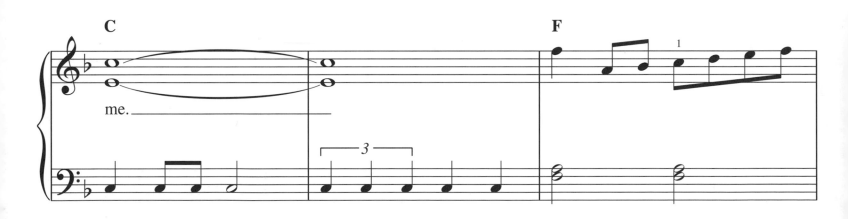

me. _____

48

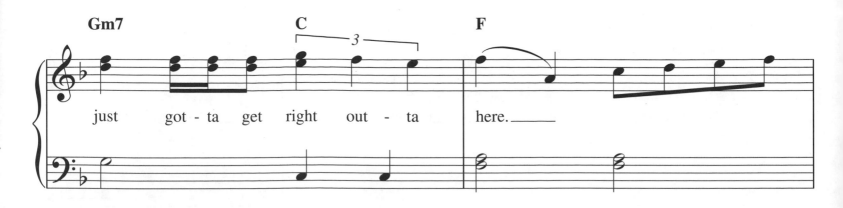

just got - ta get right out - ta here._____

rit.

Slowly, a tempo

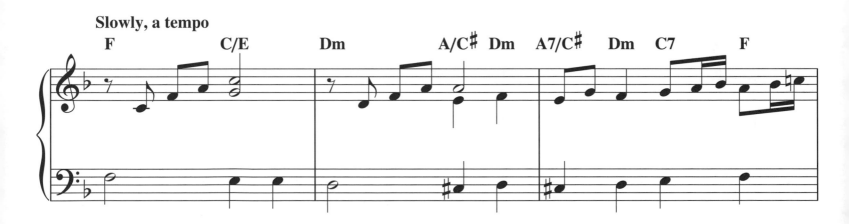

Noth-ing real - ly mat - ters,

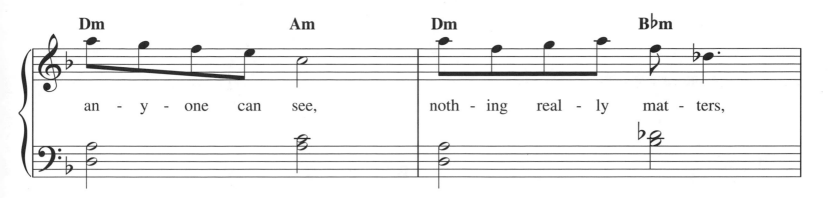

an - y - one can see, noth - ing real - ly mat - ters,

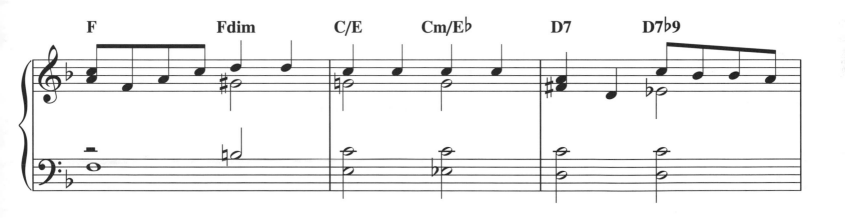

noth - ing real - ly mat - ters to me.

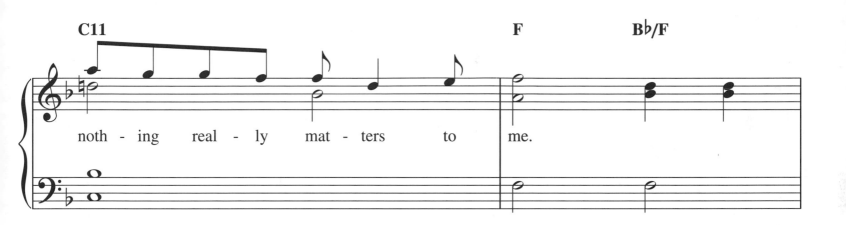

rit.

An - y way the wind blows.

BORN TO BE WILD

Words and Music by
MARS BONFIRE

Moderate Rock

Get your mo - tor run - ning.
I like smoke and light - ning,

Head out on the high - way,
heav - y met - al thun - der

look-ing for ad - ven - ture
rac-ing in the wind

in what - ev - er comes our way. ___
and the feel-ing that I'm un - der.

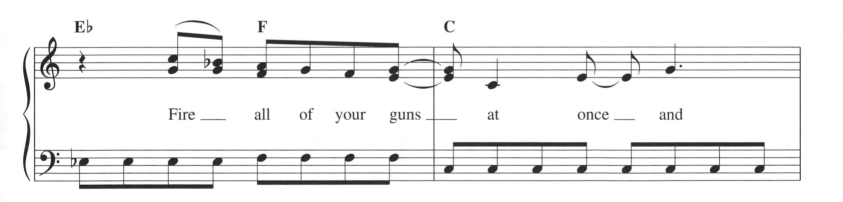

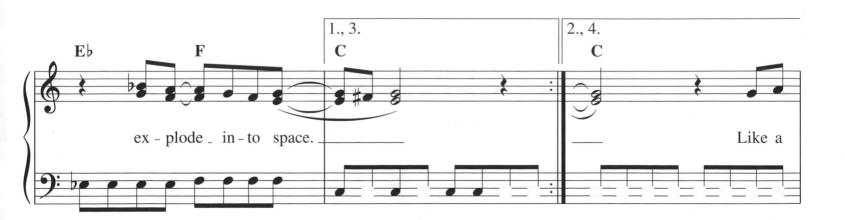

Lyrics:
Yeah, dar-ling, gon-na make it hap-pen, take the world in a love em-brace. Fire all of your guns at once and ex-plode in-to space. Like a

true na-ture child ___ we were born, born to be wild.

___ We have climbed so high, ___

nev - er want to die.

Born to be wild, _____

born   to   be   wild.

1.

2.

Born   to   be   wild.

BORN TO RUN

Words and Music by
BRUCE SPRINGSTEEN

With a driving beat

57

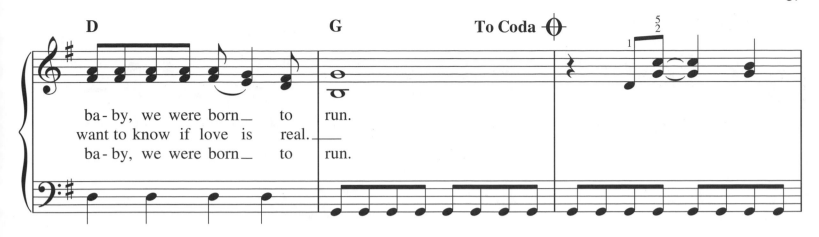

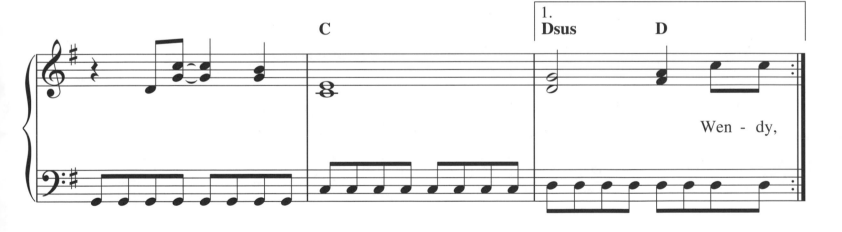

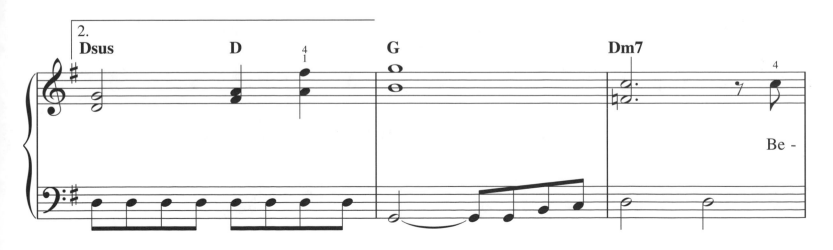

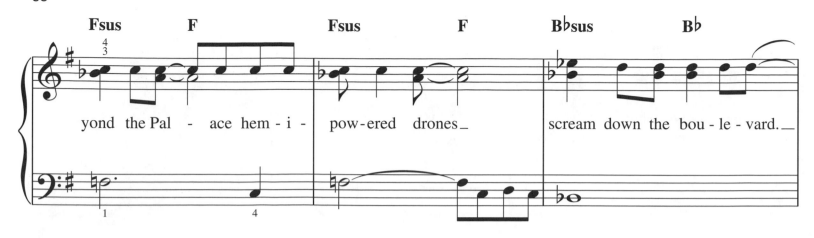

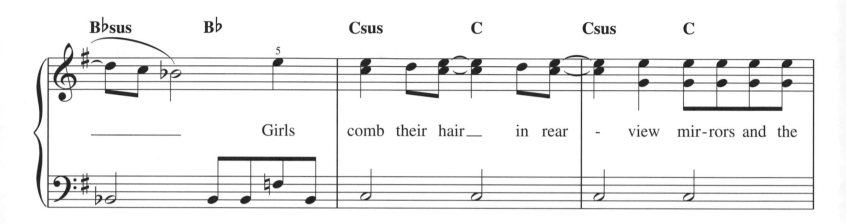

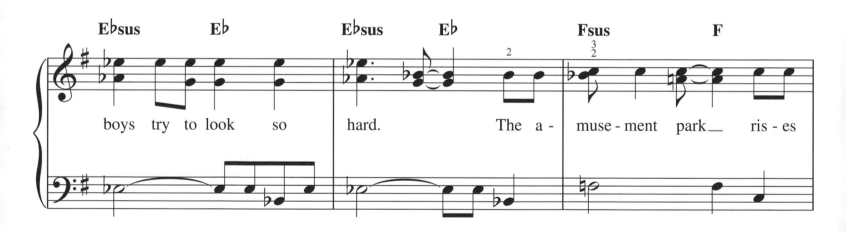

die with you, Wen - dy, on the streets to - night___ in an ev - er - last - ing

kiss.

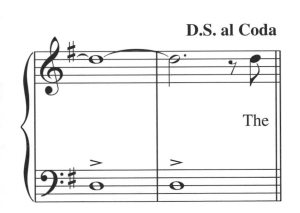

D.S. al Coda

The

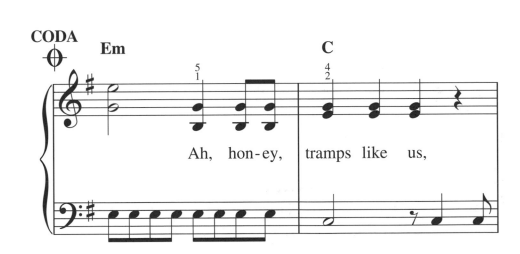

CODA

Ah, hon - ey, tramps like us,

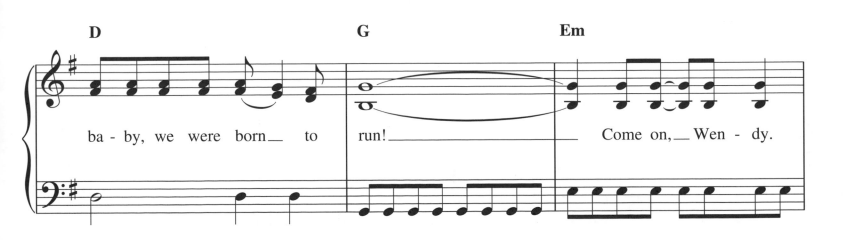

ba - by, we were born___ to run!_____ Come on,___ Wen - dy.

Tramps like us, baby, we were born to run!

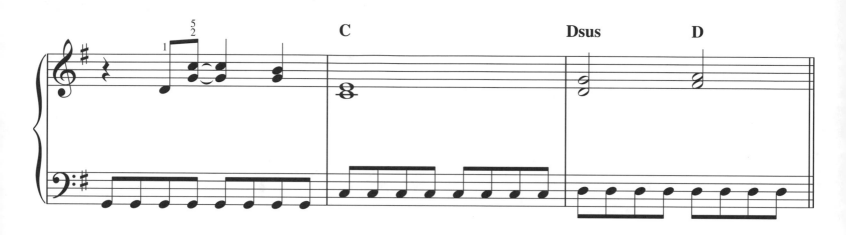

BRIDGE OVER TROUBLED WATER

Words and Music by
PAUL SIMON

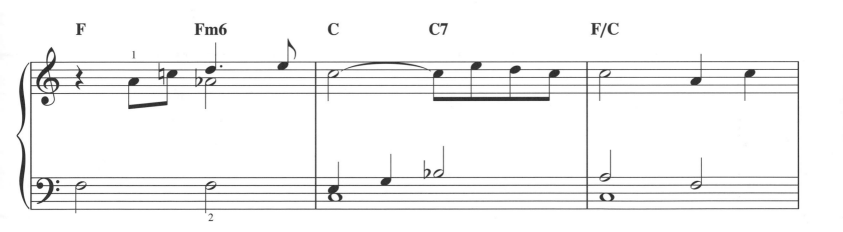

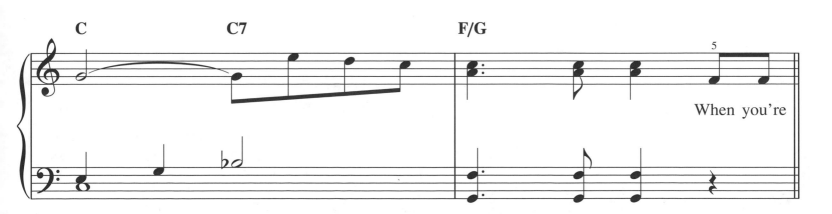

When you're

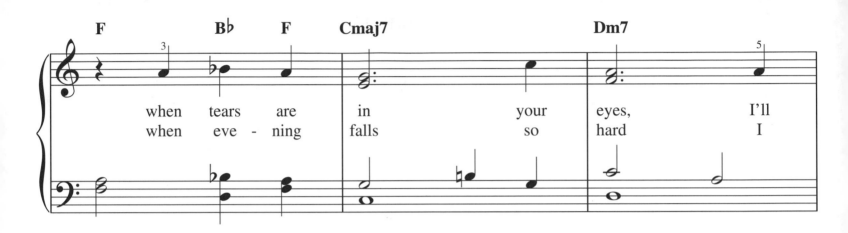

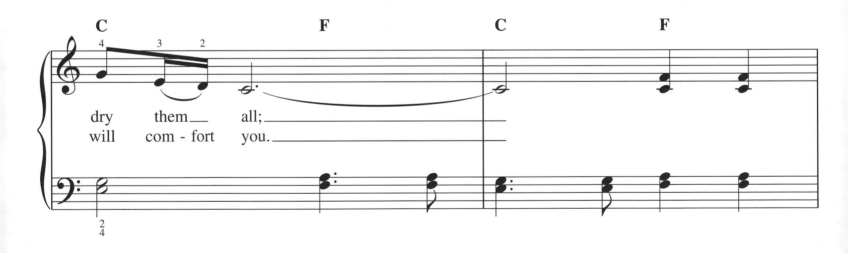

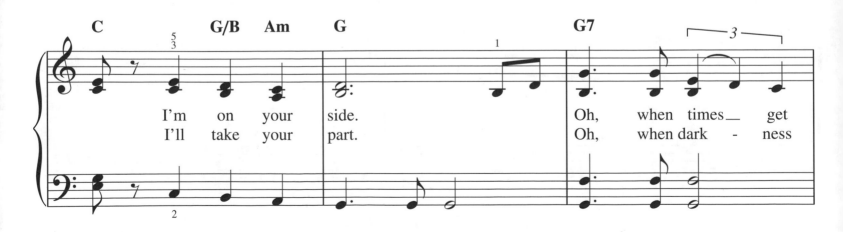

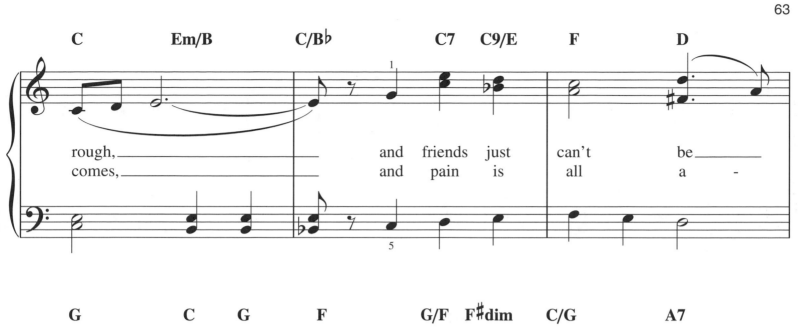

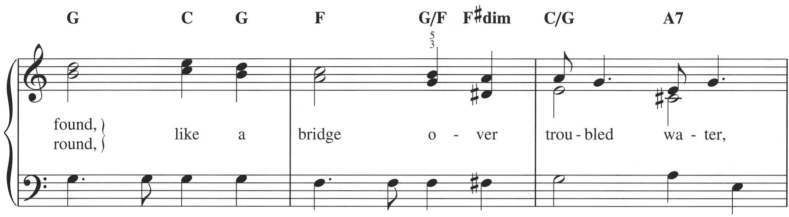

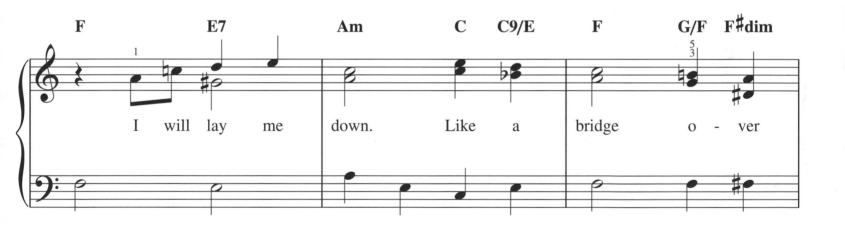

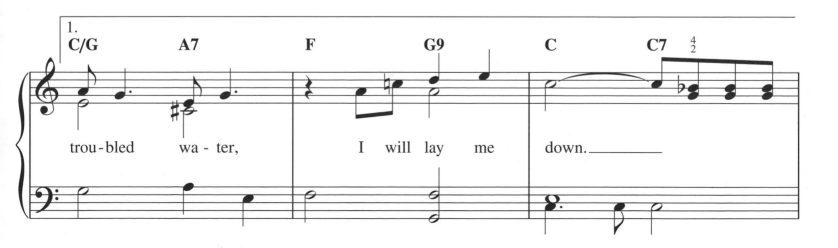

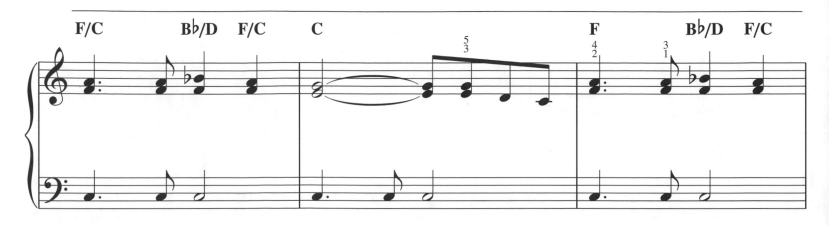

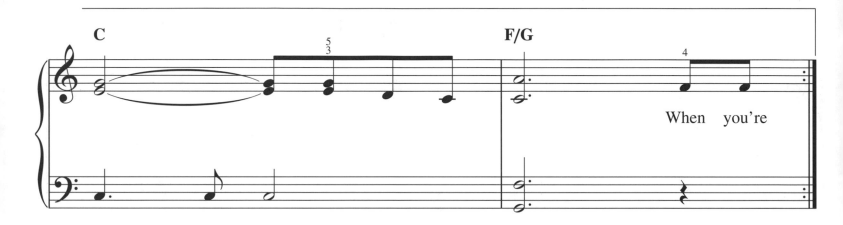

When you're

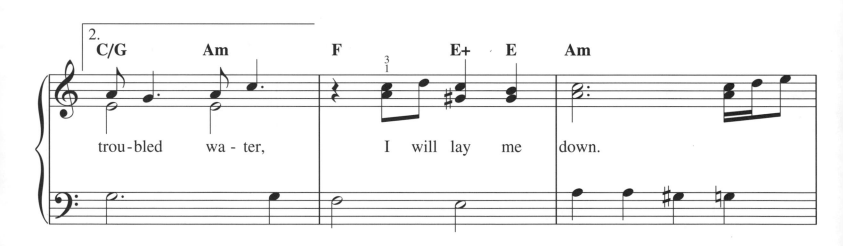

trou-bled   wa - ter,   I   will lay me   down.

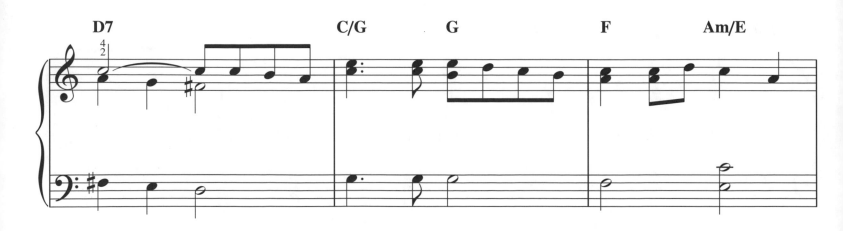

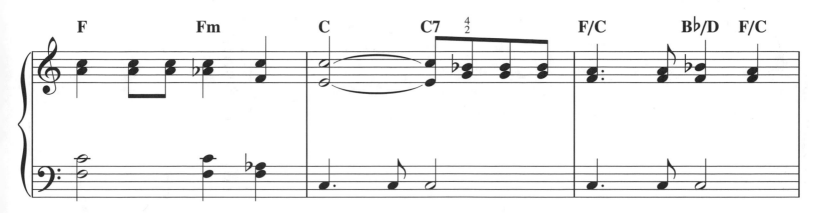

Sail on, sil - ver girl, sail on

by. Your time has come to

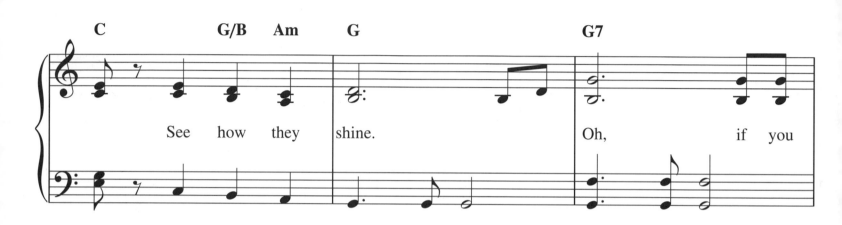

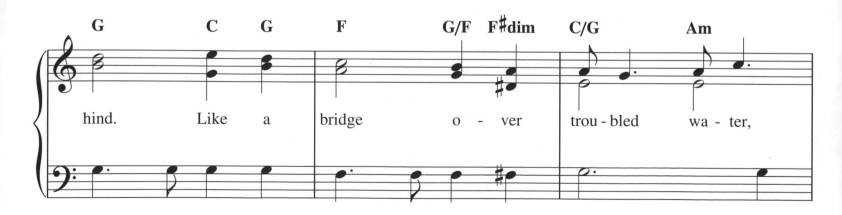

I will ease your mind. Like a bridge o - ver

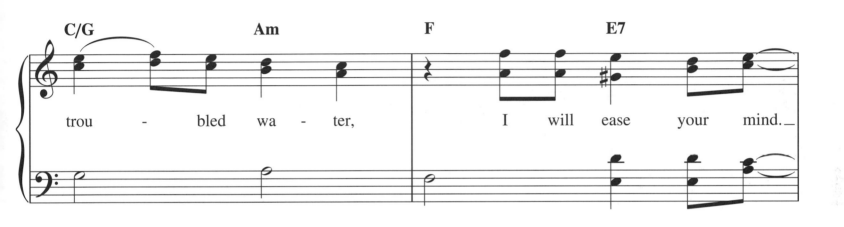

trou - bled wa - ter, I will ease your mind.

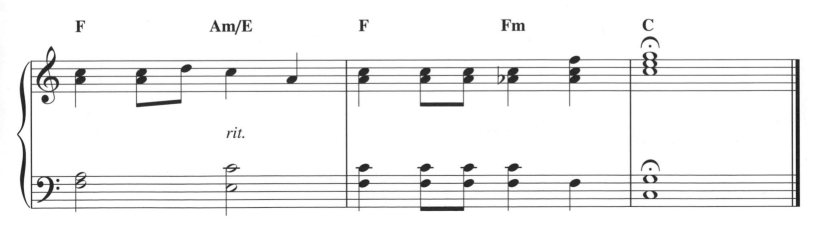

rit.

BROWN EYED GIRL

Words and Music by
VAN MORRISON

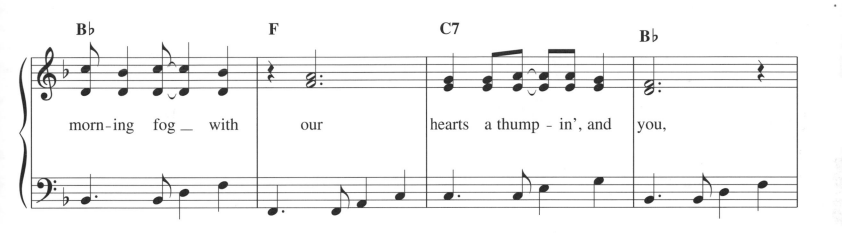

Chorus

we used to sing: sha la la la la la la la la la la te da.

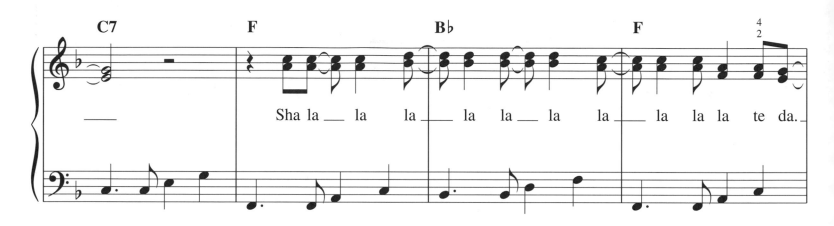

Sha la la la la la la la la la la te da.

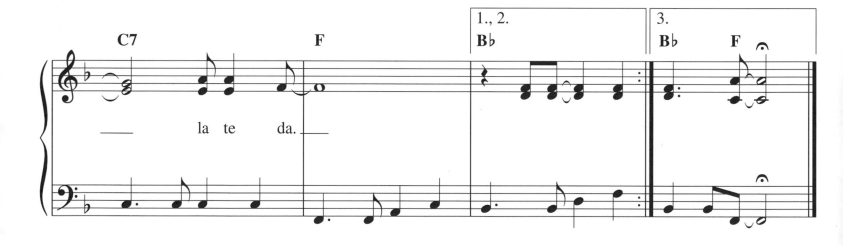

la te da.

Additional Lyrics

2. Whatever happened to Tuesday and so slow
   Going down the old mine with a transistor radio
   Standing in the sunlight laughing
   Hiding behind a rainbow's wall
   Slipping and a-sliding
   All along the waterfall
   With you, my brown eyed girl
   You, my brown eyed girl.
   Do you remember when we used to sing:
   Chorus

3. So hard to find my way, now that I'm all on my own
   I saw you just the other day, my, how you have grown
   Cast my memory back there, Lord
   Sometime I'm overcome thinking 'bout
   Making love in the green grass
   Behind the stadium
   With you, my brown eyed girl
   With you, my brown eyed girl.
   Do you remember when we used to sing:
   Chorus

CALIFORNIA GIRLS

Words and Music by BRIAN WILSON
and MIKE LOVE

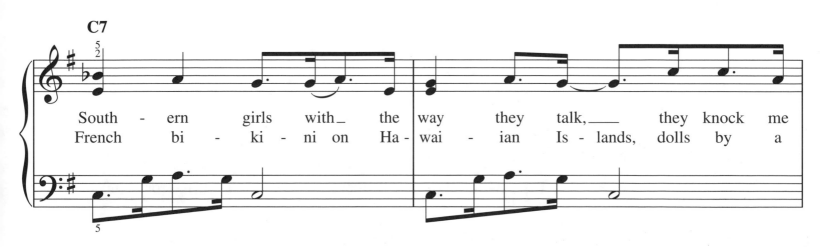

D7   **G**

out when I'm down there.___   The mid-west farm-er's
palm tree in the sand.___   I've been all around this

                              G7

daugh-ters real-ly   make you feel al-   right.___   And__
great big world, and I've   seen all kinds of   girls.___   But I

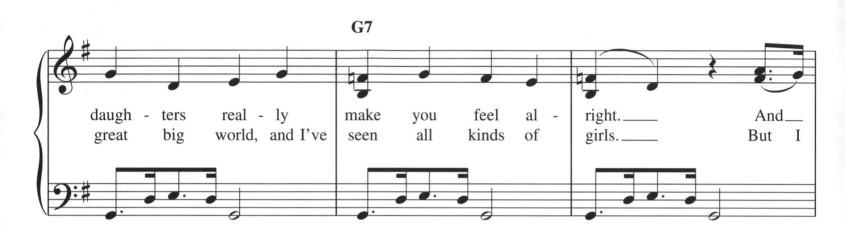

C7   **D7**

north-ern girls with the   way they kiss they keep their   boy-friends warm at night.__
could-n't wait to get   back to the states, back to the   cutest girls in the world.__

                                  𝄋 G   **Am7**

            I wish they all could be Cal-i-for-nia, I

wish they all could be Cal - i - for - nia, I wish they all could

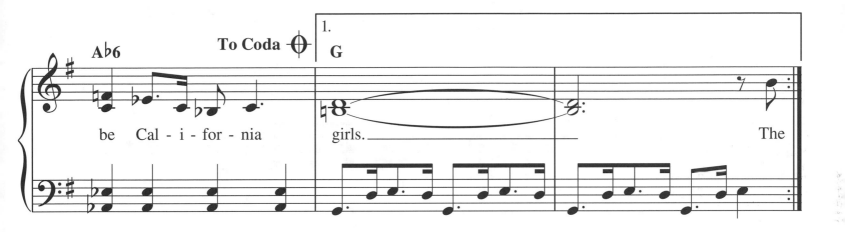

be Cal - i - for - nia girls. The

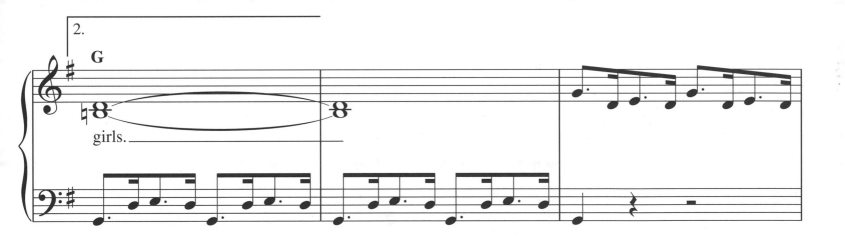

girls.

D.S. al Coda

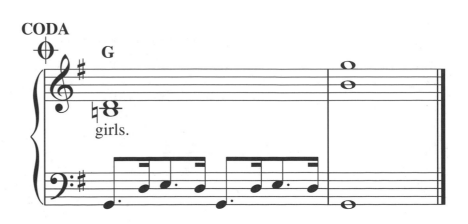

CODA

girls.

CALIFORNIA DREAMIN'

Words and Music by JOHN PHILLIPS
and MICHELLE PHILLIPS

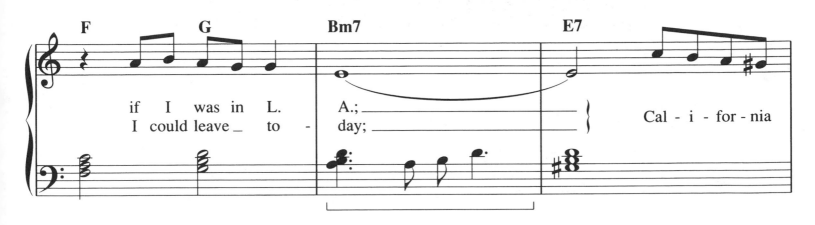

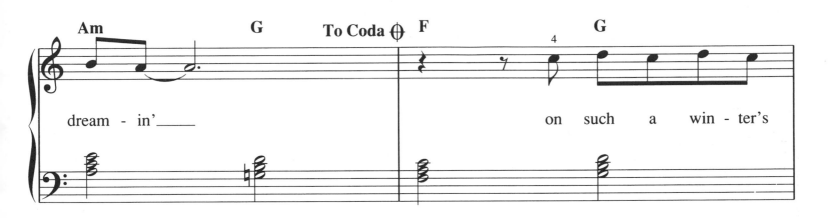

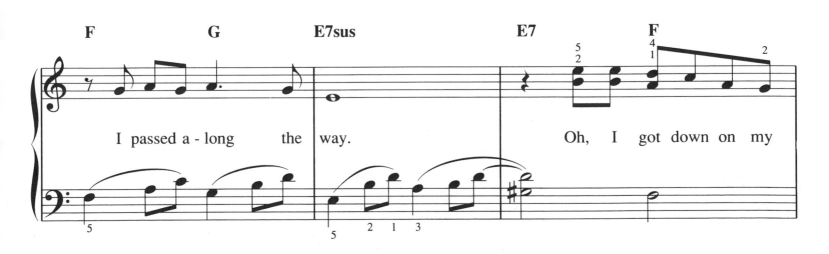

76

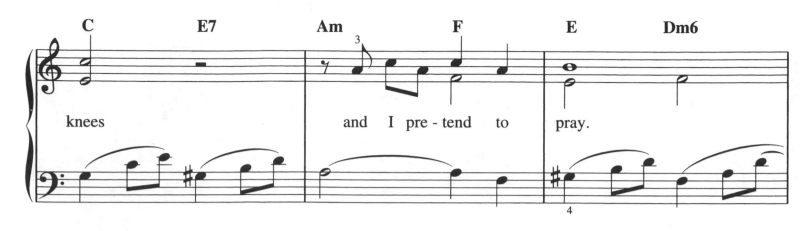

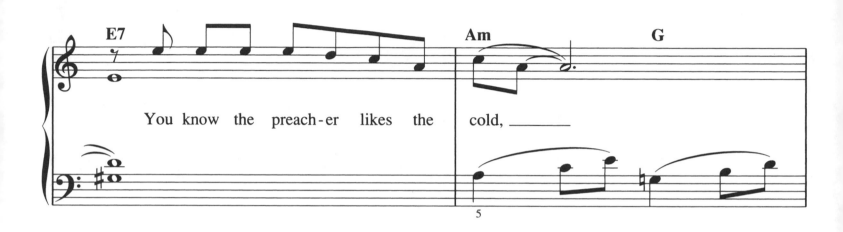

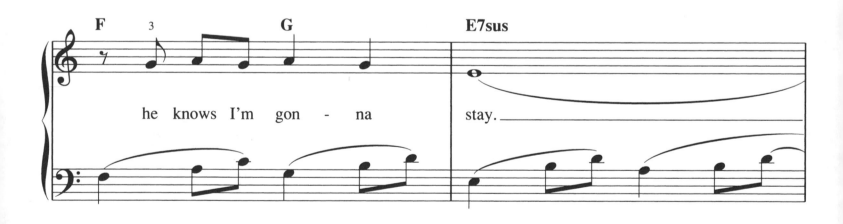

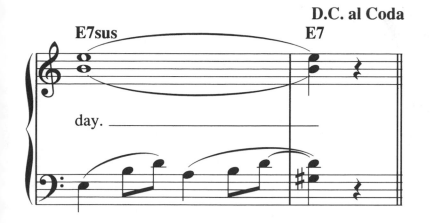

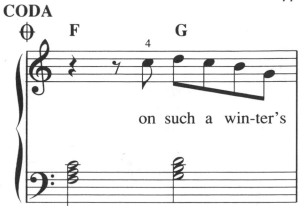

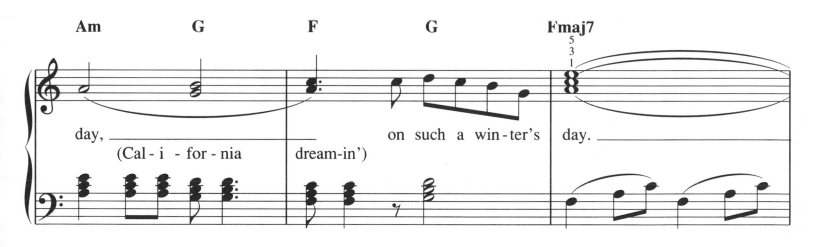

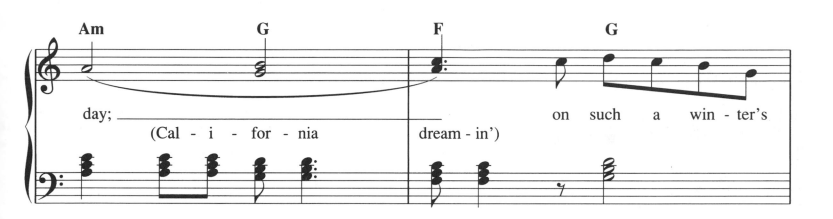

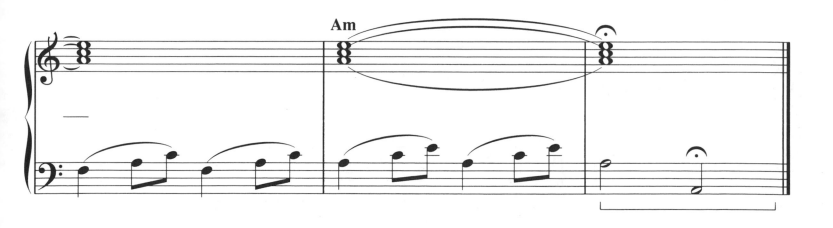

CRAZY

Words and Music by
WILLIE NELSON

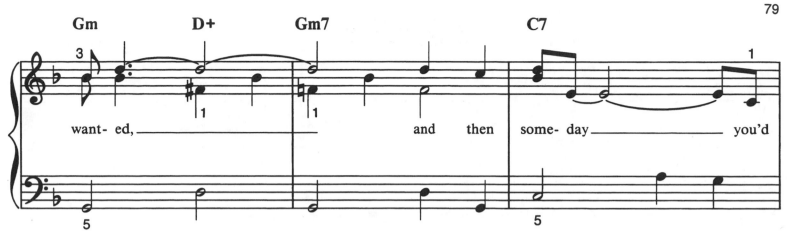

want- ed, _____ and then some- day _____ you'd

leave me for some - bod - y new. _____

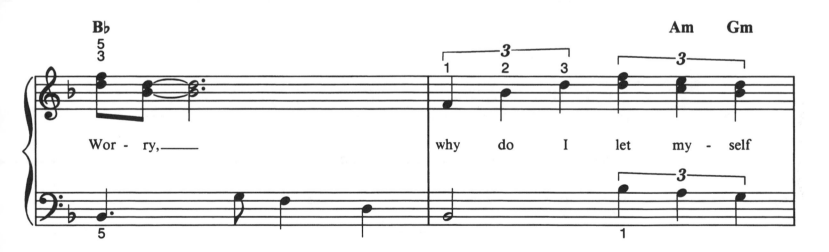

Wor - ry, _____ why do I let my - self

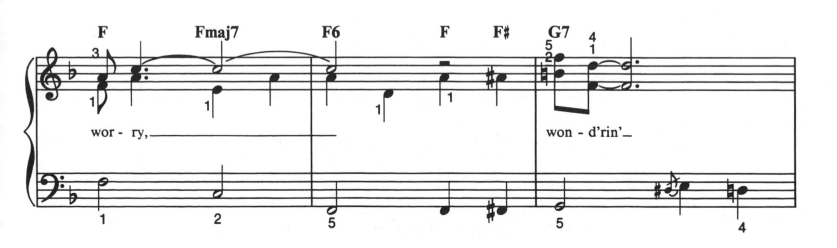

wor - ry, _____ won - d'rin' _

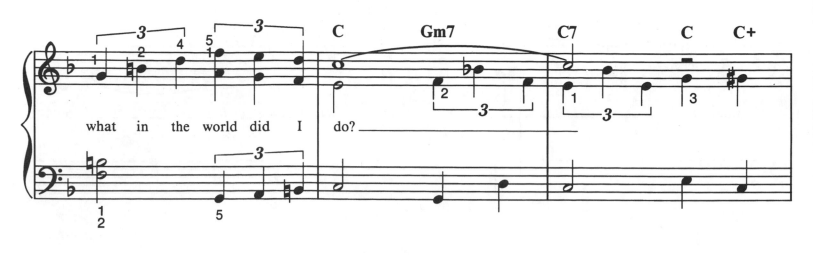

what in the world did I do?

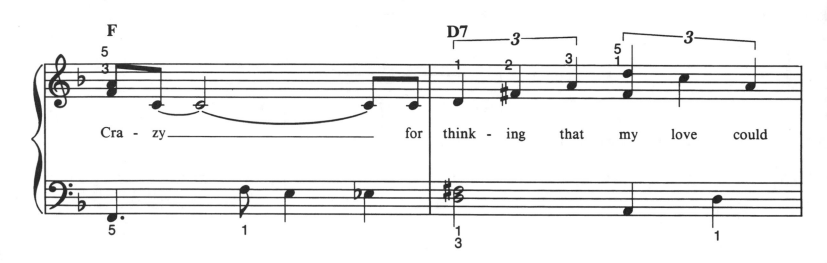

Cra - zy for think - ing that my love could

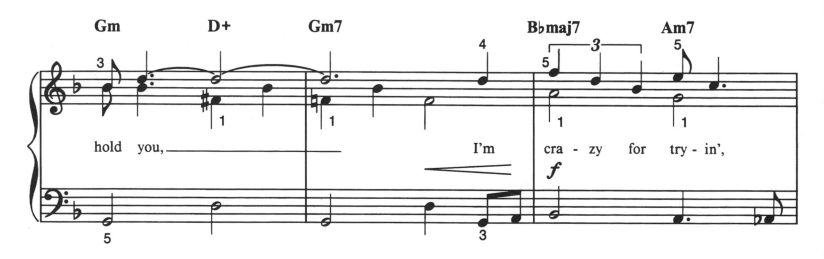

hold you, I'm cra - zy for try - in',

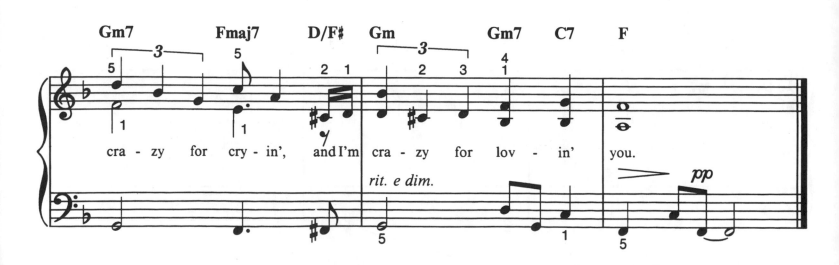

cra - zy for cry - in', and I'm cra - zy for lov - in' you.

rit. e dim.

(Sittin' On)
THE DOCK OF THE BAY

Words and Music by STEVE CROPPER
and OTIS REDDING

_____ roll _ a - way. _ Ooh, I'm just sit - tin' on the dock of the bay,

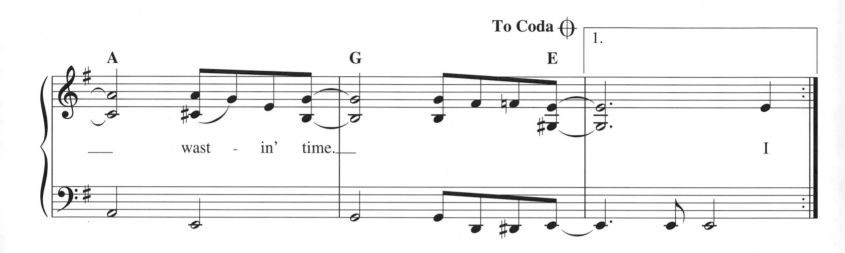

_ wast - in' time. _

1.
I

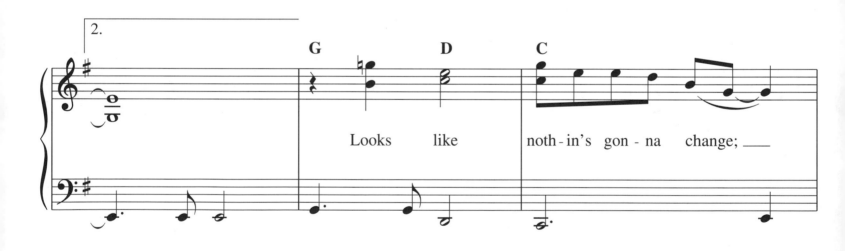

2.

Looks like noth - in's gon - na change; ___

ev - 'ry-thing still re-mains the same. ___ I can't do what

D.S. al Coda

ten peo-ple tell me to do, so I guess I'll re - main _ the same. _

CODA

(whistle)

A DAY IN THE LIFE

Words and Music by JOHN LENNON
and PAUL McCARTNEY

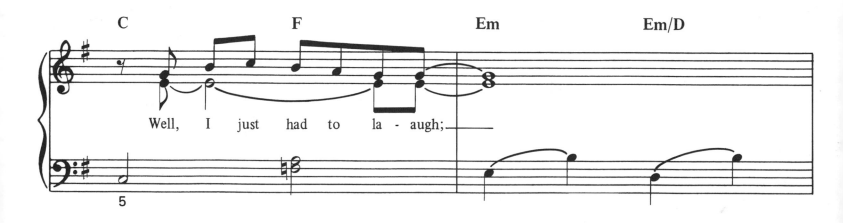

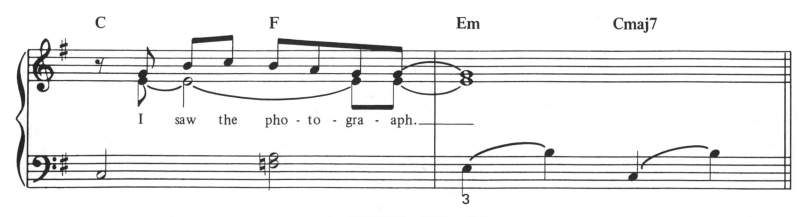

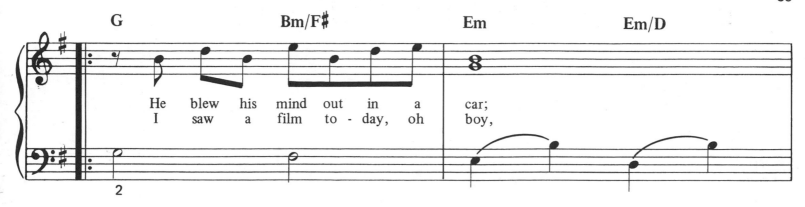

He blew his mind out in a car;
I saw a film to-day, oh boy,

He did-n't no-tice that the lights had changed.
The Eng-lish Ar-my had just won the war.

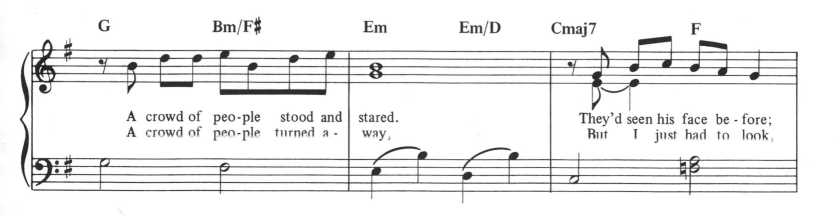

A crowd of peo-ple stood and stared.
A crowd of peo-ple turned a-way,

They'd seen his face be-fore;
But I just had to look,

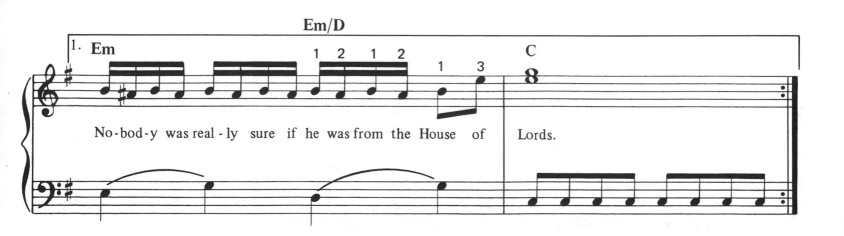

No-bod-y was real-ly sure if he was from the House of Lords.

Hav-ing read the book, I'd love to turn

you _____ on. _____

Twice as fast (♪=♩)

Woke up, got out of bed; Dragged a comb a-cross my

head. Found my way down stairs and

87

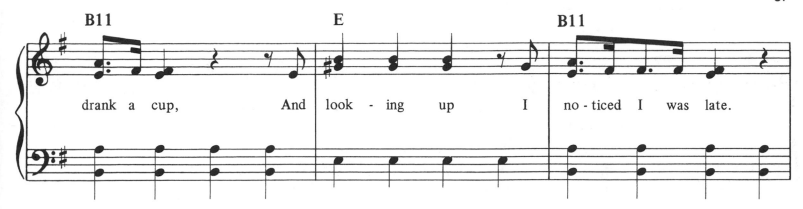

drank a cup, And look - ing up I no - ticed I was late.

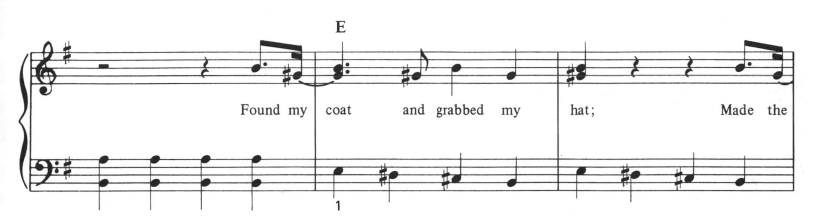

Found my coat and grabbed my hat; Made the

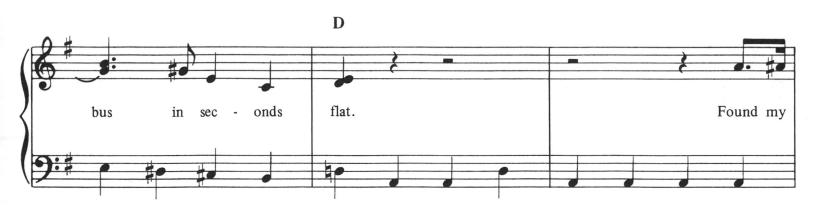

bus in sec - onds flat. Found my

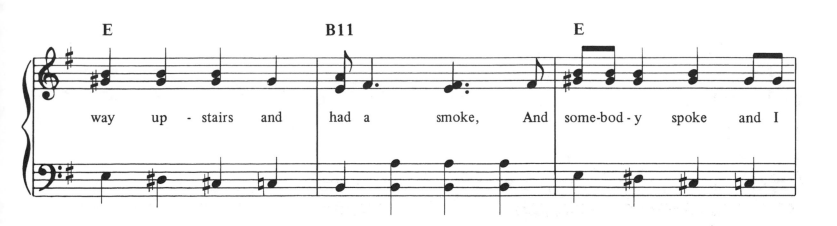

way up - stairs and had a smoke, And some-bod - y spoke and I

88

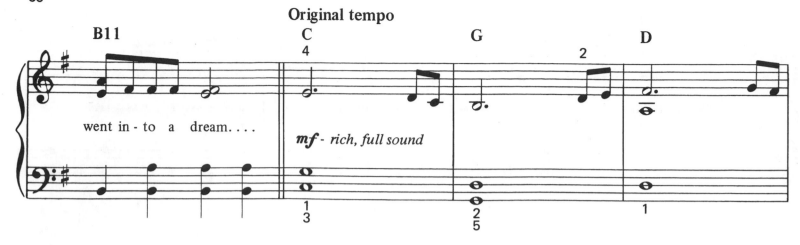

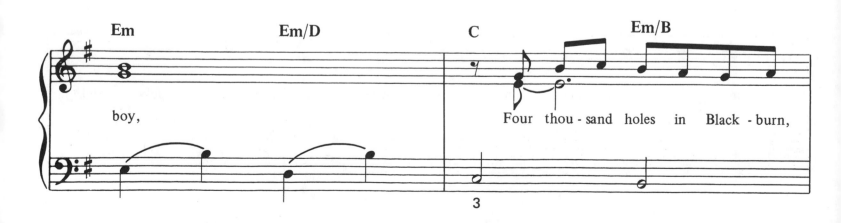

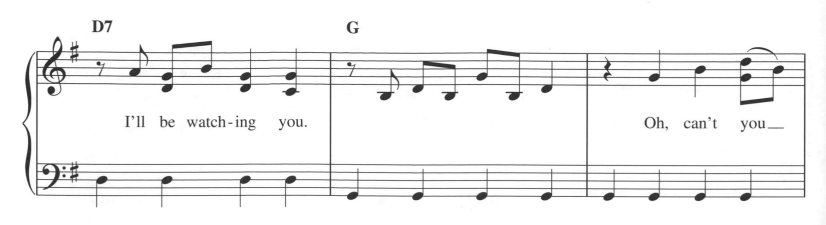

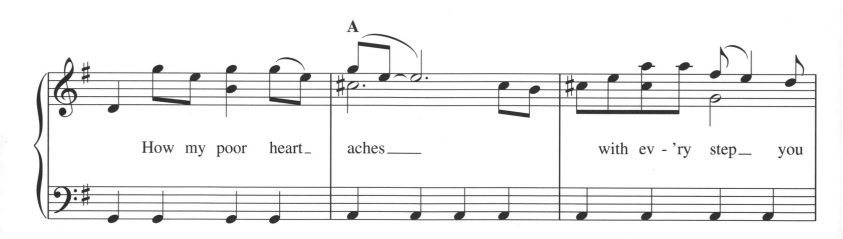

102

you I can't_ re-place, I feel so cold and I long for your_ em-brace.

I keep cry - ing ba - by, ba - by, please.

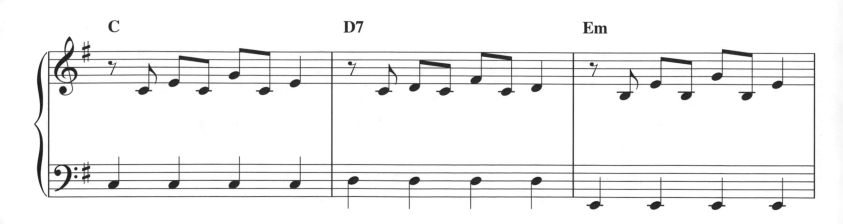

103

FIRE AND RAIN

Words and Music by
JAMES TAYLOR

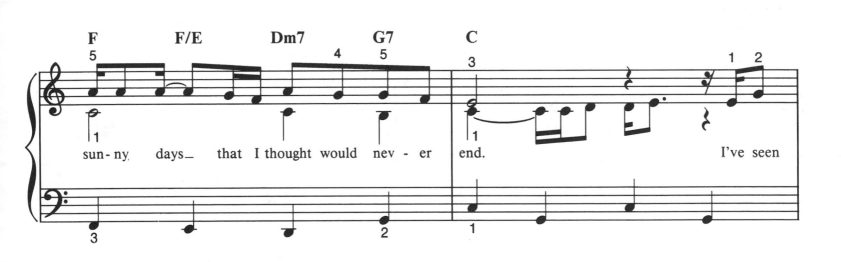

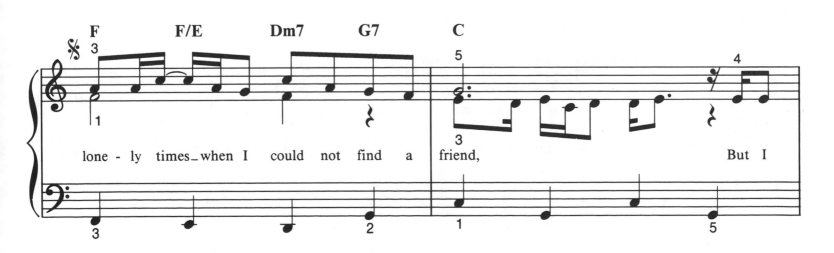

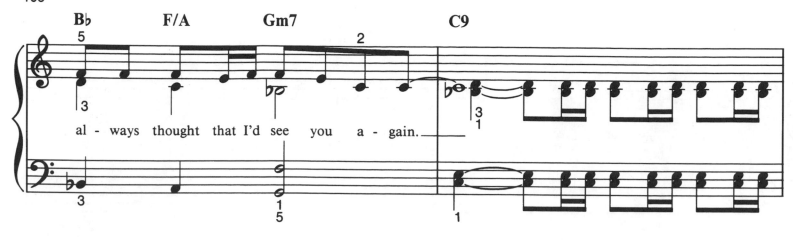

Bb   **F/A**   **Gm7**   **C9**

al - ways thought that I'd see you a - gain.

1.,2.   **2nd time to Verse 3**   **Bb/D C**   **Fine**

2. Won't you
3. Now I'm

Verse 3

C   **Bb/C**   **F/C**   **C**

walk - ing my mind to an eas - y time, my back turned towards the sun.

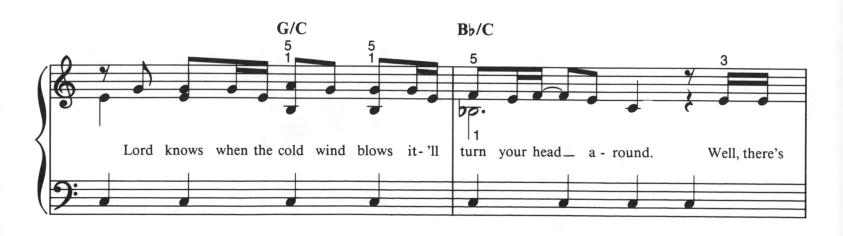

G/C   **Bb/C**

Lord knows when the cold wind blows it - 'll turn your head a - round. Well, there's

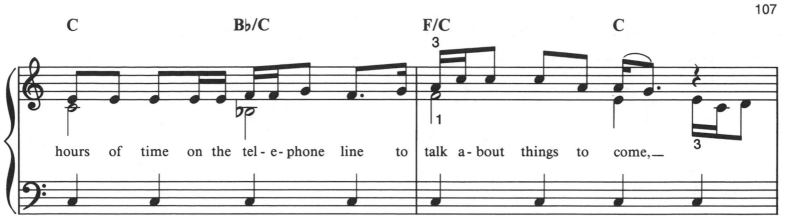

hours of time on the tel - e - phone line to talk a - bout things to come,—

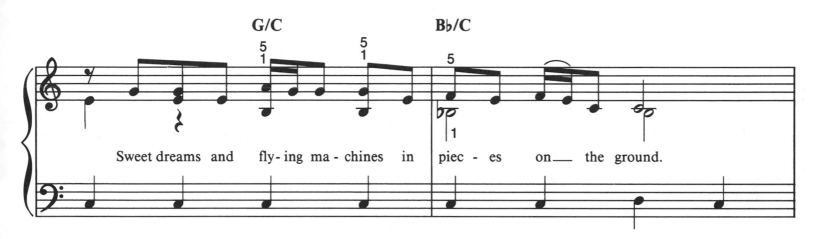

Sweet dreams and fly - ing ma - chines in piec - es on—— the ground.

Chorus

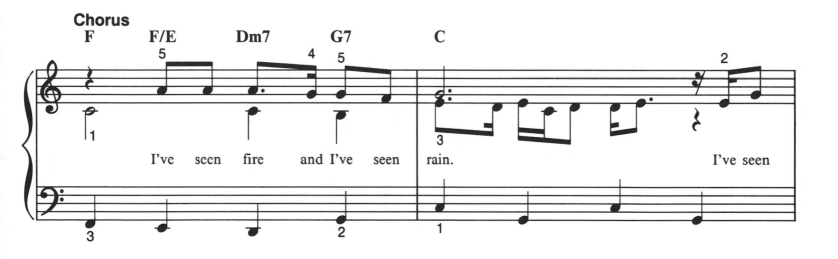

I've seen fire and I've seen rain. I've seen

D.S. al Fine

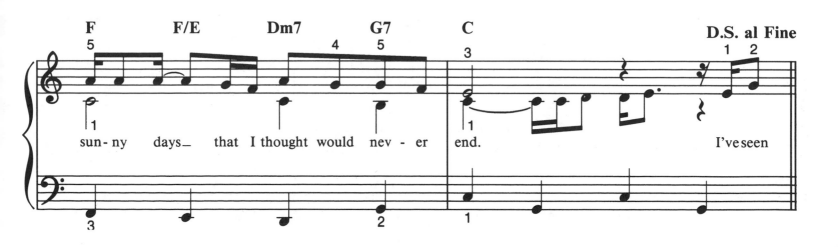

sun - ny days— that I thought would nev - er end. I've seen

FOR WHAT IT'S WORTH

Words and Music by
STEPHEN STILLS

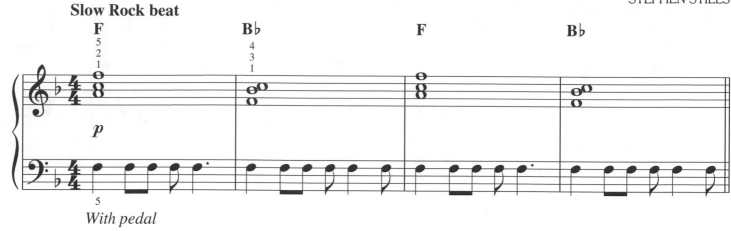

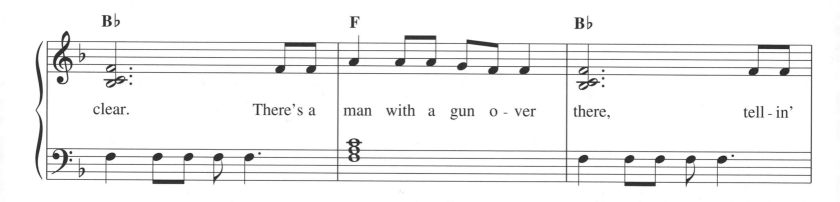

Ev-'ry-bod-y look what's go-in' down.

There's bat-tle lines   be-in'
What a field day for the
Pa - ra - noi - a strikes_

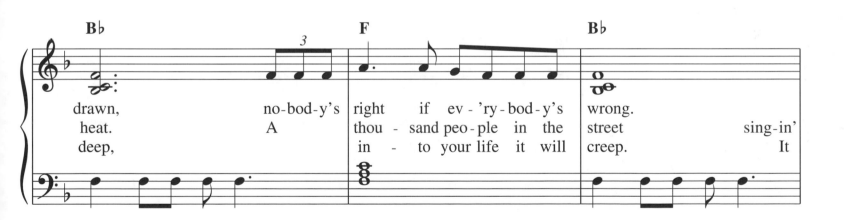

drawn,   no-bod-y's   right   if   ev-'ry-bod-y's   wrong.
heat.   A   thou - sand peo-ple in the   street   sing-in'
deep,   in - to your life it will   creep.   It

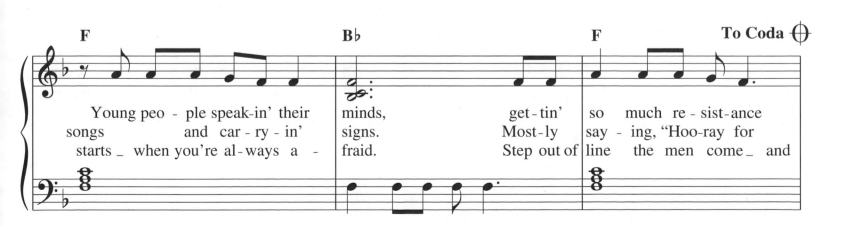

To Coda

Young peo - ple speak-in' their   minds,   get-tin'   so   much re-sist-ance
songs   and car-ry - in'   signs.   Most-ly   say - ing, "Hoo-ray for
starts _ when you're al-ways a -   fraid.   Step out of line   the men come_ and

from be - hind. I think it's time we stop, chil - dren, what's that sound? _
our side." Stop, chil - dren, what's that sound? _

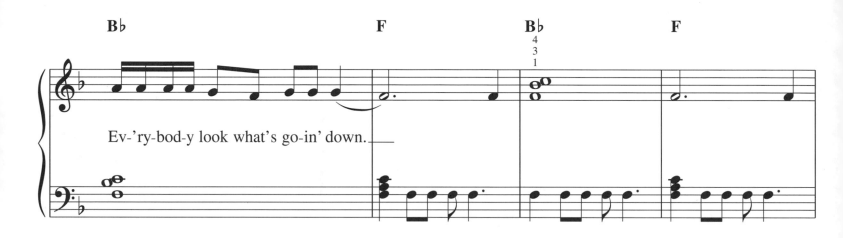

Ev-'ry-bod-y look what's go-in' down. _

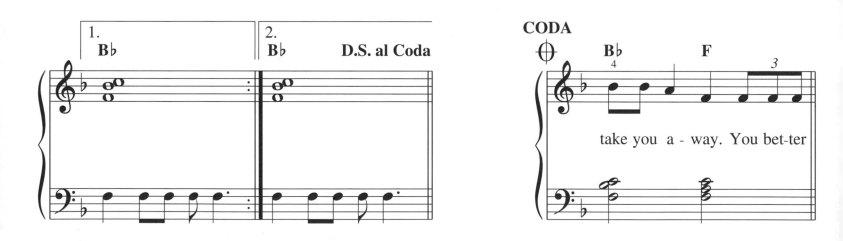

1.
B♭

2.
B♭   D.S. al Coda

CODA
B♭   F

take you a - way. You bet-ter

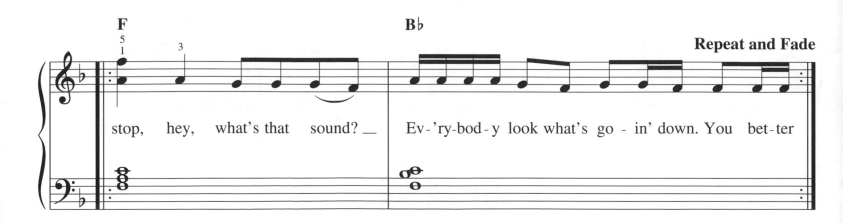

F
stop, hey, what's that sound? _

Repeat and Fade

B♭
Ev-'ry-bod-y look what's go - in' down. You bet-ter

GOOD VIBRATIONS

Words and Music by BRIAN WILSON
and MIKE LOVE

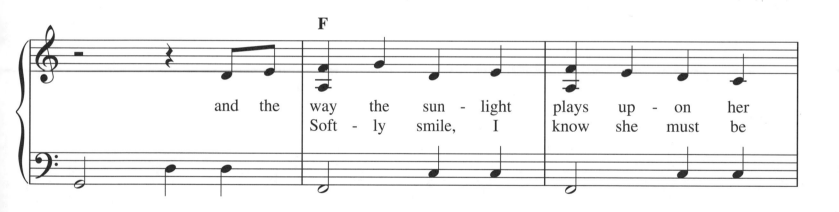

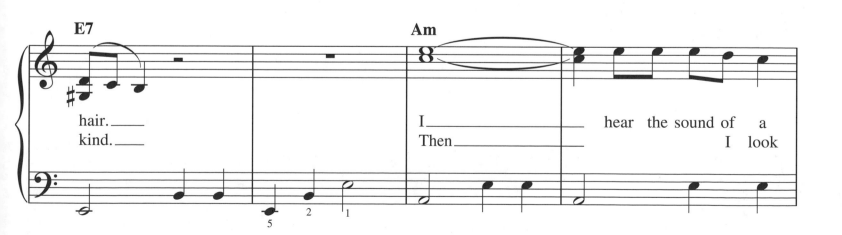

G **F**

gen - tle word,_____ on the wind that lifts her

in her eyes,_____ she goes with me to a

E7 **G7**

per - fume through the air._____

blos - som___ world.___

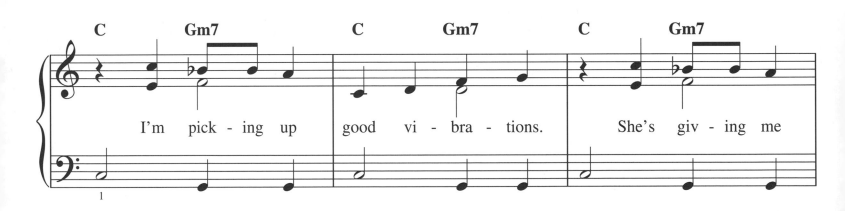

C **Gm7** **C** **Gm7** **C** **Gm7**

I'm pick - ing up good vi - bra - tions. She's giv - ing me

C **Gm7** **C** **Gm7** **C** **Gm7**

ex - ci - ta - tions. I'm pick - ing up good vi - bra - tions.

113

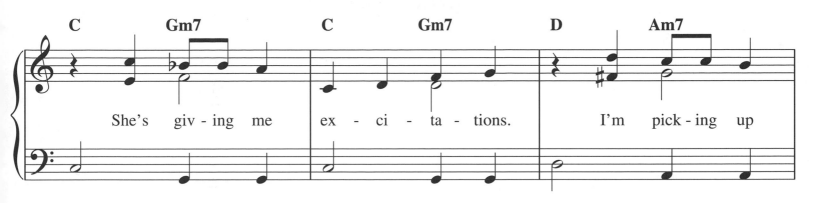

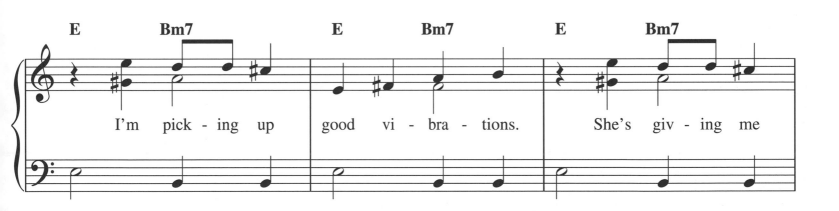

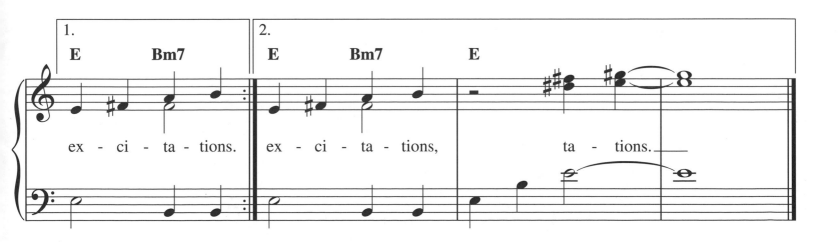

FREE BIRD

Words and Music by ALLEN COLLINS
and RONNIE VAN ZANT

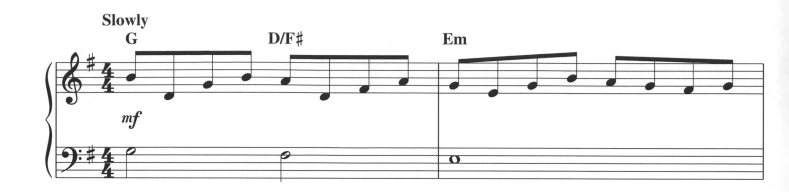

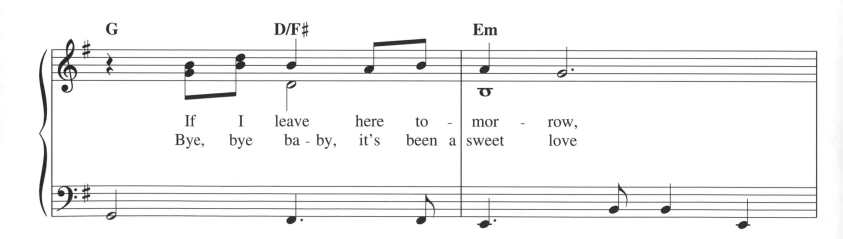

If I leave here to-mor-row,
Bye, bye ba-by, it's been a sweet love

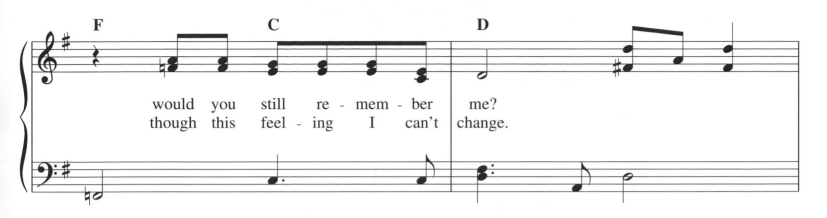

would you still re - mem - ber me?
though this feel - ing I can't change.

For I must be ____ trav - 'ling on now
But please don't take ____ it so bad - ly

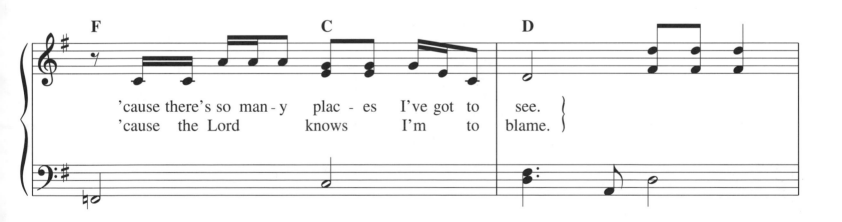

'cause there's so man - y plac - es I've got to see.
'cause the Lord knows I'm to blame.

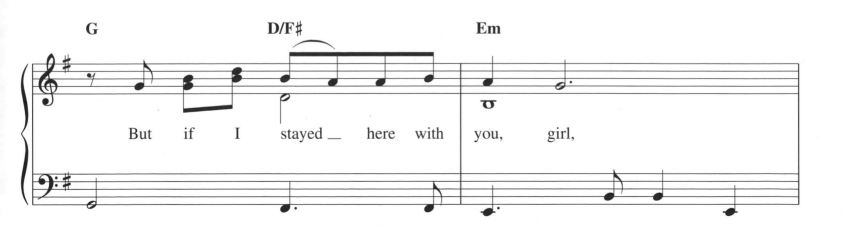

But if I stayed __ here with you, girl,

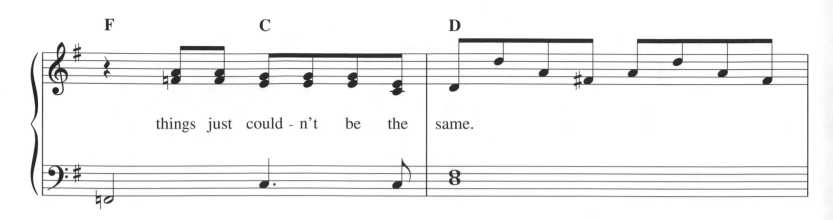

things just could-n't be the same.

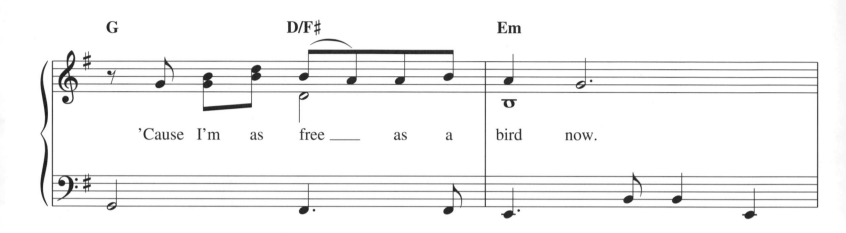

'Cause I'm as free ___ as a bird now.

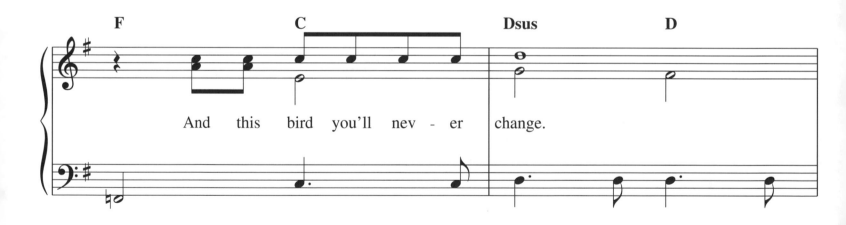

And this bird you'll nev - er change.

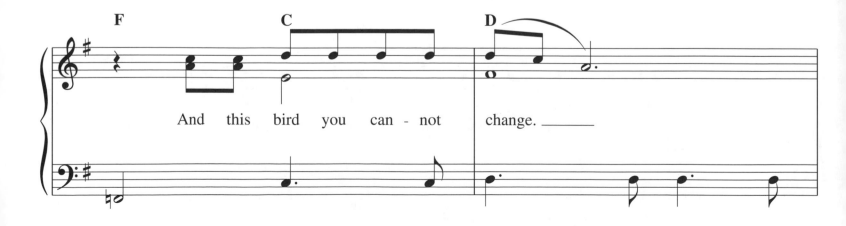

And this bird you can - not change. ___

GIMME SOME LOVIN'

Words and Music by STEVE WINWOOD,
MUFF WINWOOD and SPENCER DAVIS

Moderately bright

Well, my

tem - p'ra - ture's ris - ing and my
feel so good; __ ev - 'ry -
feel so good; __ ev - 'ry -

feet on the floor.
thing is sound - ing hot.
bod - y's get - tin' high.

Twen - ty peo - ple knock - in' 'cause they're
Bet - ter take it eas - y, 'cause the
Bet - ter take it eas - y, 'cause the

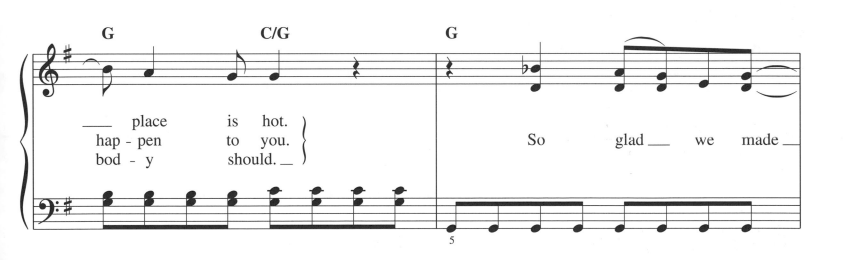

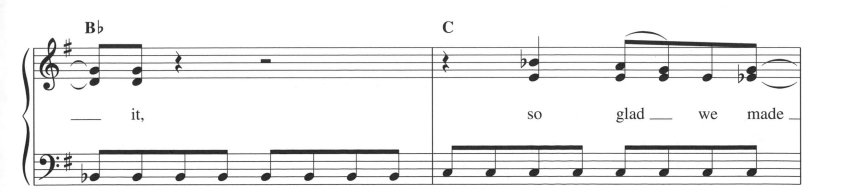

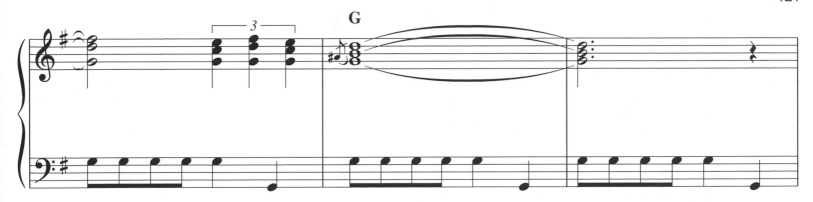

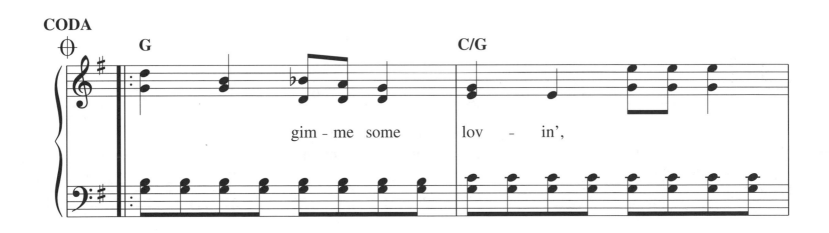

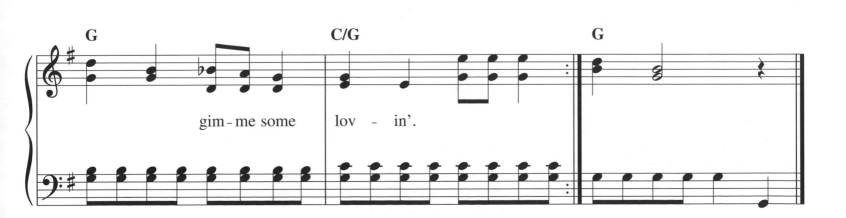

GLORIA

Words and Music by
VAN MORRISON

Steady rock beat

Like to tell you 'bout my ba - by.
here,

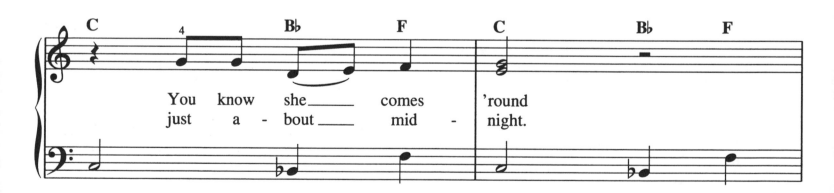

You know she_____ comes 'round
just a - bout_____ mid - night.

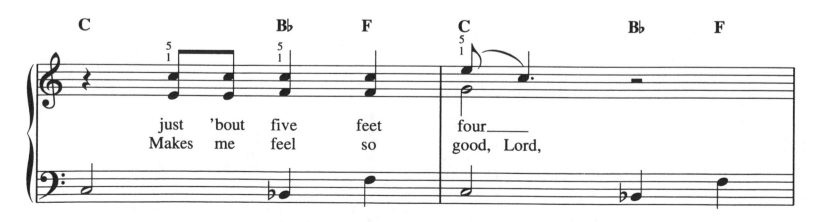

just 'bout five feet four_____
Makes me feel so good, Lord,

123

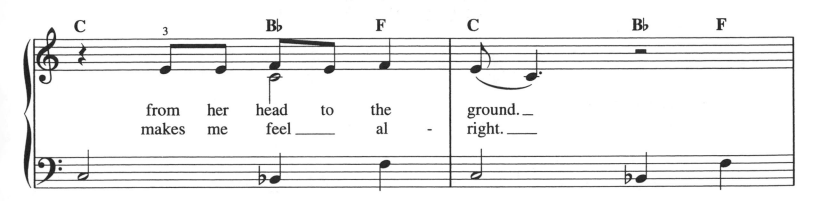

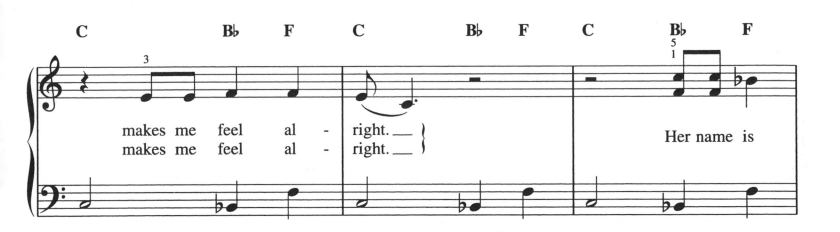

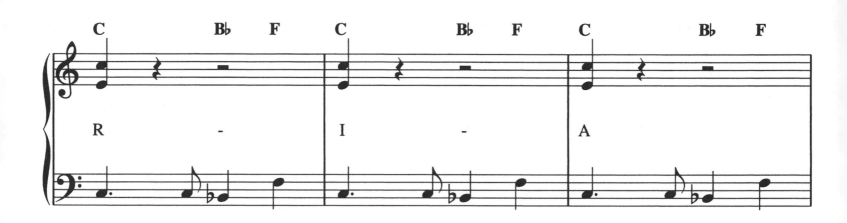

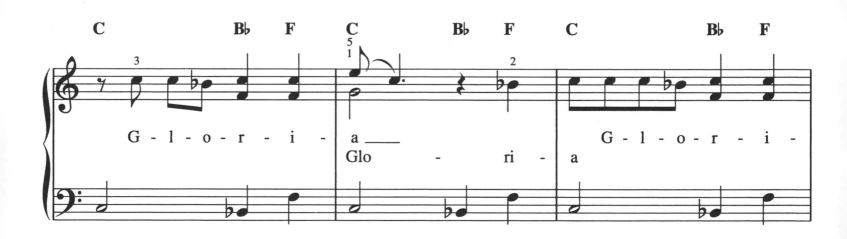

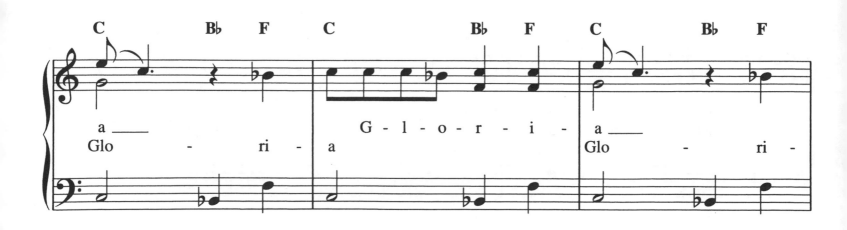

125

Al - right one time. __
a
Glo - ri - a

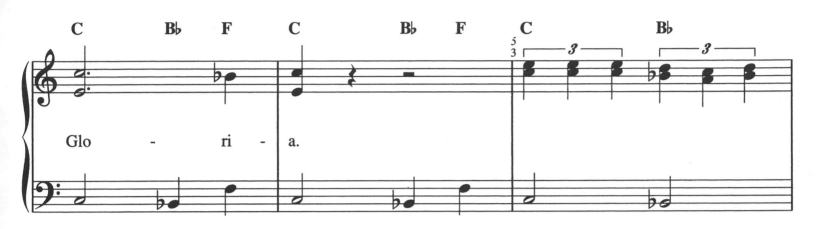

Glo - ri - a.

1.

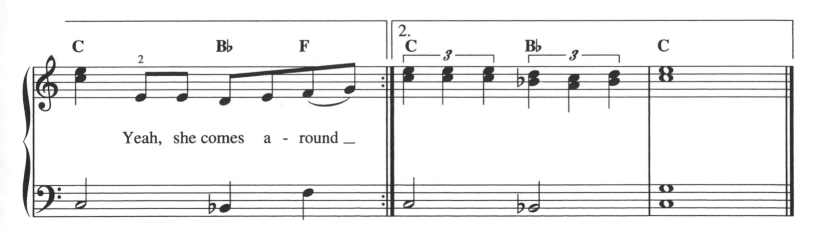

Yeah, she comes a - round __

2.

GOD ONLY KNOWS

Words and Music by BRIAN WILSON
and TONY ASHER

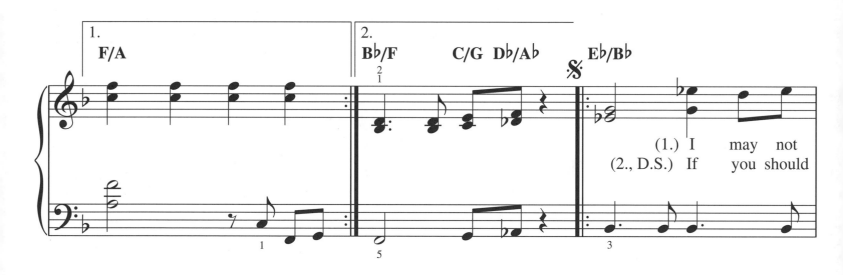

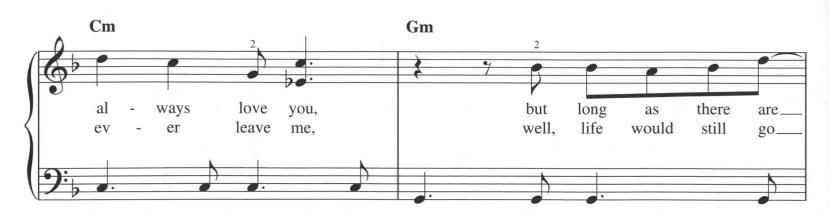

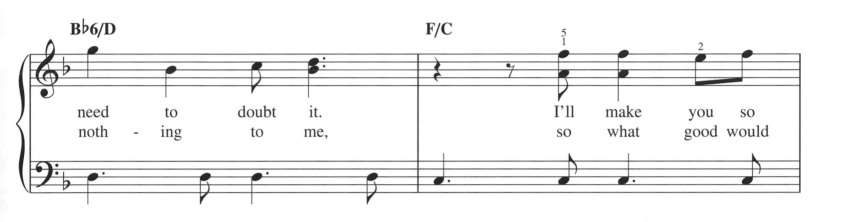

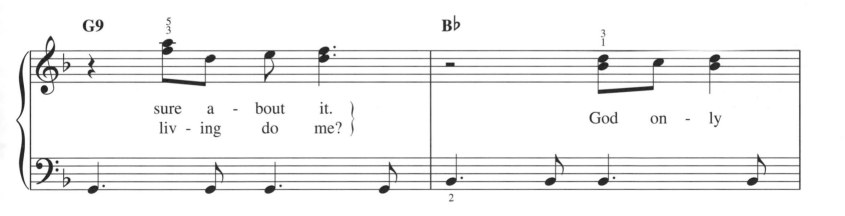

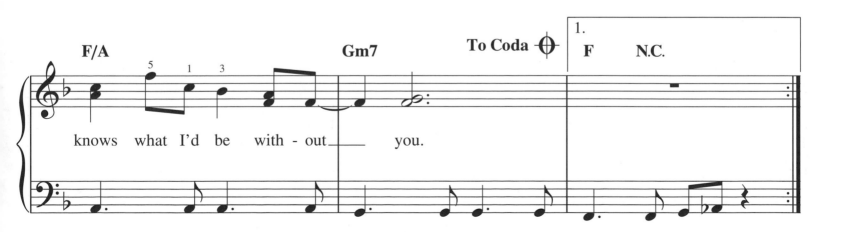

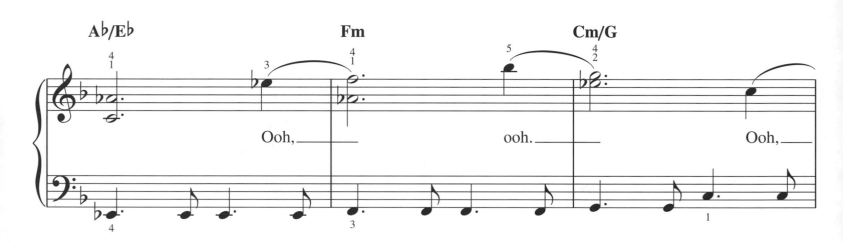

Ooh,_____ ooh._____ Ooh,

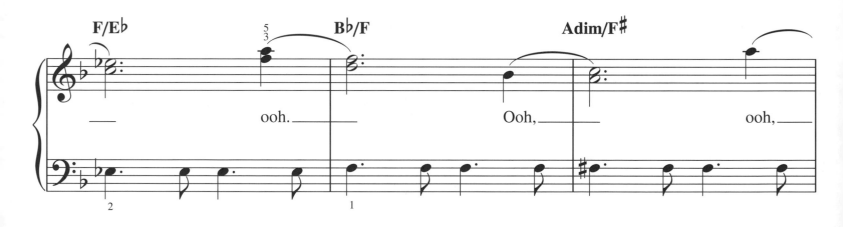

_____ ooh._____ Ooh,_____ ooh,

_____ ooh._____ And God on - ly knows___

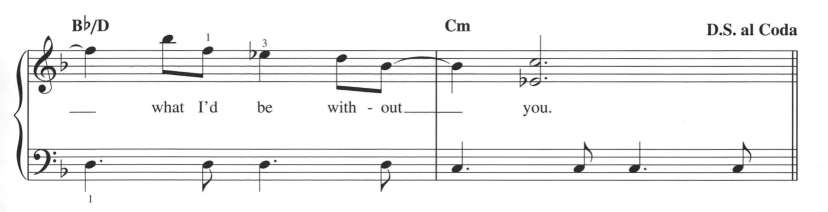

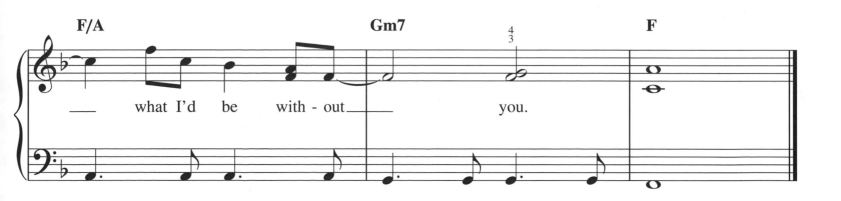

GOOD GOLLY MISS MOLLY

Words and Music by ROBERT BLACKWELL
and JOHN MARSCALCO

Good gol - ly Miss

Mol - ly,   yeah, you sure___ like a

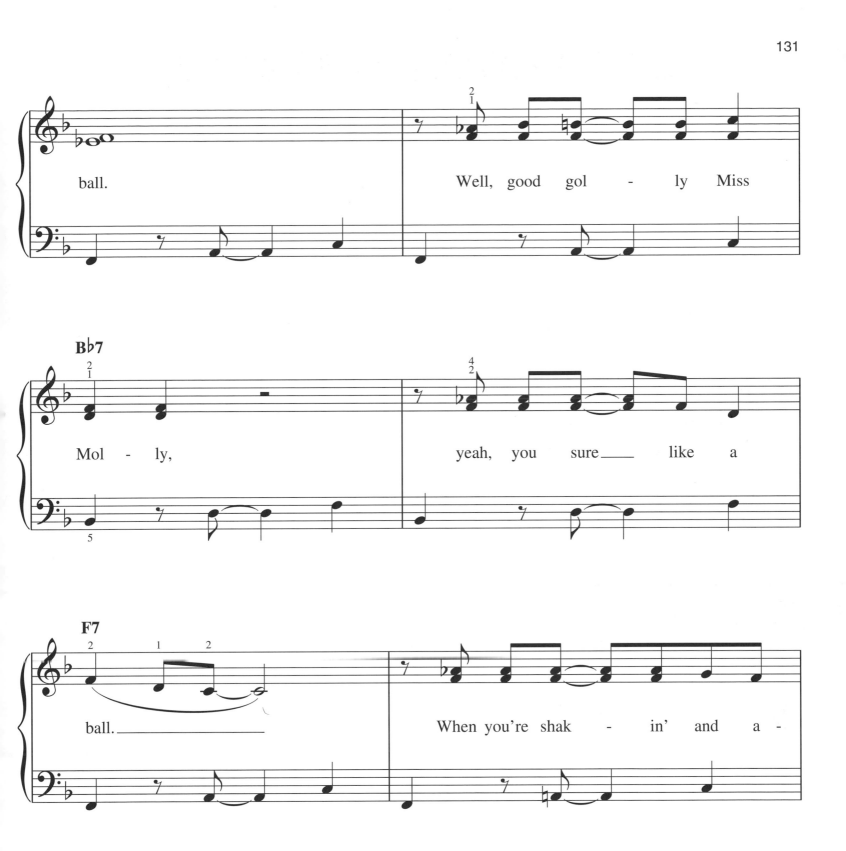

ball.

Well, good gol - ly Miss

B♭7

Mol - ly,

yeah, you sure___ like a

F7

ball.___

When you're shak - in' and a -

C7

shout - in',

B♭7

can't you hear___ your mom - ma

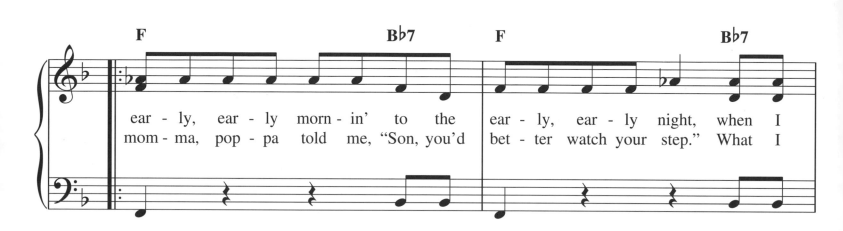

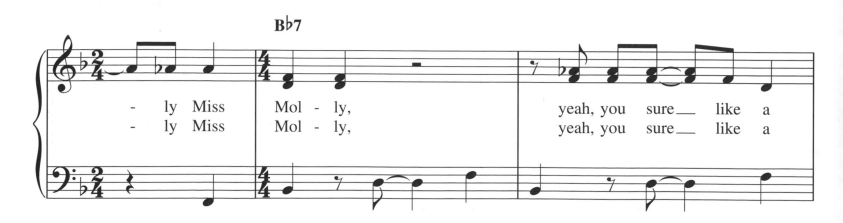

GREAT BALLS OF FIRE

Words and Music by OTIS BLACKWELL
and JACK HAMMER

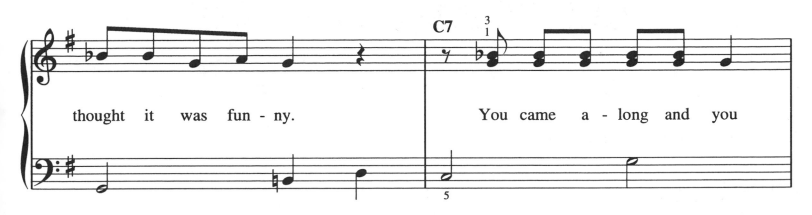

thought it was fun - ny.   You came a - long and you

moved me, hon-ey.   I changed my mind,   love's just fine.

Good - ness gra - cious,   great balls of fire!
(Instrumental ends)   Kiss me, ba - by,

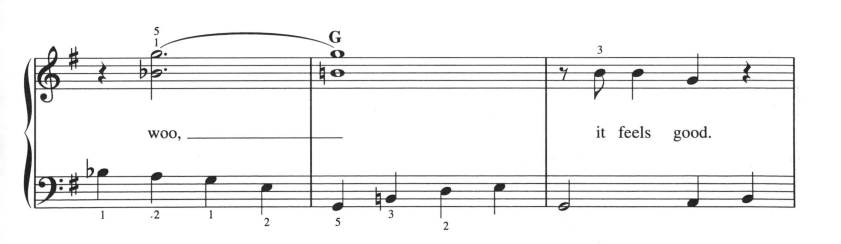

woo, _____   it feels good.

C7   **D**

Hold me ba - by.

Girl, just let me love you like a
I want to love you like a

lov - er should.
lov - er should.

You're fine, ___

so kind, ___

I'm gon-na tell the world that you're

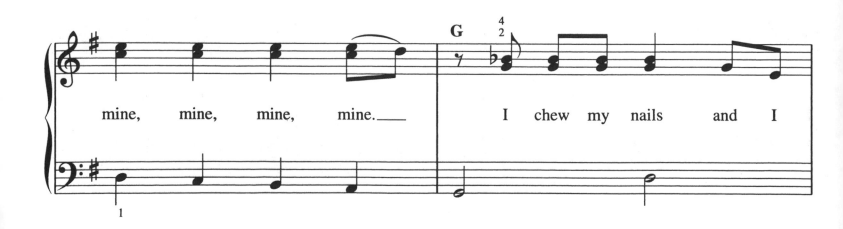

mine, mine, mine, mine. ___

G

I chew my nails and I

twid - dle my thumb. ___   I'm real ner - vous but it

sure is fun. ___   Come on, ba - by, you're

driv-ing me cra - zy.   Good - ness gra - cious,   great balls of fire!

Good - ness gra - cious,   great balls of fire!

A HARD DAY'S NIGHT

Words and Music by JOHN LENNON
and PAUL McCARTNEY

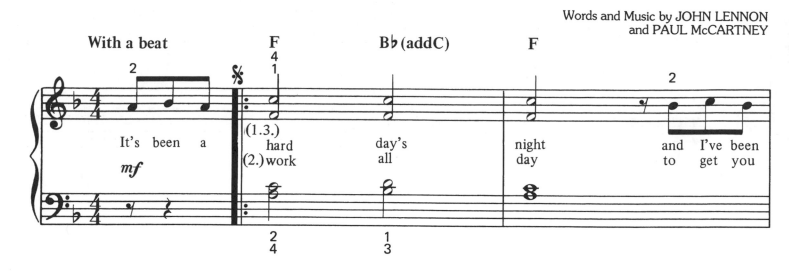

It's been a
hard (1.3.) day's night
work (2.) all day
and I've been
to get you

work-ing like a dog. It's been a hard day's
mon-ey to buy you things. And it's worth it just to hear you

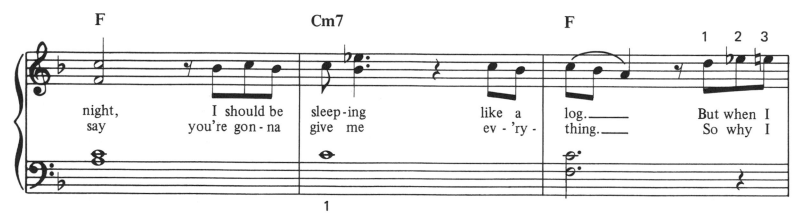

night, I should be sleep-ing like a log. But when I
say you're gon-na give me ev-'ry-thing. So why I

get home to you____ I find the thing that you do____ will make me
love to come home____ 'cause when I get you a-lone____ you know I'll

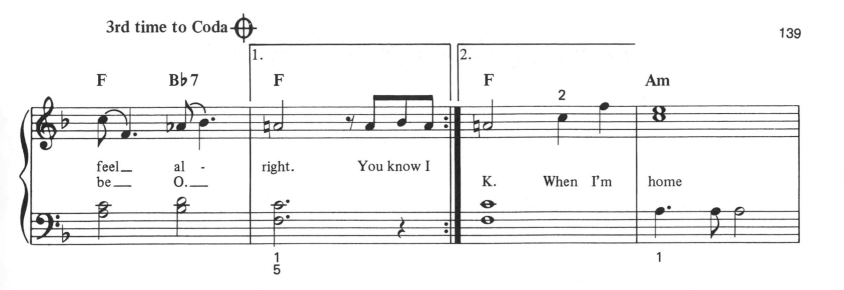

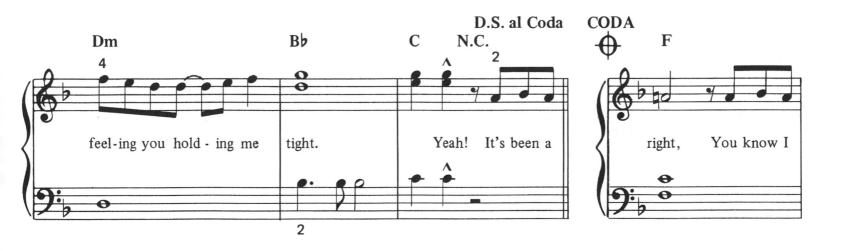

HEARTBREAK HOTEL

Words and Music by MAE BOREN AXTON,
TOMMY DURDEN and ELVIS PRESLEY

Steady Blues beat

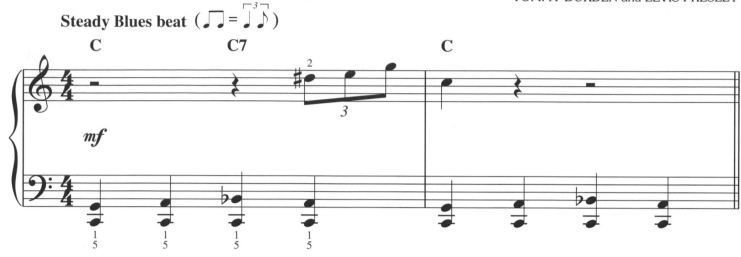

Since my ba-by left me, I found a new place to dwell. Well, it's

if your ba-by leaves ya, and you've got a tale to tell, well, just

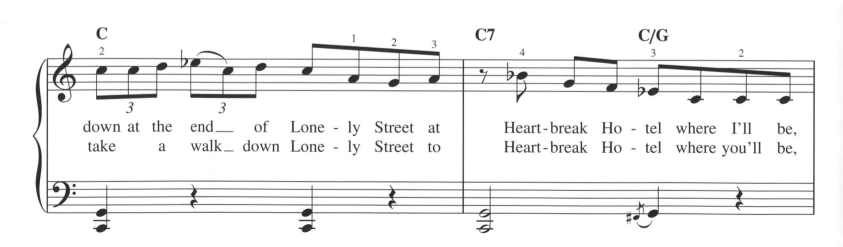

down at the end___ of Lone-ly Street at Heart-break Ho-tel where I'll be,

take a walk___ down Lone-ly Street to Heart-break Ho-tel where you'll be,

HOUND DOG

Words and Music by JERRY LEIBER
and MIKE STOLLER

G7

nev - er caught a rab - bit and you **F7** ain't no friend __ of

C

mine. **N.C.** When they said you was **C7** high - classed,

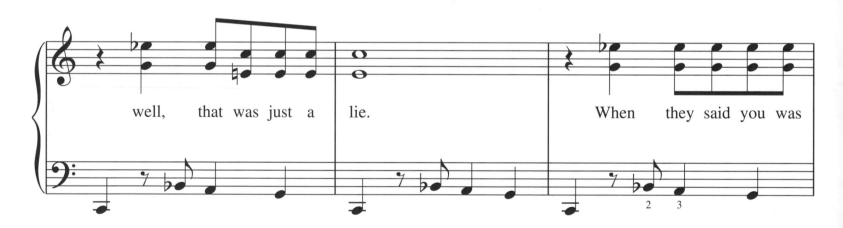

well, that was just a lie. When they said you was

F7

high - classed, well, that was just a

145

HEY JUDE

Words and Music by JOHN LENNON
and PAUL McCARTNEY

Slow and steady

Hey Jude, _____ don't make it bad, take a

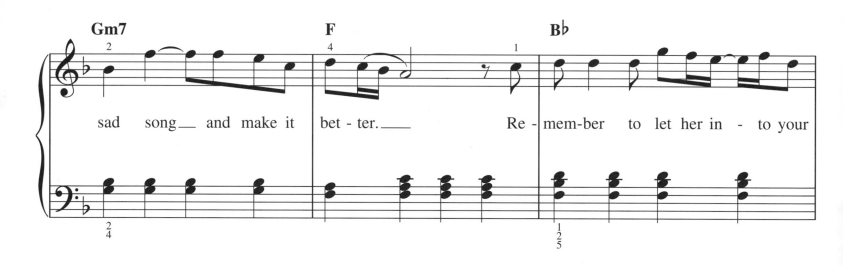

sad song__ and make it bet - ter.__ Re - mem-ber to let her in - to your

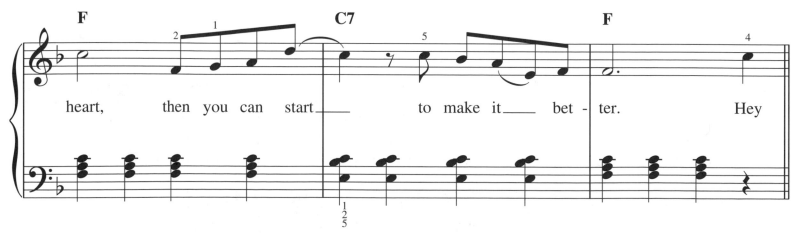

heart, then you can start___ to make it__ bet - ter. Hey

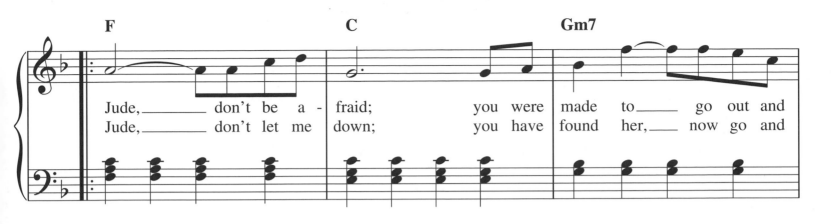

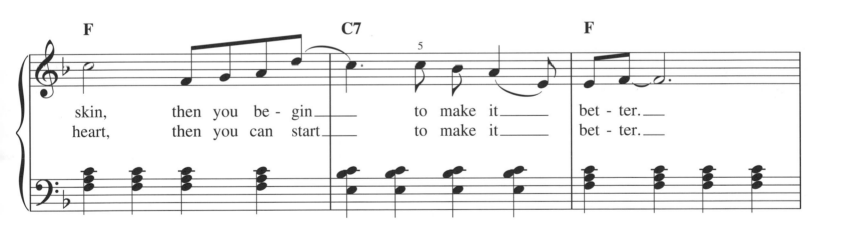

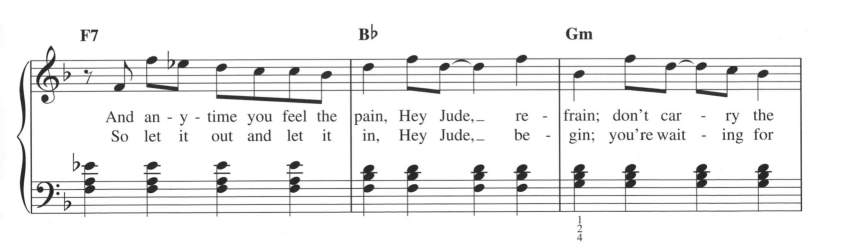

148

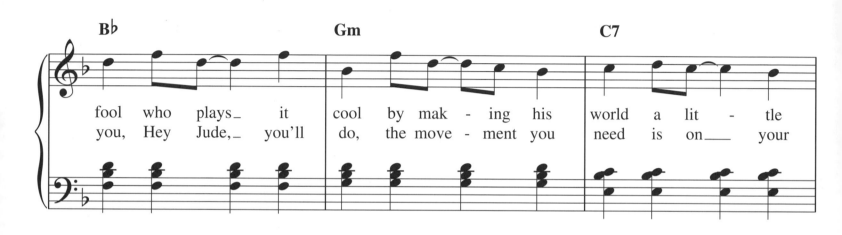

so good,
so nice,

I got ___ you.
I got ___ you.

Woh!

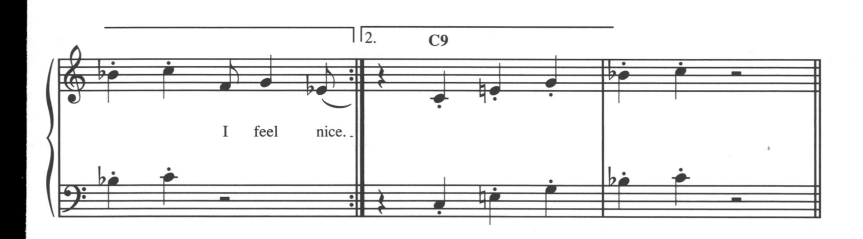

I feel nice.

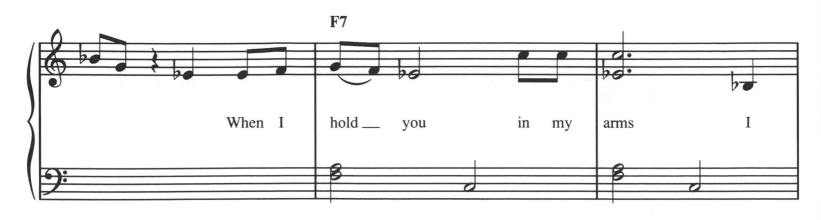

When I hold___ you in my arms I

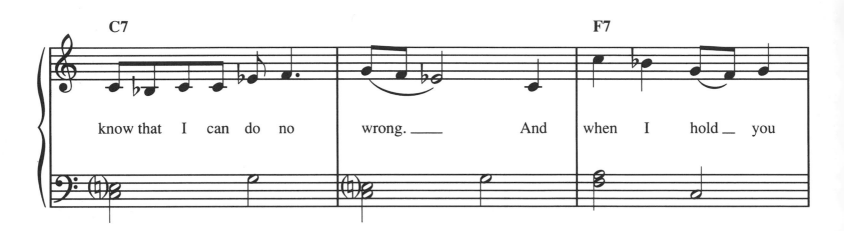

know that I can do no wrong.___ And when I hold___ you

in my arms my love won't do you no harm.___ And I feel___
love can't do me no harm.___

___ nice.___ Ah, sug - ar and spice.

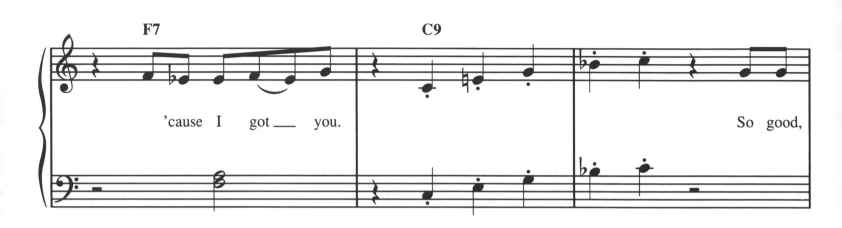

I HEARD IT THROUGH THE GRAPEVINE

Words and Music by NORMAN J. WHITFIELD
and BARRETT STRONG

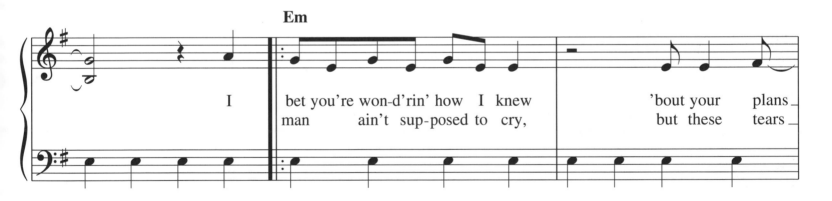

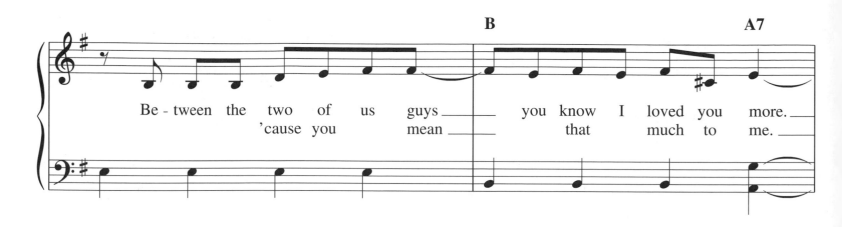

Be - tween the two of us guys _____ you know I loved you more. _____
'cause you mean _____ that much to me. _____

_____ It took me by sur - prise _____ I must say _____ when I
_____ You could have told _____ me your - self _____ that you

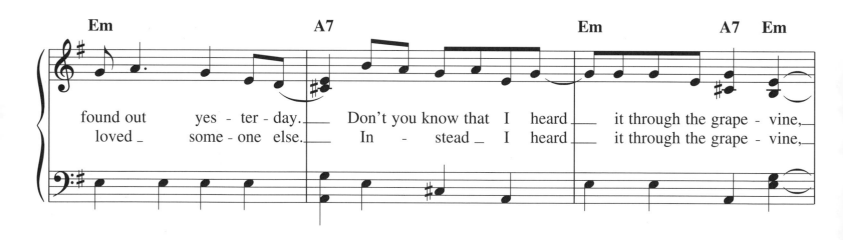

found out yes - ter - day. _____ Don't you know that I heard _____ it through the grape - vine,
loved _ some - one else. _____ In - stead _ I heard _____ it through the grape - vine,

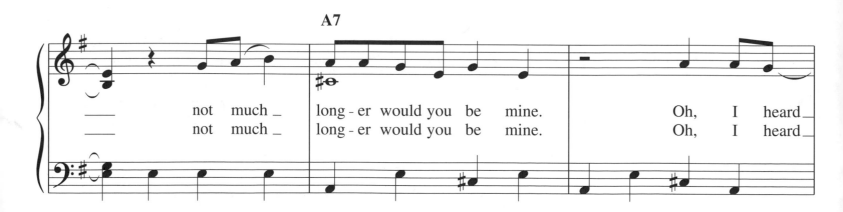

_____ not much _ long - er would you be mine. Oh, I heard _____
_____ not much _ long - er would you be mine. Oh, I heard _____

Em　　　　　**A7**　**Em**　　　　　　　　　　　　**A7**

it through the grape - vine. ____ Oh, I'm just a - bout to lose ___ my
it through the grape - vine. ____ And I'm just a - bout to lose ___ my

Em

mind. } Hon - ey, hon - ey, I heard it through the grape - vine, not much
mind.

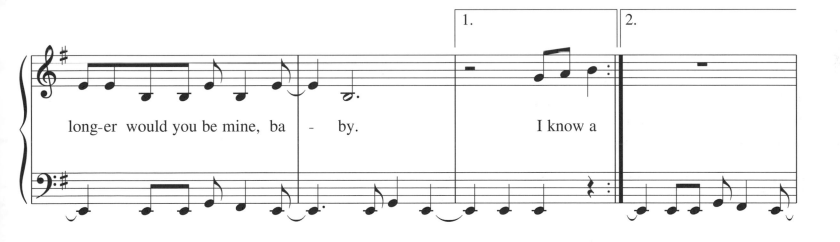

1.　　　　　　　　　2.

long-er would you be mine, ba - by.　　　　　I know a

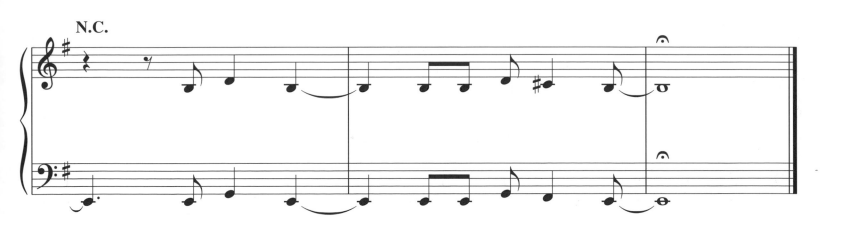

N.C.

I WANT TO HOLD YOUR HAND

Words and Music by JOHN LENNON
and PAUL McCARTNEY

It's such a feel - ing that my love I can't hide, _

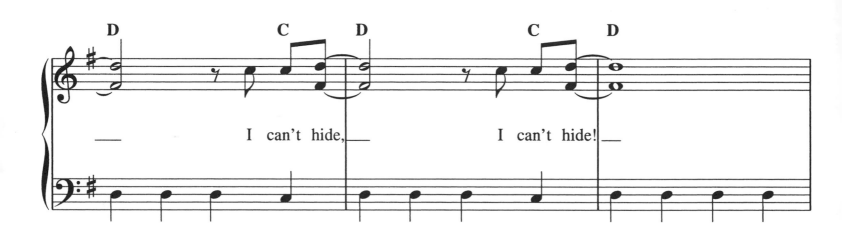

_ I can't hide, __ I can't hide! __

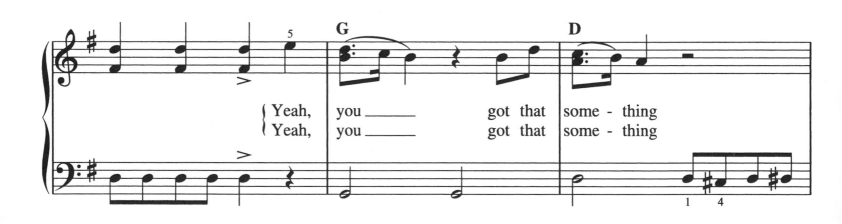

Yeah, you _____ got that some - thing
Yeah, you _____ got that some - thing

I think you'll un - der - stand. When I _____ say that
I think you'll un - der - stand. When I _____ feel that

IMAGINE

Words and Music by
JOHN LENNON

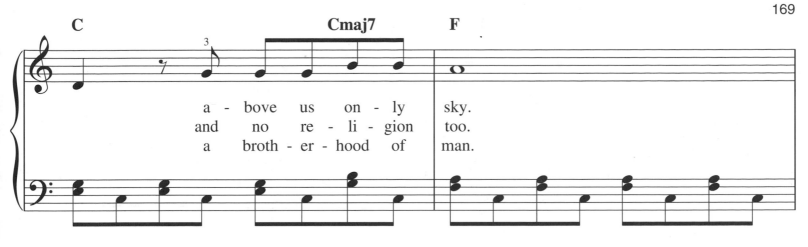

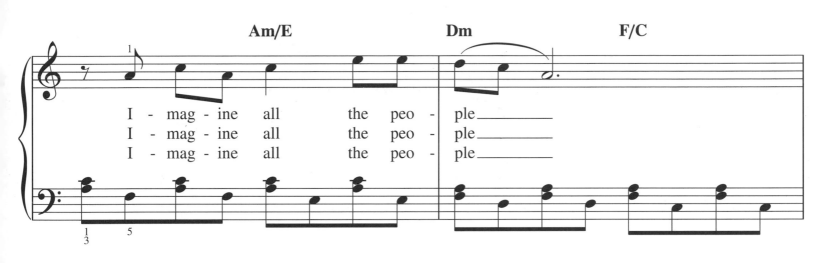

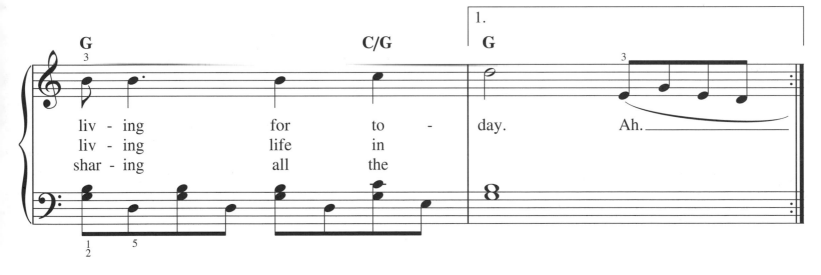

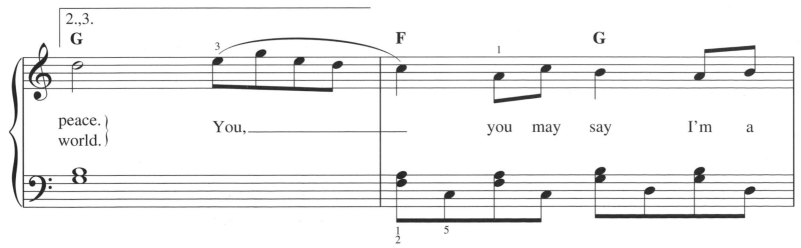

170

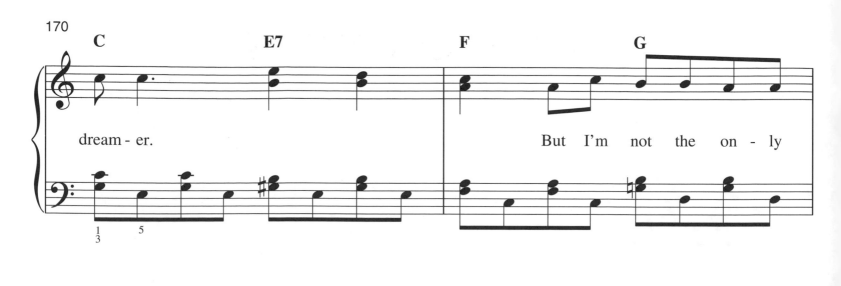

dream - er.   But I'm not the on - ly

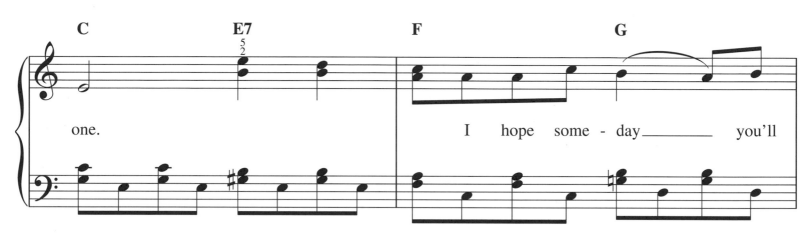

one.   I   hope some - day_____ you'll

To Coda $\oplus$ D.S. al Coda
                                                        (take 2nd ending)

join us___   and the world___ will be as one.

CODA
$\oplus$

rit.   and the world_____ will   be as one.

JAILHOUSE ROCK

Words and Music by JERRY LEIBER
and MIKE STOLLER

Chorus

F7 **N.C.**

should -'ve heard those knocked - out jail - birds sing. ___} Let's
whole ___ rhy - thm sec - tion was the pur - ple gang. ___}

Bb7

rock! Let's

F7

rock! Ev - 'ry -

C7 **C11** **Bb7**

bod - y in the whole cell block ___ was a -

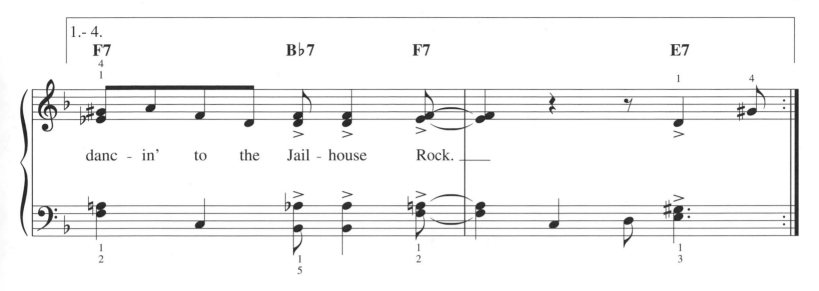

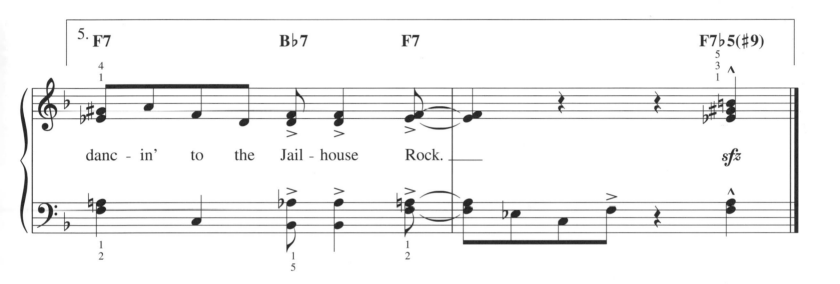

Additional Lyrics

3. Number Forty-seven said to Number Three:
   You're the cutest jailbird I ever did see.
   I sure would be delighted with your company.
   Come on and do the Jailhouse Rock with me.
   To Chorus:

4. The sad sack was a-sittin' on a block of stone,
   Way over in the corner weeping all alone.
   The warden said: Hey, buddy, don't you be no square.
   If you can't find a partner, find a wooden chair!
   To Chorus:

5. Shifty Henry said to Bugs: For heaven's sake.
   No one's lookin'; now's our chance to make a break.
   Bugsy turned to Shifty and said: Nix, nix:
   I wanna stick around a while and get my kicks.
   To Chorus:

IN THE MIDNIGHT HOUR

Words and Music by STEVE CROPPER
and WILSON PICKETT

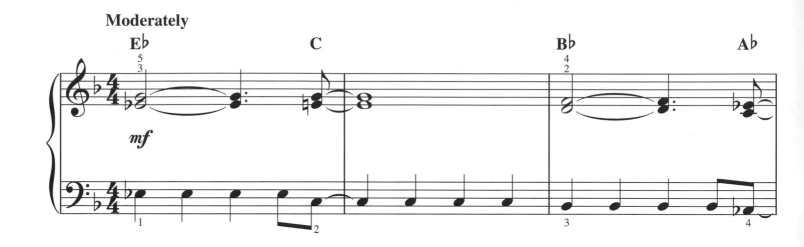

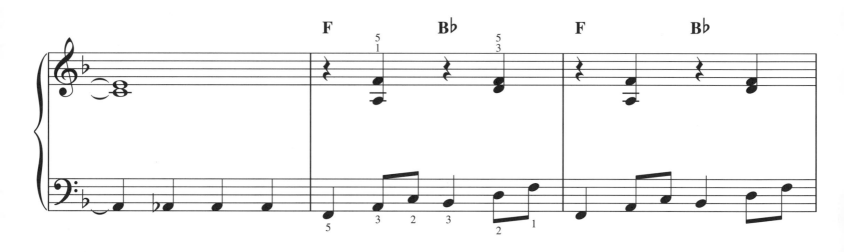

I'm gon - na (1.,3.) wait till the mid - night hour,_
(2.) wait till the stars come out,_

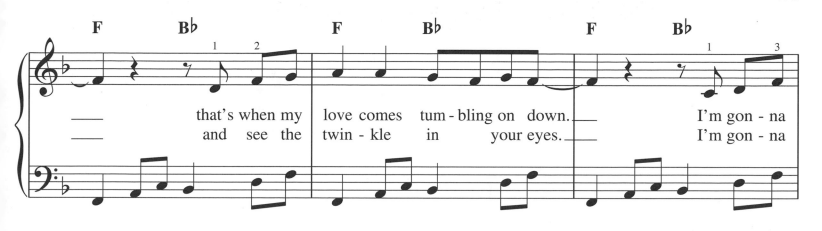

that's when my love comes tum - bling on down.___ I'm gon - na
and see the twin - kle in your eyes.___ I'm gon - na

wait till the mid - night hour,___ when there's no one else__ a - round.__
wait till the mid - night hour,___ that's when my love will be - gin to shine.__

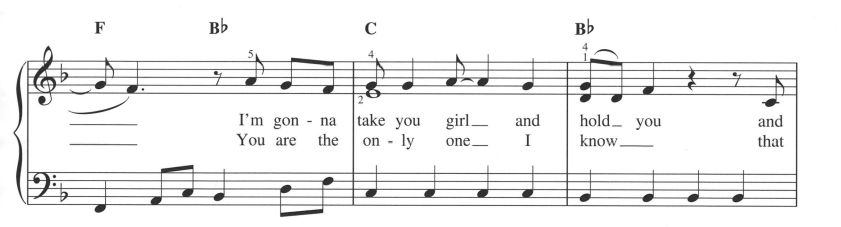

_____ I'm gon - na take you girl__ and hold__ you and
_____ You are the on - ly one__ I know_____ that

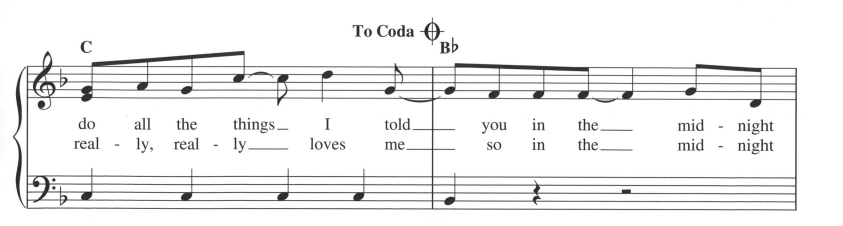

do all the things__ I told___ you in the___ mid - night
real - ly, real - ly___ loves me___ so in the___ mid - night

To Coda

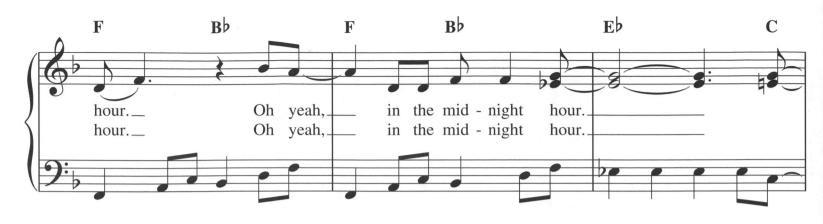

hour.__   Oh   yeah,__   in   the   mid - night   hour.__
hour.__   Oh   yeah,__   in   the   mid - night   hour.__

Gon - na

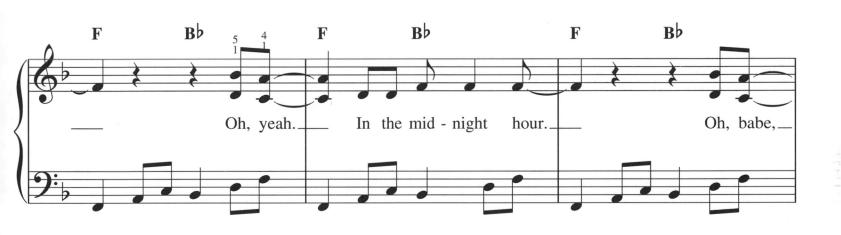

JOHNNY B. GOODE

Words and Music by
CHUCK BERRY

stood an old___ cab-in made of earth and wood,__ where
en-gineer in the train__ sit-tin' in the shade,__

lived a coun-try boy__ named__ John-ny B. Goode.. Who'd
strum-min' with the rhy-thm that the driv-ers made.__ The

nev - er ev - er learned to read or write so well,__ but he could
peo - ple pass - in' by,__ they would stop and say

play a gui-tar__ just like a ring-in' a bell.__ } Go!
oh my, but that lit-tle coun-try boy__ could play.__ }

Go!

Go! John - ny! Go! Go!

Go!

Go! John - ny! Go! Go!

Bb7

Go!

Go! John - ny! Go! Go!

F

Go!

Go! John - ny! Go! Go!

182

LA BAMBA

By RITCHIE VALENS

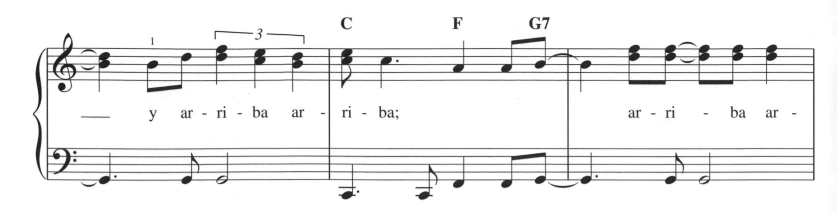

y ar - ri - ba ar - ri - ba;   ar - ri - ba ar -

ri - ba por ti se re____ por ti se re se - re.

Yo no soy mar - i - ne - ro.   Yo no soy mar - i -

ne - ro, soy cap - i - tan;____ yo no soy mar - i - ne - ro, soy cap - i - tan.____

JUMP

Words and Music by DAVID LEE ROTH, EDWARD VAN HALEN,
ALEX VAN HALEN and MICHAEL ANTHONY

Bright Rock

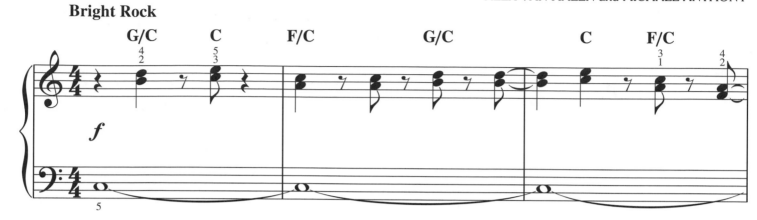

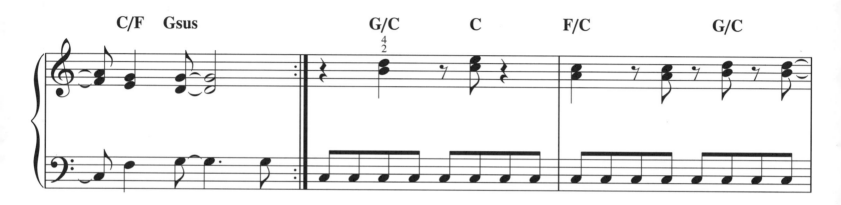

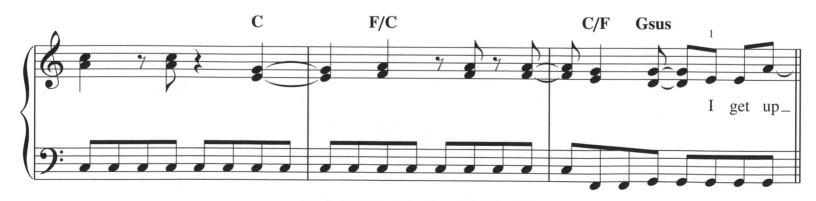

I get up

187

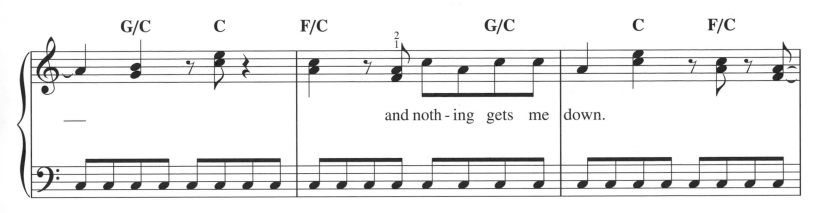

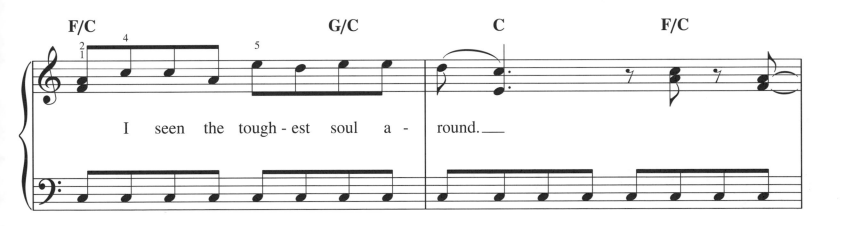

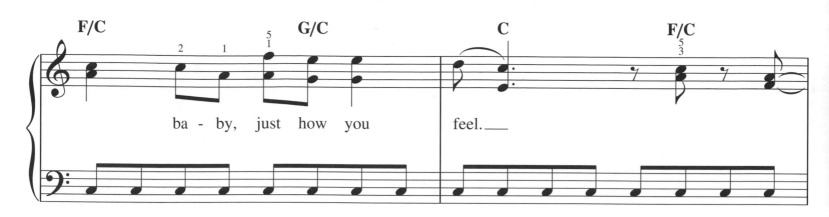

F/C   G/C   C   F/C

ba - by, just how you   feel.___

C/F   Gsus   G/C   C

You got to   roll_____   with the

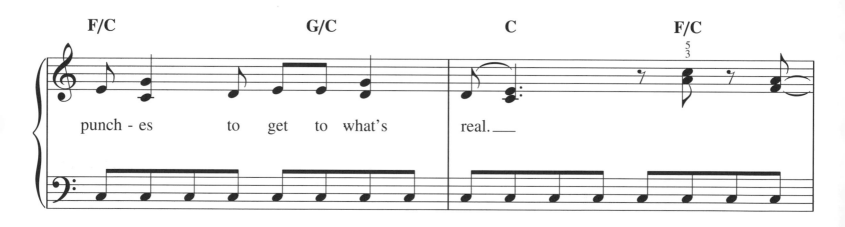

F/C   G/C   C   F/C

punch - es   to get to what's   real.___

C/F   Gsus   Am

Ah, can't you   see me stand - ing here? I got my

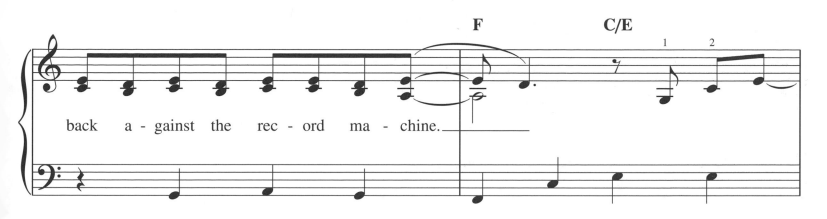

back a-gainst the rec-ord ma-chine.

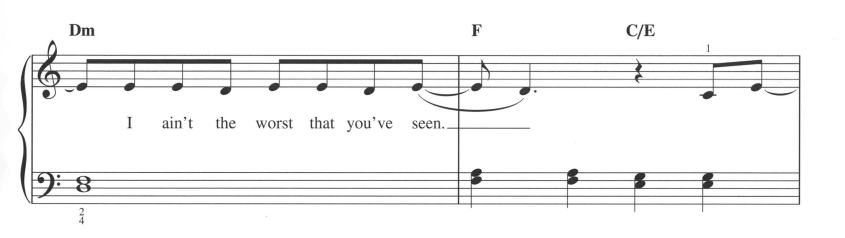

Dm

I ain't the worst that you've seen.

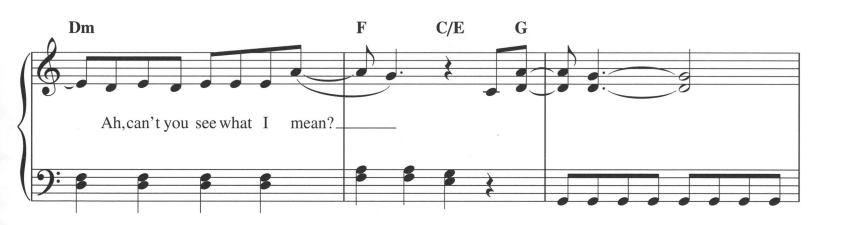

Dm

Ah, can't you see what I mean?

To Coda ⊕

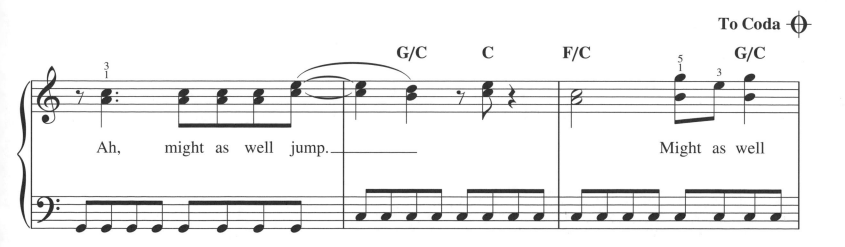

Ah,   might as well jump.

Might as well

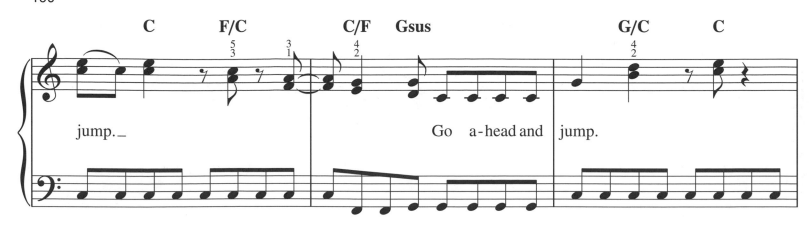

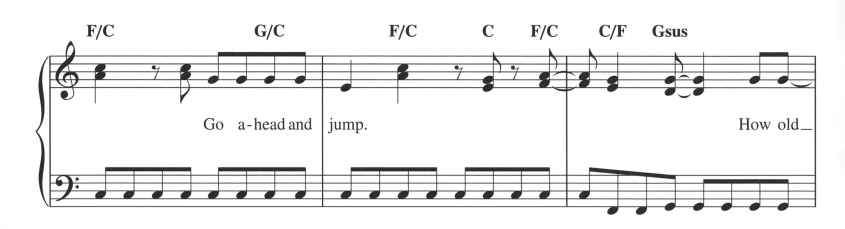

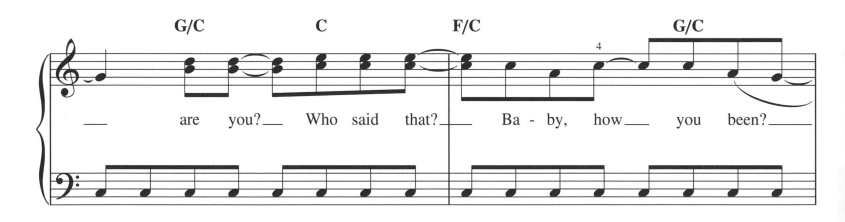

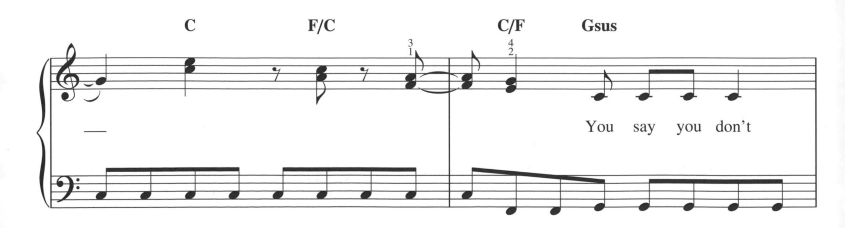

know. _____ You won't know_ un-til you be - gin. _

D.S. al Coda

So can't you

CODA

jump. _

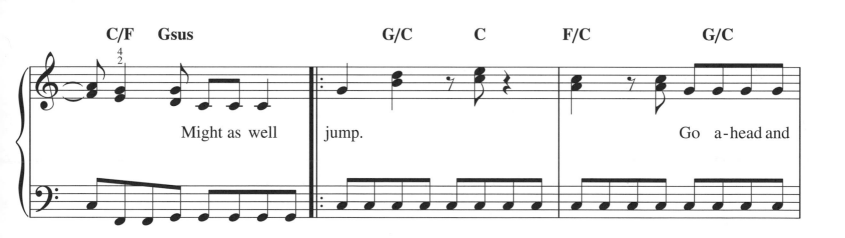

Might as well jump. Go a-head and

jump. _ Might as well jump.

LAYLA

Words and Music by ERIC CLAPTON
and JIM GORDON

Moderately fast Rock

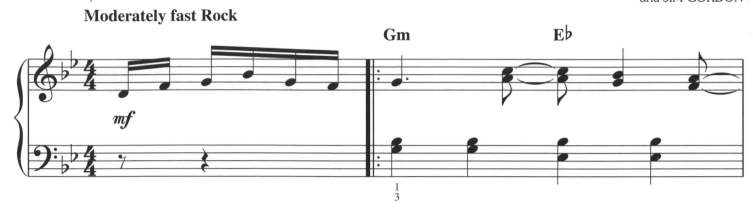

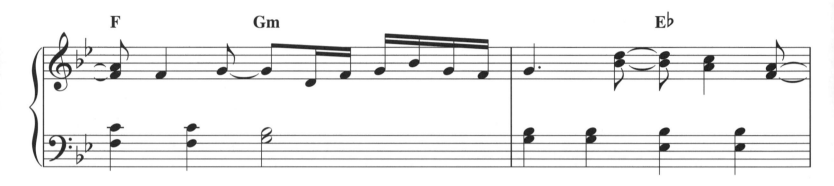

What will you   do   when you   get   lone - ly_____
I tried to   give you con - so -   la - tion_____
So make the   best of the sit - u -   a - tion_____

193

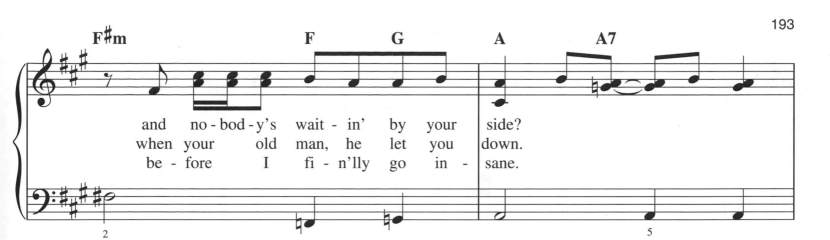

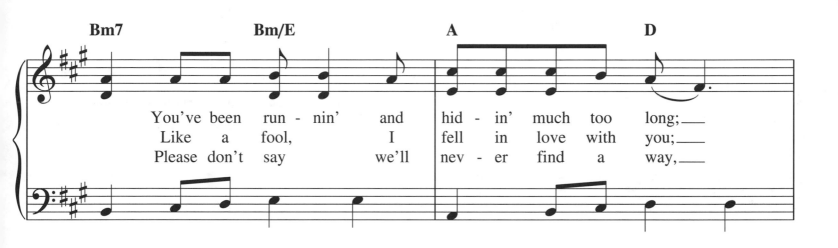

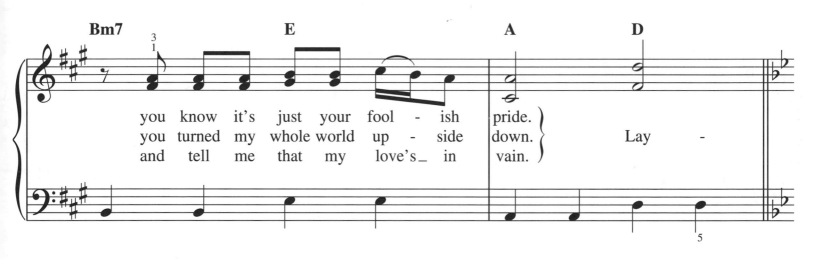

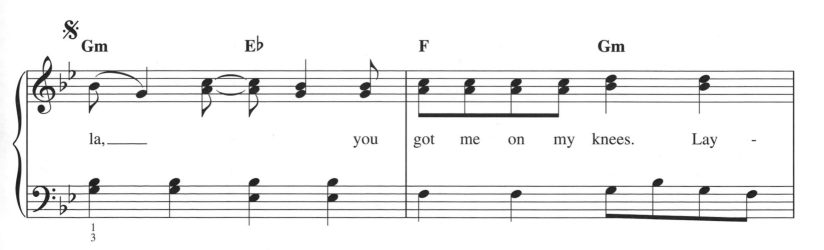

194

la,_____   I'm   beg - gin', dar - lin,'   please._   Lay -

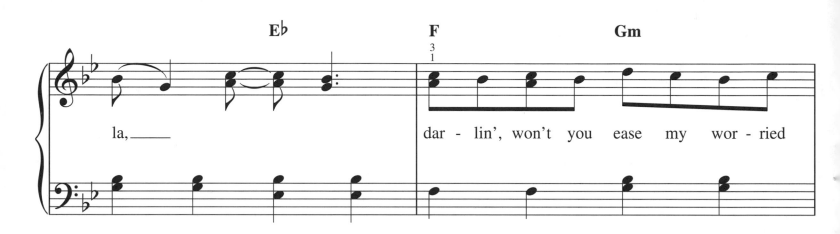

la,_____   dar - lin', won't you ease my wor - ried

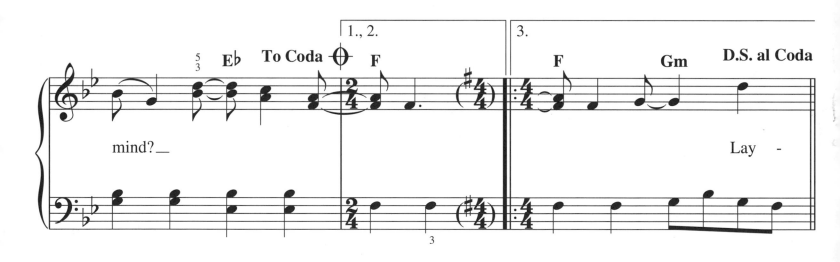

mind?_   Lay -

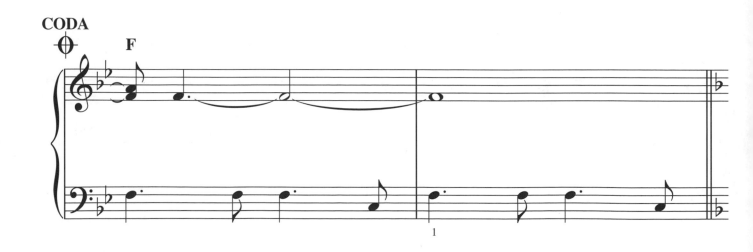

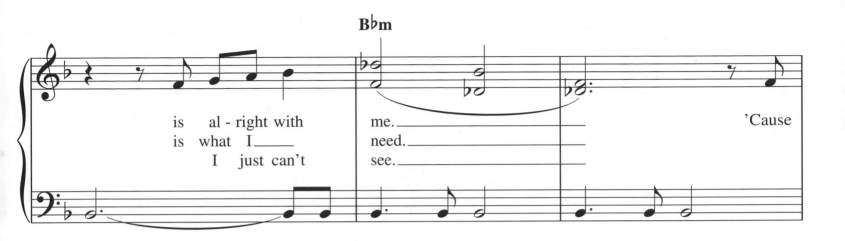

is   al - right with   me. _____   'Cause
is   what I_____   need. _____
     I just can't   see. _____

you   make me   feel_____ so___ brand   new,_____
Let   me   be the   one you come run - ning   to._____
You'd   nev - er   do   that__ to   me,_____

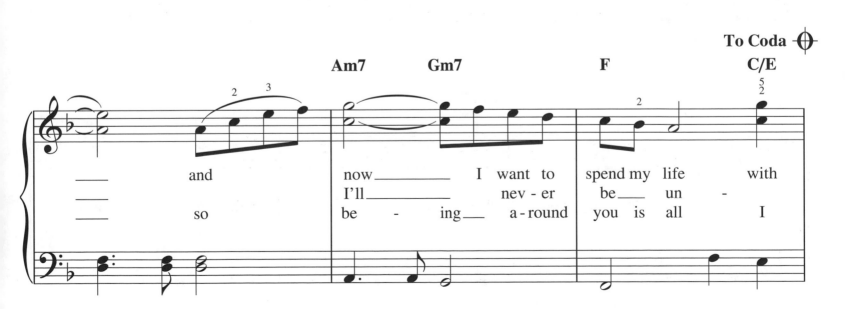

__   and   now_____ I want to   spend my life   with
__   so   I'll_____ nev - er be__ un -   be__ un -
__   so   be - ing__ a - round   you is all   I

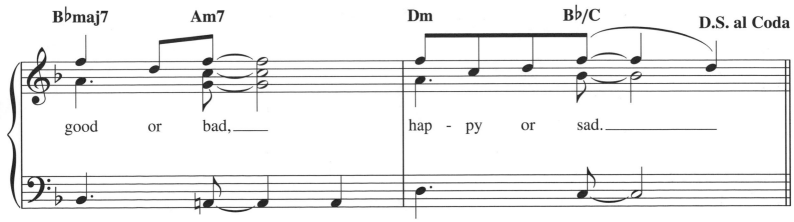

204

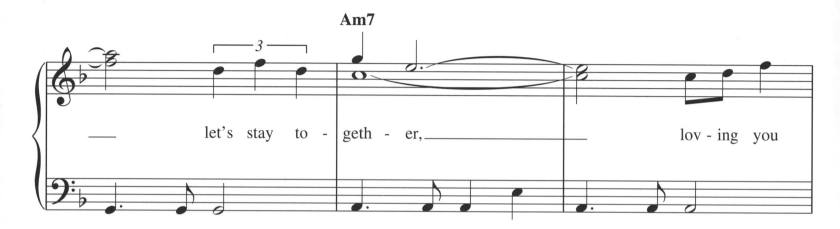

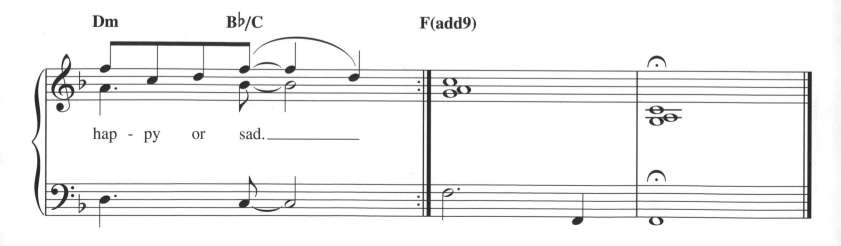

LOUIE, LOUIE

Words and Music by
RICHARD BERRY

Moderate Rock

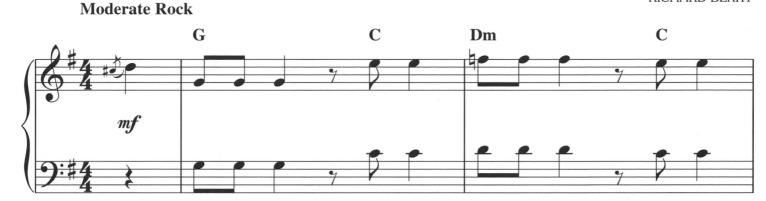

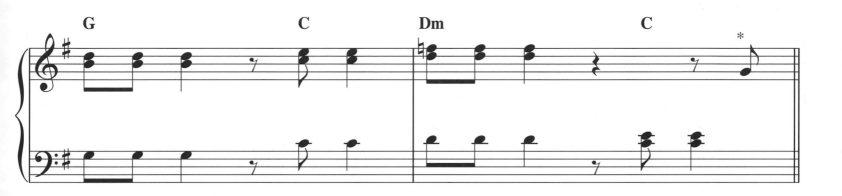

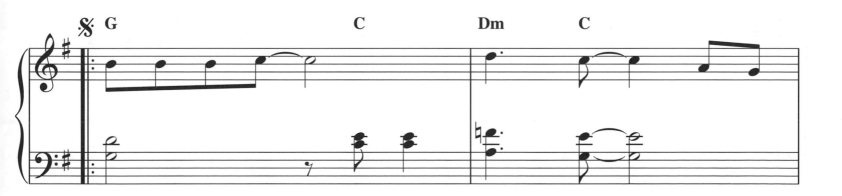

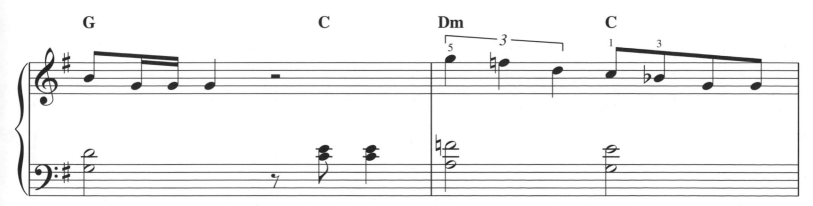

Lyrics not printed at the request of the publisher.

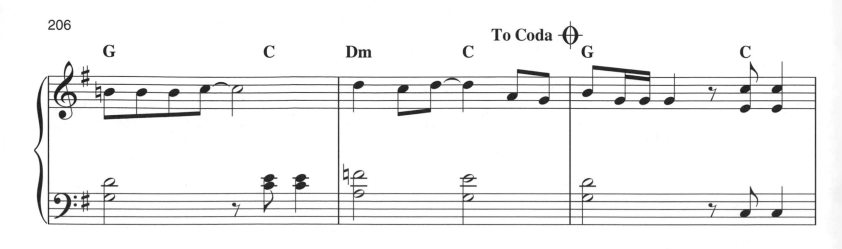

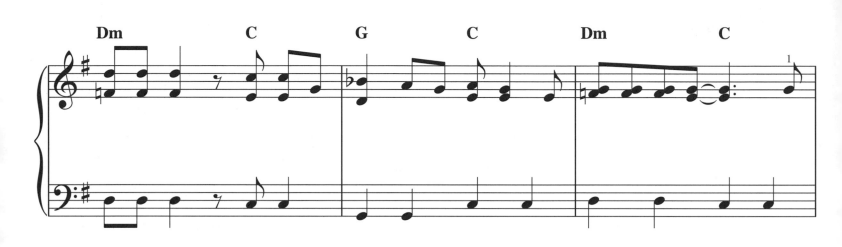

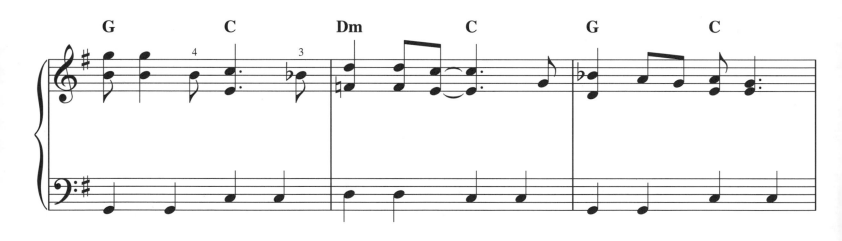

207

LIGHT MY FIRE

Words and Music by
THE DOORS

You know that it would be un - true,
time to hes - i - tate is through;

you know that I would be a liar,
no time to wal-low in the mire.

Am7   F#m7   Am7

if I was to say to you, _____   girl, we could-n't get much   higher.

Try now, we can on - ly lose, _____   and our love be-come a fun-'ral   pyre.

F#m7   G   A   D

Come on, ba - by, light my   fire. _____

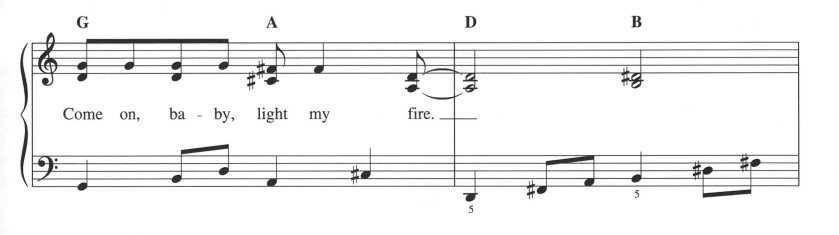

G   A   D   B

Come on, ba - by, light my   fire. _____

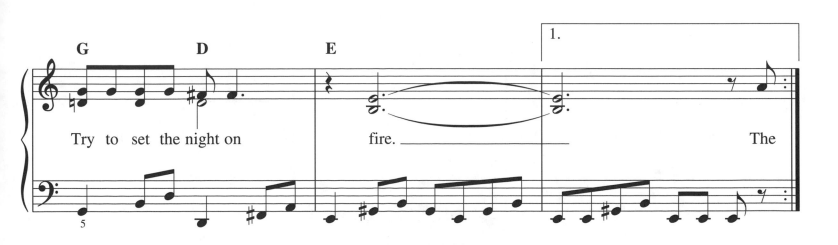

G   D   E

1.

Try to set the night on   fire. _____   The

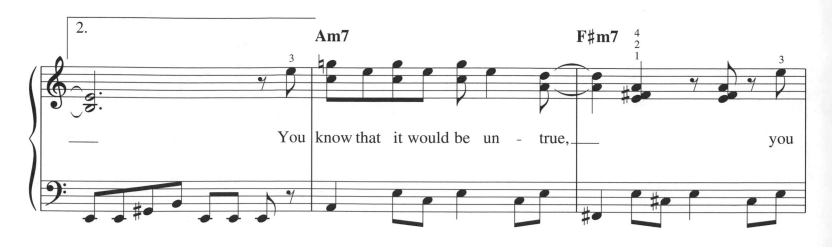

You know that it would be un - true,_____ you

know that I would be a liar,_____ if I was to say to you,

_____ girl, we could-n't get much higher._____

Come on, ba - by, light my fire. Come on, ba - by, light my fire.

Play 3 times

Try to set the night on   fire.

Try   to   set   the   night   on   fire.

L.H.

R.H.

LIKE A ROLLING STONE

Words and Music by
BOB DYLAN

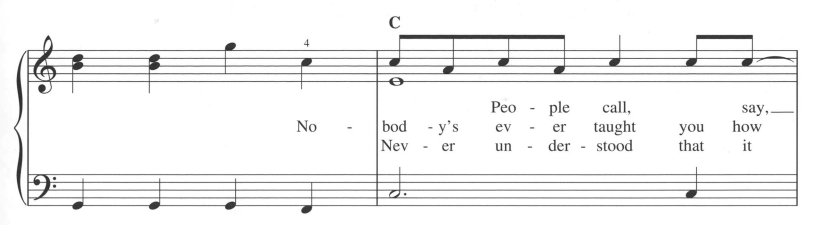

C

Peo - ple call, say,___
No - bod - y's ev - er taught you how
Nev - er un - der - stood that it

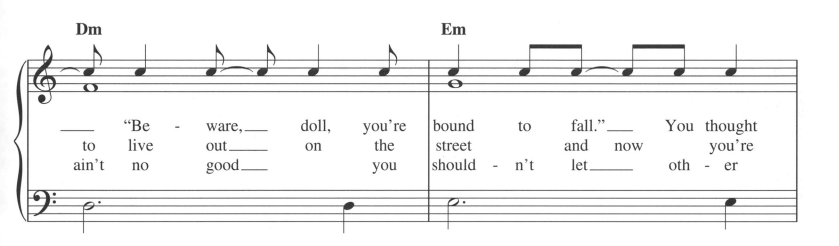

Dm   Em

___ "Be - ware,___ doll, you're bound to fall." ___ You thought
to live out___ on the street and now you're
ain't no good___ you should - n't let___ oth - er

F   G

they were all   a - kid - din' you.
gon - na have   to get   used to it.
peo - ple get your   kicks for you.

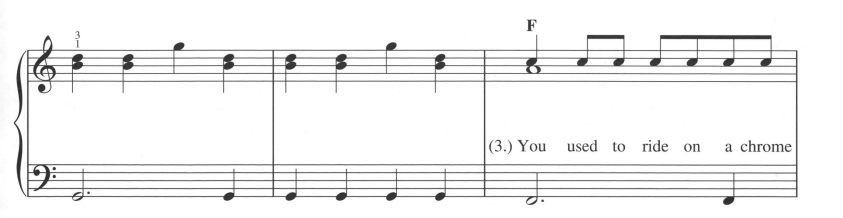

F

(3.) You used to ride on a chrome

214

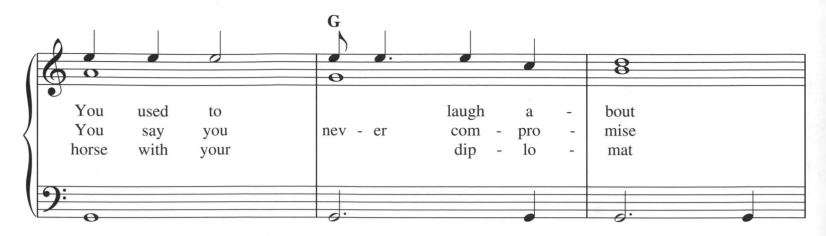

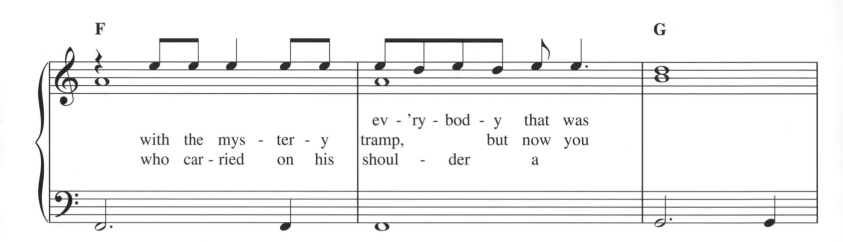

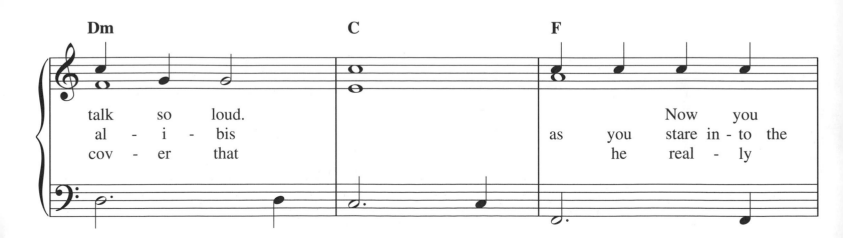

215

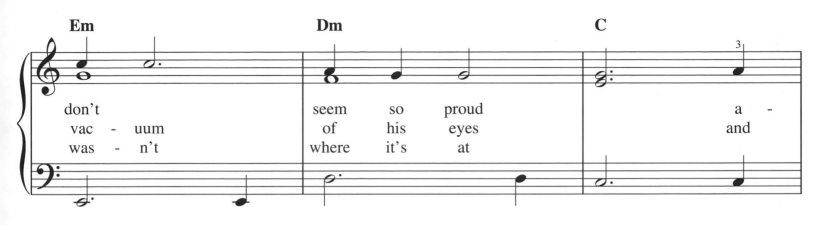

don't · · · · · seem so proud · · a -
vac - uum · · · of his eyes · · and
was - n't · · · where it's at

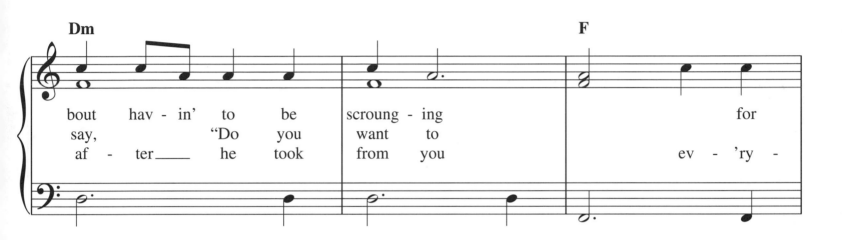

bout hav - in' to be scroung - ing · · for
say, "Do you want to · · ev - 'ry -
af - ter he took from you

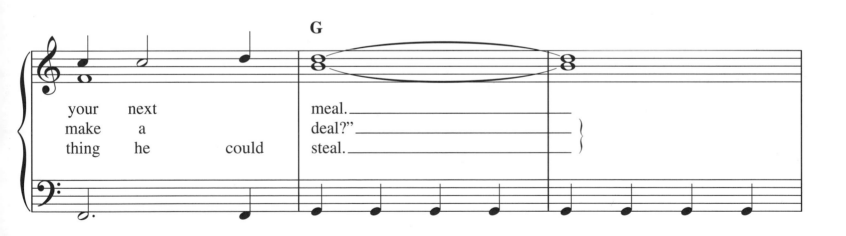

your next meal.
make a deal?"
thing he could steal.

Chorus

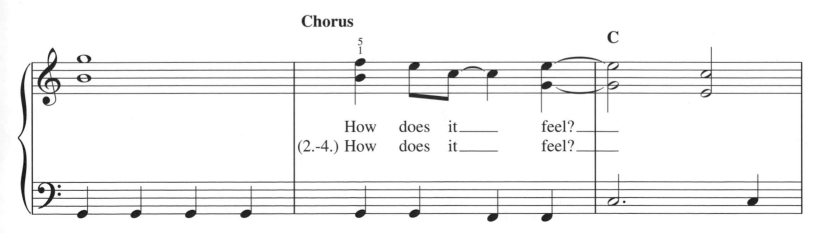

How does it feel?
(2.-4.) How does it feel?

How does it_____ feel_____
How does it_____ feel_____

_____ to be
_____ to be

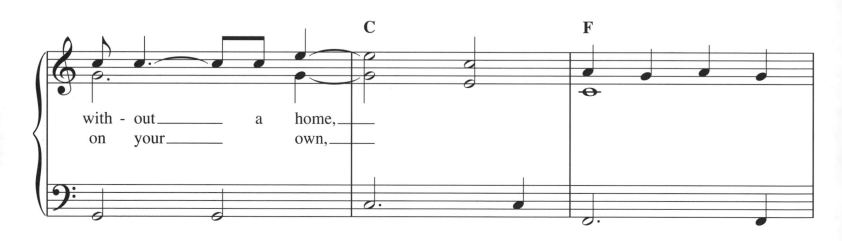

with - out_____ a home,_____
on your_____ own,_____

like   a com - plete un - _____ known,
with   no di - rec - tion _____ home,

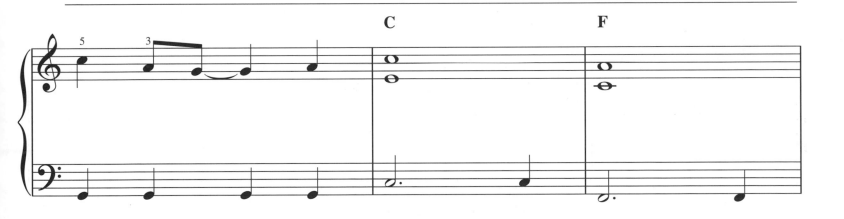

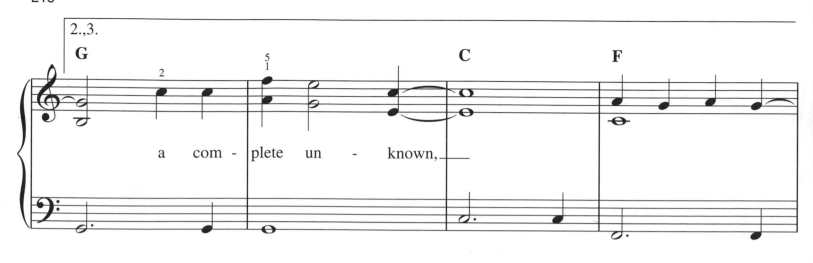

a com- plete un - known,__

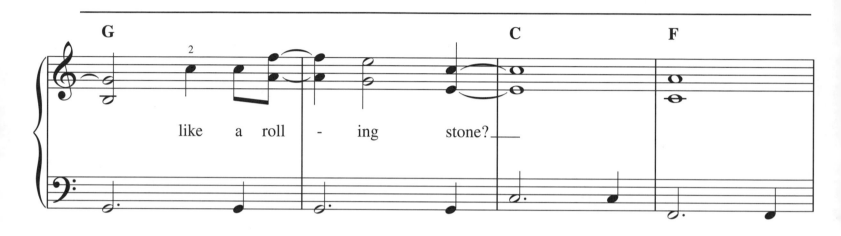

like a roll - ing stone?__

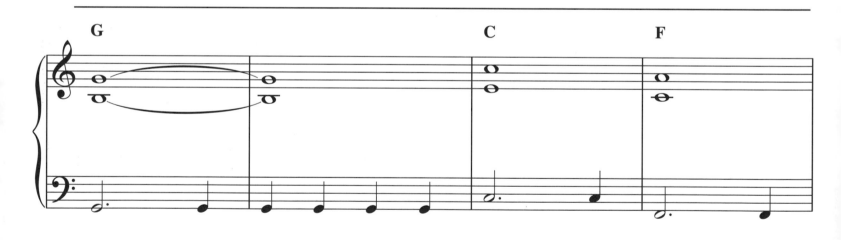

(3.) Oh, you

a com - plete un - known,____

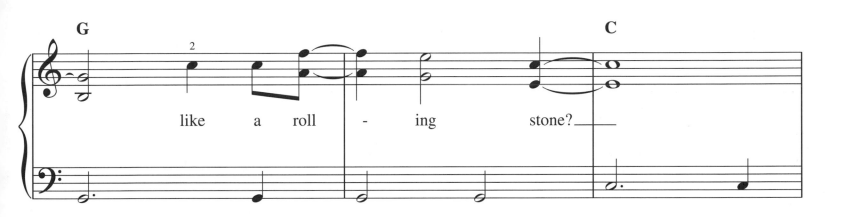

like a roll - ing stone?____

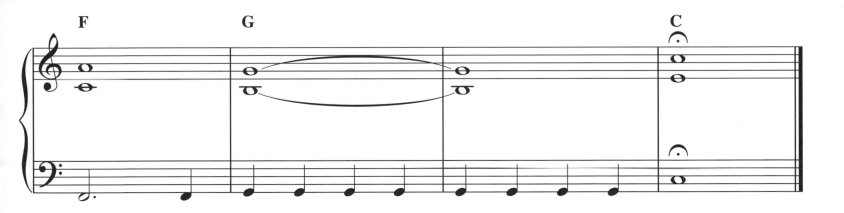

Additional Lyrics

4. Princess on the steeple and all the pretty people
They're all drinkin', thinkin' that they got it made.
Exchanging all precious gifts,
But you better take your diamond ring,
You'd better pawn it, babe.
You used to be so amused
At Napoleon in rags and the language that he used.
Go to him now, he calls you, you can't refuse.
When you got nothin', you got nothin' to lose.
You're invisible now, you got no secrets to conceal.
Chorus

LONDON CALLING

Words and Music by JOE STRUMMER, MICK JONES,
PAUL SIMONON and TOPPER HEADON

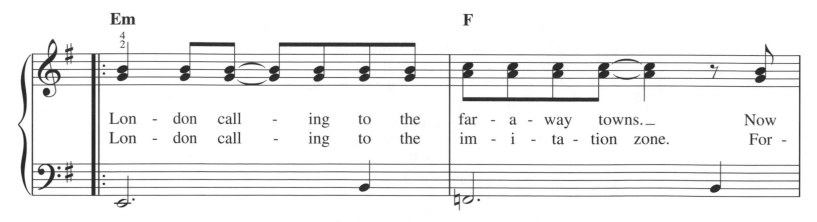

Lon - don call - ing to the far - a - way towns.___ Now
Lon - don call - ing to the im - i - ta - tion zone. For -

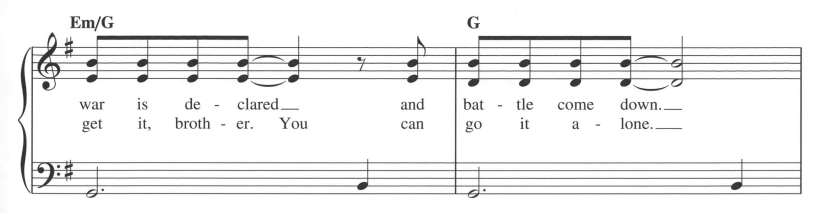

war is de - clared____ and bat - tle come down.____
get it, broth - er. You can go it a - lone.____

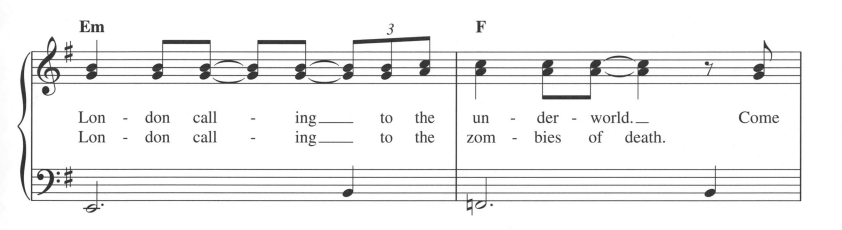

Lon - don call - ing____ to the un - der - world.__ Come
Lon - don call - ing____ to the zom - bies of death.

out of the cup - board, you boys and girls.____
Quit hold - ing out____ and draw an - oth - er breath.

Lon - don call - ing.____ Now, don't look to us.____
Lon - don call - ing. And I don't want to shout. But

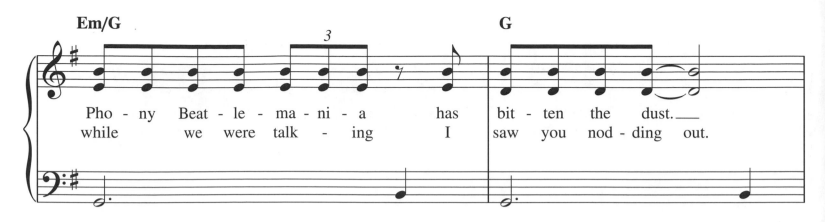

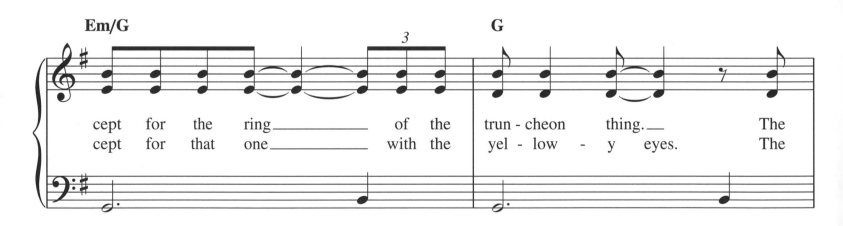

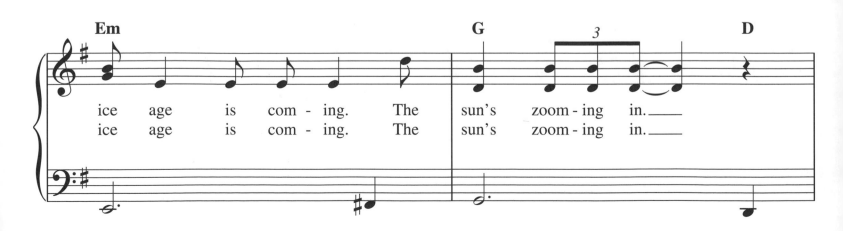

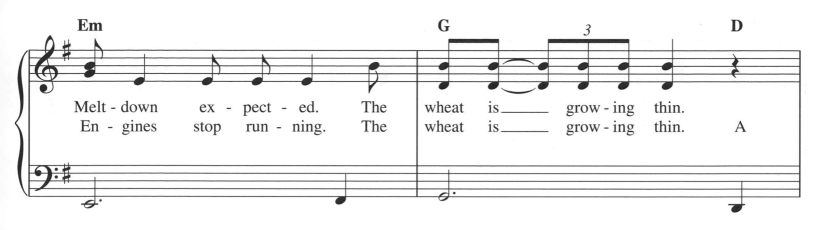

Melt - down ex - pect - ed. The wheat is_____ grow - ing thin.
En - gines stop run - ning. The wheat is_____ grow - ing thin. A

En - gines stop run - ning. But I have no fear, 'cause
nu - cle - ar er - ror. But I have no fear, 'cause

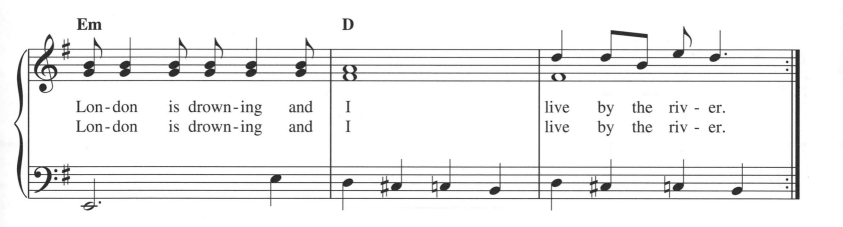

Lon - don is drown - ing and I live by the riv - er.
Lon - don is drown - ing and I live by the riv - er.

Lon - don call - ing. Yes,

I was there, too.___ And you know what they said? Well,

some of it was true! Lon - don call - ing at the

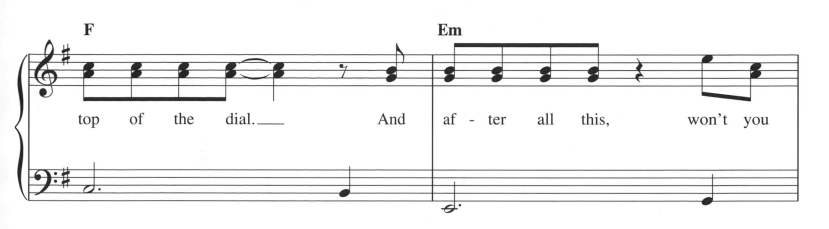

top of the dial.___ And af - ter all this, won't you

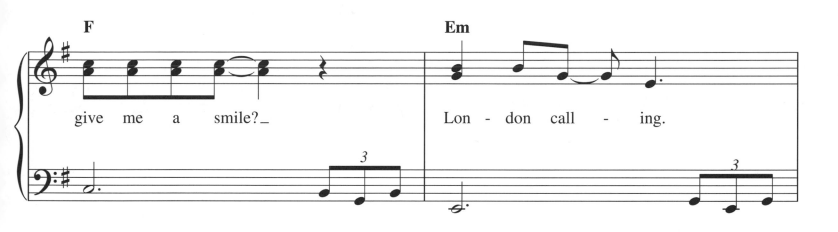

give me a smile?_ Lon - don call - ing.

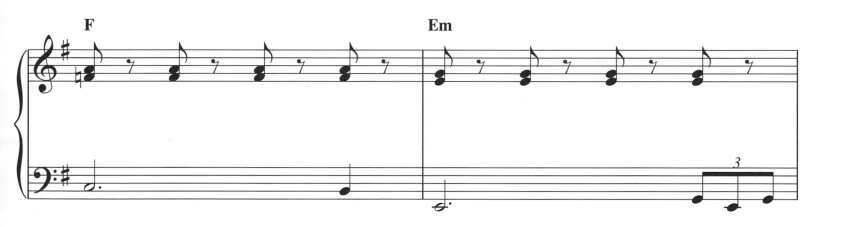

I nev - er felt so much a - like...___

MAGGIE MAY

Words and Music by ROD STEWART
and MARTIN QUITTENTON

227

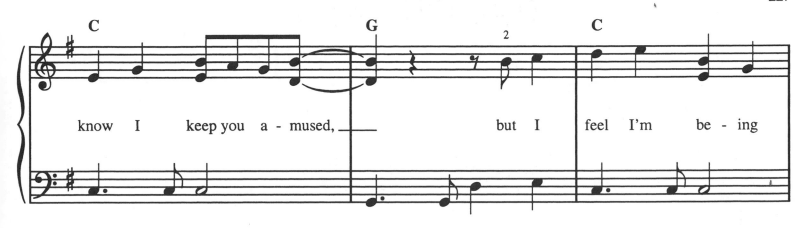

know I keep you a - mused, _____ but I feel I'm be - ing

used, Oh, Mag - gie, I could-n't have tried _____ an - y

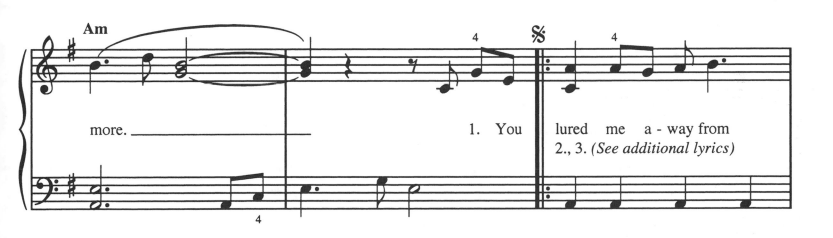

more. _____ 1. You lured me a - way from
2., 3. *(See additional lyrics)*

home, just to save you from be - ing a - lone. You

stole my heart __ and | that's what real - ly | hurts. _____

____ | The morn - ing sun, when it's | in your face, real - ly

shows your age, _____ | But | that don't wor - ry me

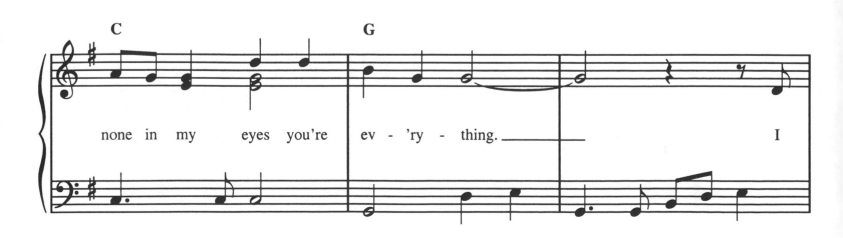

none in my eyes you're | ev - 'ry - thing. _____ | I

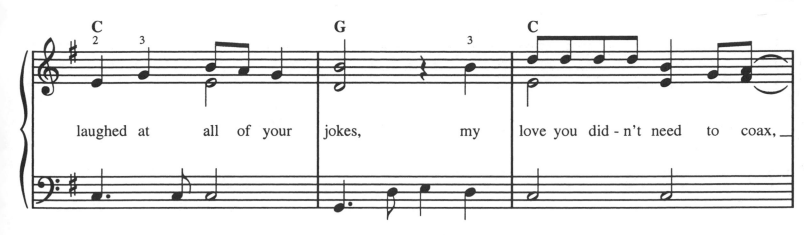

laughed at all of your jokes, my love you did-n't need to coax,_

_ Oh, Mag-gie, I could-n't have tried_____ an - y

more._____ 2. You 3. You

face._____ You made a first - class fool out of

230

Additional Lyrics

2. You lured me away from home, just to save you from being alone.
You stole my soul, that's a pain I can do without.
All I needed was a friend to lend a guiding hand.
But you turned into a lover, and, Mother, what a lover! You wore me out.
All you did was wreck my bed, and in the morning kick me in the head.
Oh, Maggie, I couldn't have tried any more.

3. You lured me away from home, 'cause you didn't want to be alone.
You stole my heart, I couldn't leave you if I tried.
I suppose I could collect my books and get back to school.
Or steal my Daddy's cue and make a living out of playing pool,
Or find myself a rock and roll band that needs a helpin' hand.
Oh, Maggie, I wish I'd never seen your face. **(To Coda)**

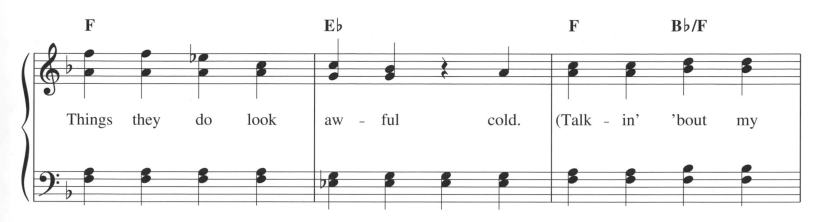

Things they do look aw - ful cold. (Talk - in' 'bout my

gen - er - a - tion.) Hope I die be - fore ___ I get old.

This is my gen - er - a - tion. ___

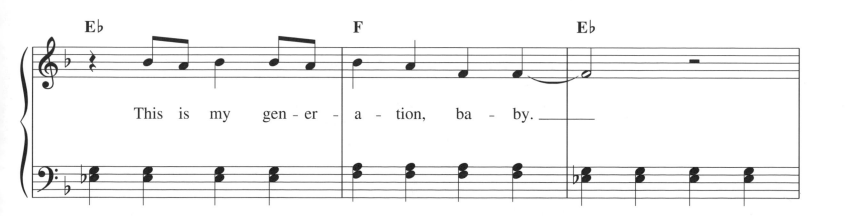

This is my gen - er - a - tion, ba - by. ___

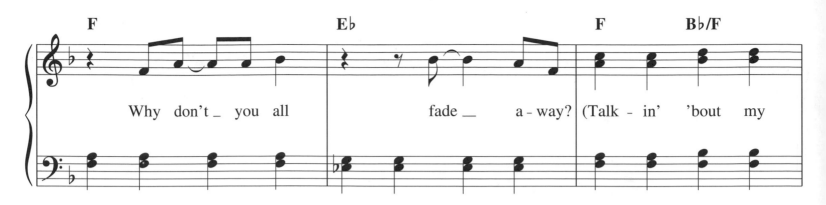

Why don't _ you all fade _ a - way? (Talk - in' 'bout my

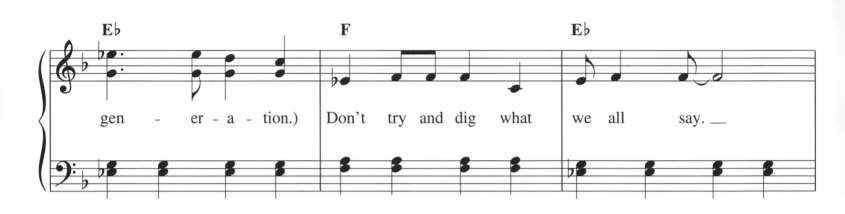

gen _ er - a - tion.) Don't try and dig what we all say. _

(Talk - in' 'bout my gen _ er - a - tion.) I'm not tryin' to cause a

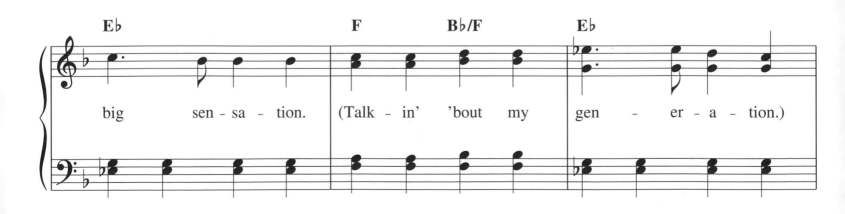

big sen - sa - tion. (Talk - in' 'bout my gen _ er - a - tion.)

239

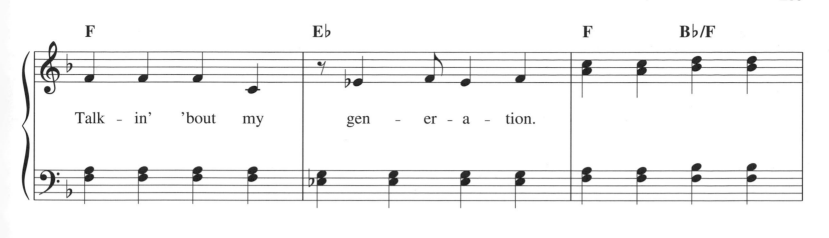

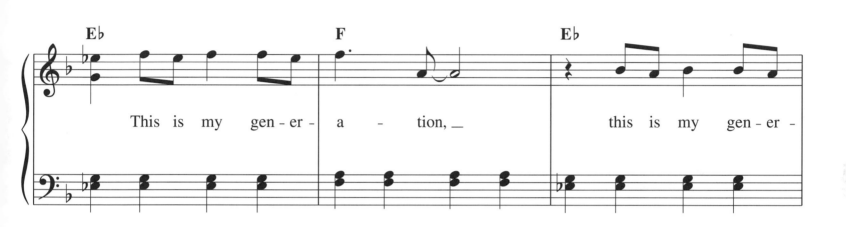

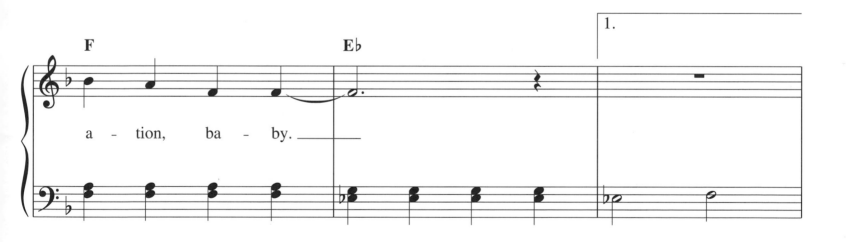

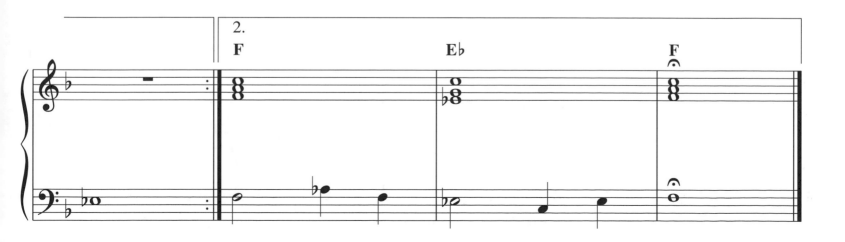

MY GIRL

Words and Music by WILLIAM "SMOKEY" ROBINSON
and RONALD WHITE

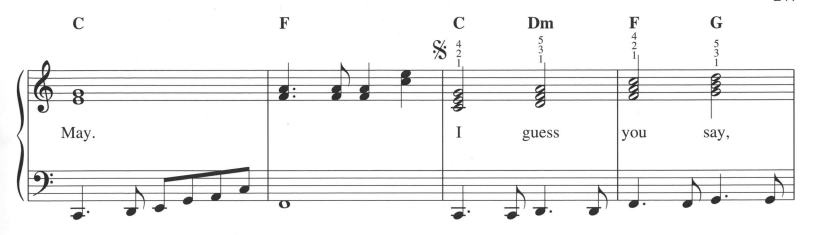

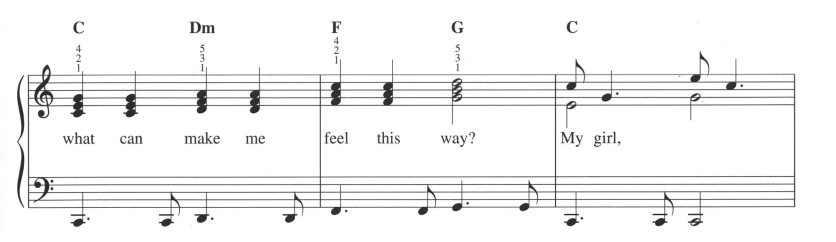

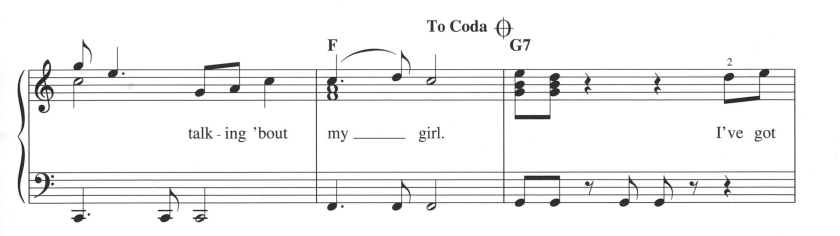

I've got a sweet-er song _____ than the birds in the

trees. Well,

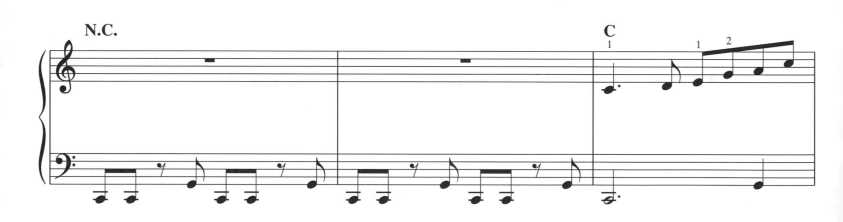

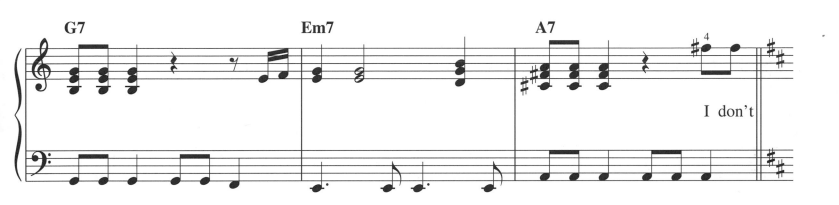

I don't

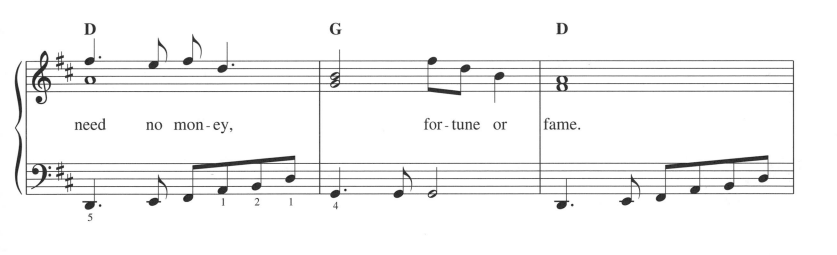

need   no mon-ey,   for-tune or   fame.

I've got   all the rich-es, ba - by,   one man can

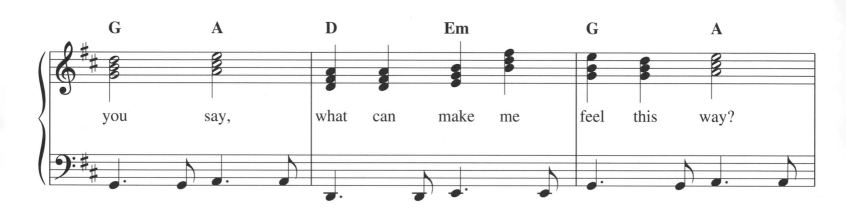

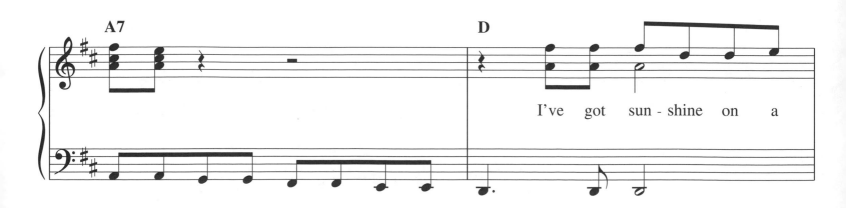

cloud - y day with my girl. _____ I've e - ven got the month of May with

my girl. _____ Talk-ing 'bout, _ talk-ing 'bout, _ talk-ing 'bout _

my girl. _____ Woo, my girl. _____

That's all I can talk a-bout is my girl. _____

NO WOMAN NO CRY

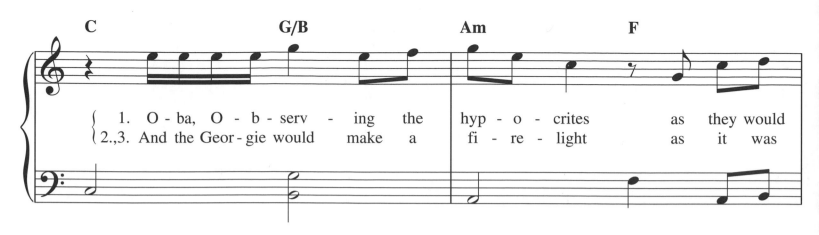

C   G/B   Am   F

1. O - ba, O - b - serv - ing the hyp - o - crites as they would
2.,3. And the Geor - gie would make a fi - re - light as it was

C   G/B   Am   F

min - gle with the good peo - ple we meet,
log wood burn - in' through the night.

C   G/B   Am   F

good friends we had, oh good friends we've lost
Then we would cook corn - meal por - ridge

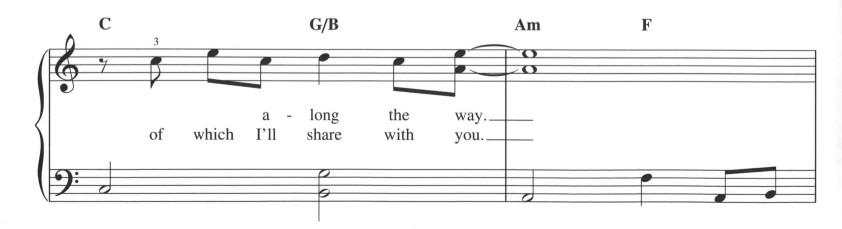

C   G/B   Am   F

a - long the way.
of which I'll share with you.

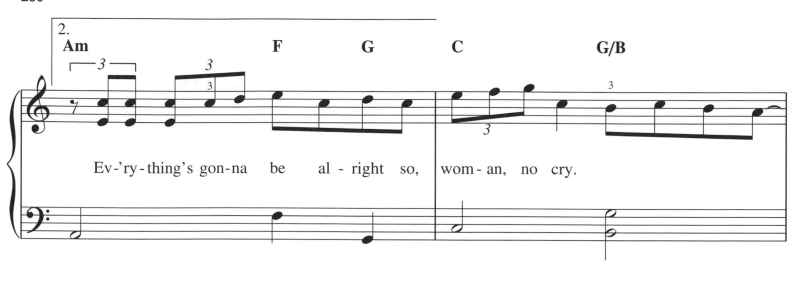

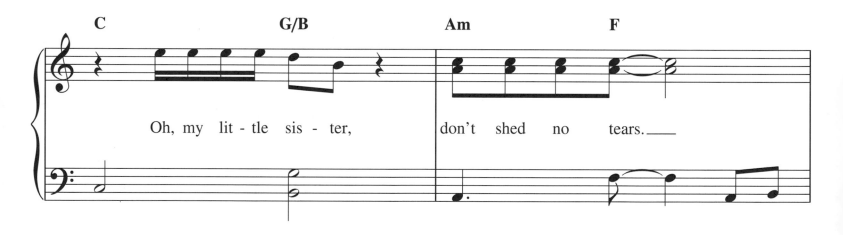

CODA

No wom-an, no cry.

No wom-an, no cry.

Oh, my lit-tle dar-lin', I say don't shed no tears.

No wom-an, no cry. Yeah.

PIANO MAN

Words and Music by
BILLY JOEL

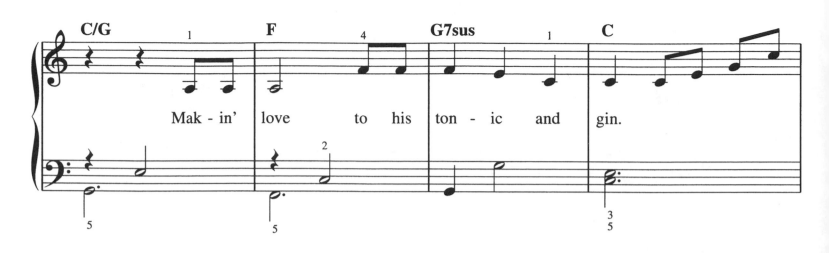

Mak - in' love to his ton - ic and gin.

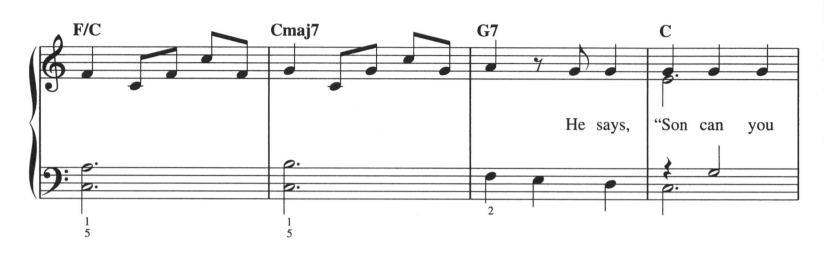

He says, "Son can you

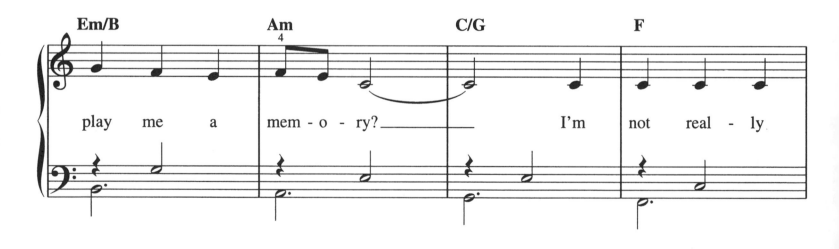

play me a mem - o - ry?____ I'm not real - ly

sure how it goes, But it's sad and it's

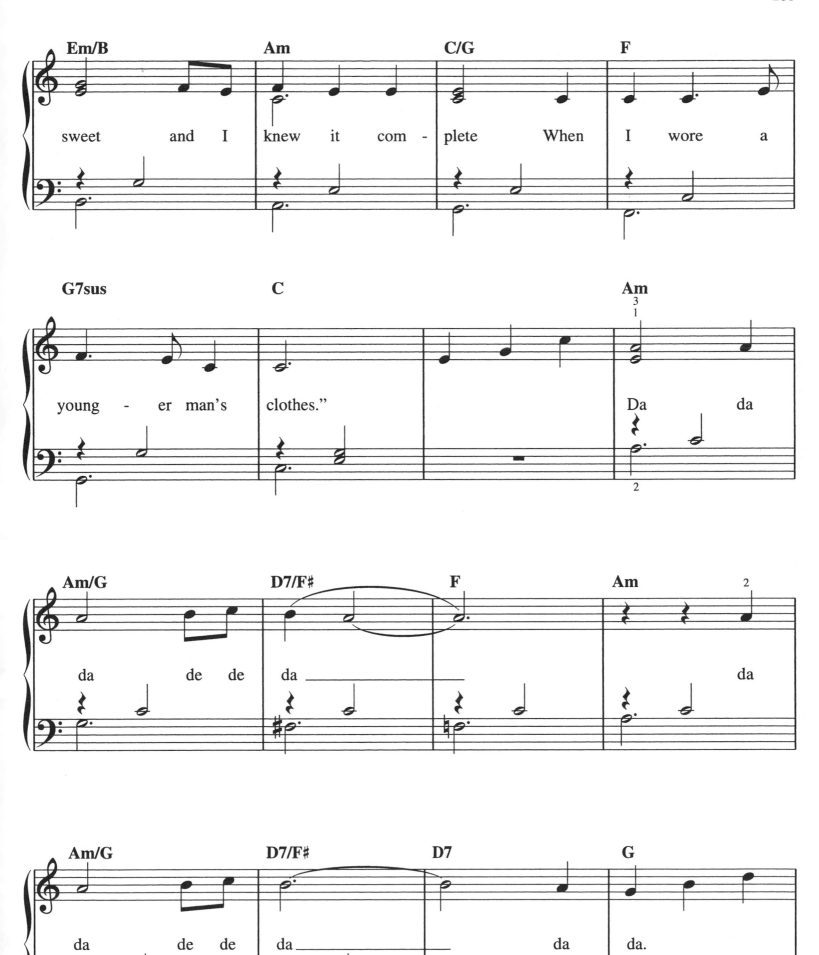

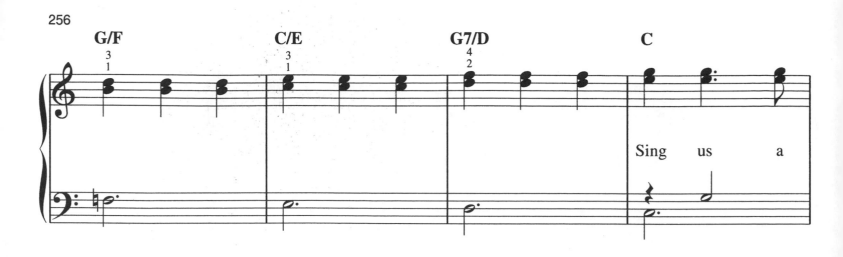

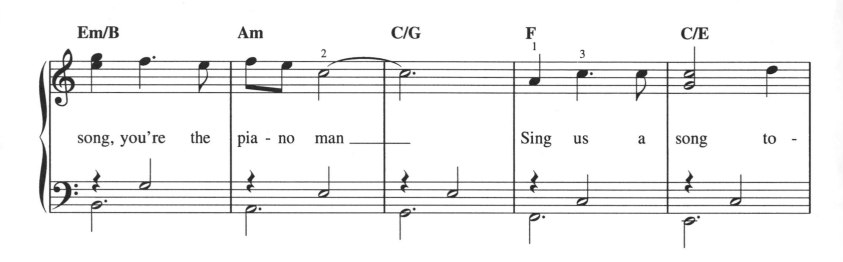

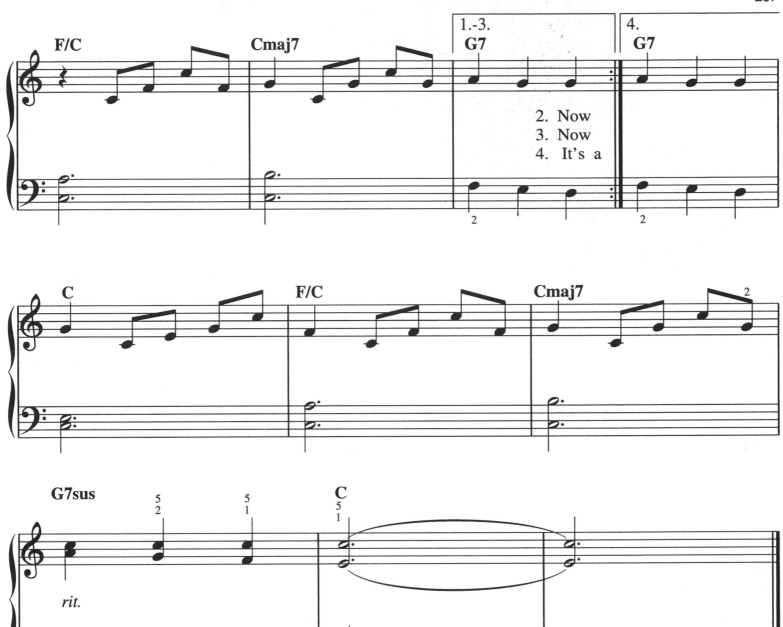

Additional Lyrics

2. Now John at the bar is a friend of mine,
   He gets me my drinks for free,
   And he's quick with a joke or to light up your smoke
   But there's someplace that he'd rather be.
   He says, "Bill, I believe this is killing me,"
   As a smile ran away from his face
   "Well, I'm sure that I could be a movie star
   If I could get out of this place."

3. Now Paul is a real estate novelist
   Who never had time for a wife
   And he's talkin' with Davy who's still in the Navy
   And probably will be for life.
   And the waitress is practicing politics,
   As the businessmen slowly get stoned
   Yes, they're sharing a drink they call loneliness
   But it's better than drinkin' alone.

4. It's a pretty good crowd for a Saturday,
   And the manager gives me a smile
   'Cause he knows that it's me they've been comin' to see
   To forget about life for a while.
   And the piano sounds like a carnival
   And the microphone smells like a beer
   And they sit at the bar and put bread in my jar
   And say, "Man, what are you doin' here?"

OH, PRETTY WOMAN

Words and Music by ROY ORBISON
and BILL DEES

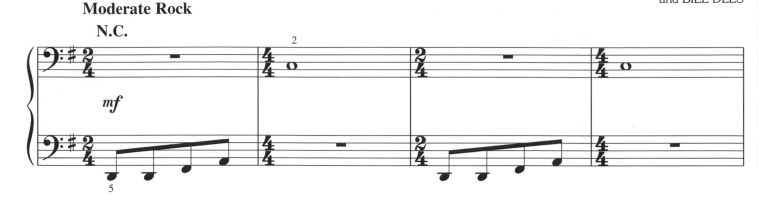

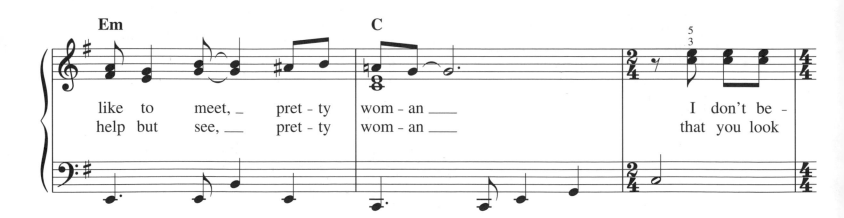

lieve you, _____ you're not the truth _____ no one could look as good as
love-ly _____ as can be _____ are you lone-ly just like

you.
me?

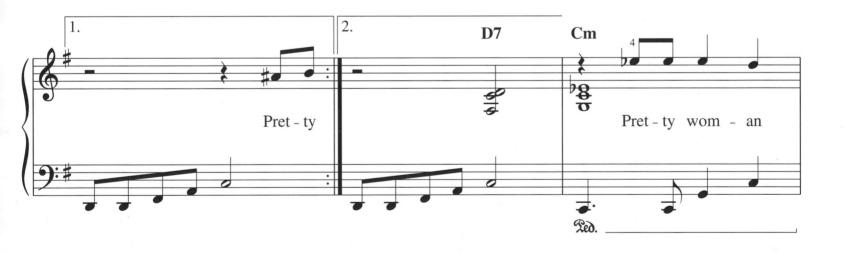

1. 2. D7 Cm

Pret-ty Pret-ty wom-an

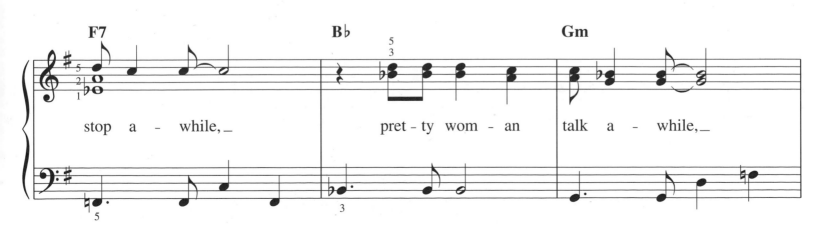

F7 B♭ Gm

stop a-while, ___ pret-ty wom-an talk a-while, ___

pret - ty wom - an   give your smile to   me.

Pret - ty wom - an   yeah, yeah,   yeah.   Pret - ty wom - an

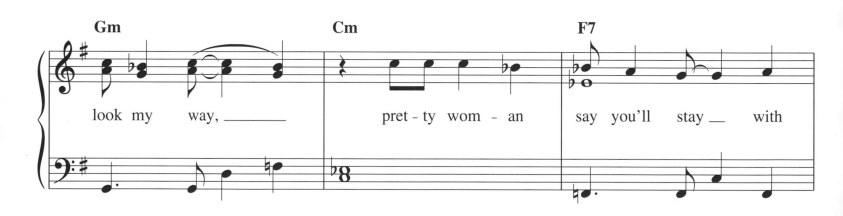

look my   way,   pret - ty wom - an   say you'll stay   with

me.   'Cause I   need   you   I'll   treat   you

right. Come with me ba - by. ___

Be mine to - night. ___

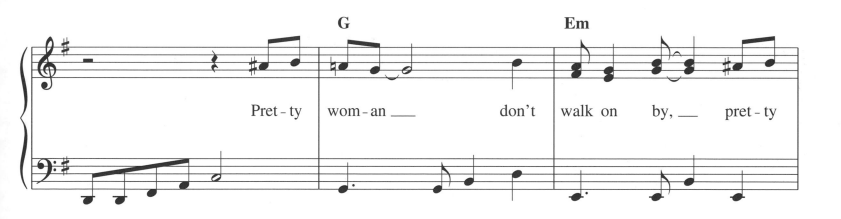

Pret - ty wom - an ___ don't walk on by, ___ pret - ty

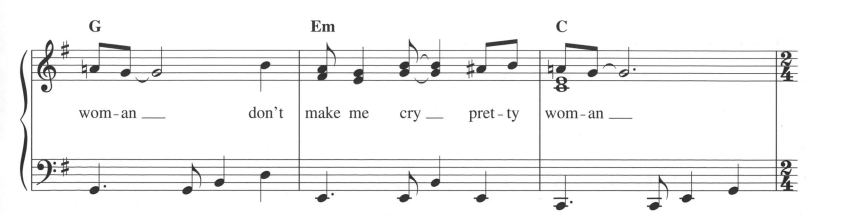

wom - an ___ don't make me cry ___ pret - ty wom - an ___

don't walk a - way. _ Hey, _____ O.

K. _____ If that's the way it must be ___ O.

K. _____ I guess I'll go on home, _ it's late _

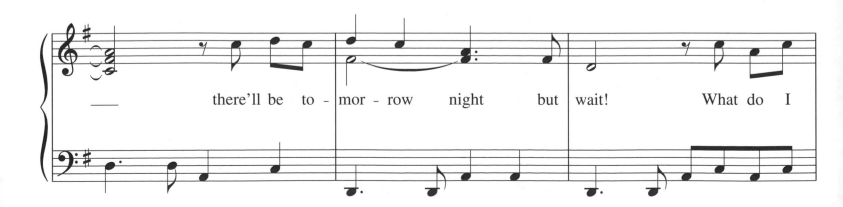

___ there'll be to - mor - row night but wait! What do I

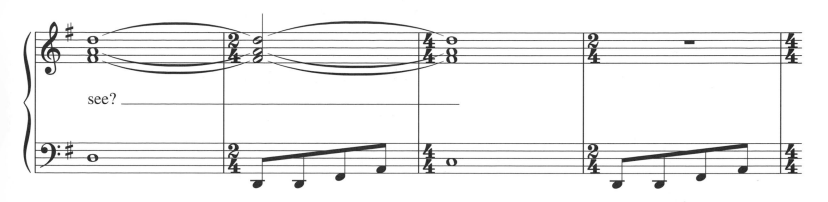

see?

Is she walk-ing back to me? ____

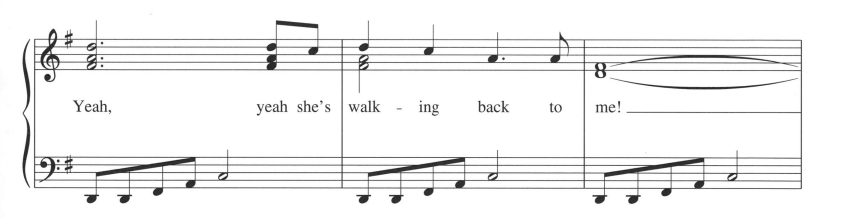

Yeah, yeah she's walk - ing back to me! ____

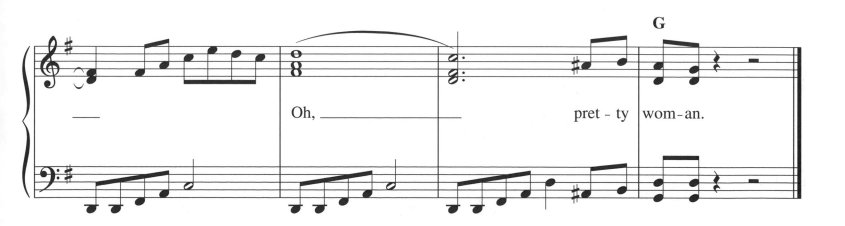

____ Oh, ____ pret - ty wom-an.

G

PAPA WAS A ROLLIN' STONE

Words and Music by NORMAN WHITFIELD
and BARRETT STRONG

Moderately fast

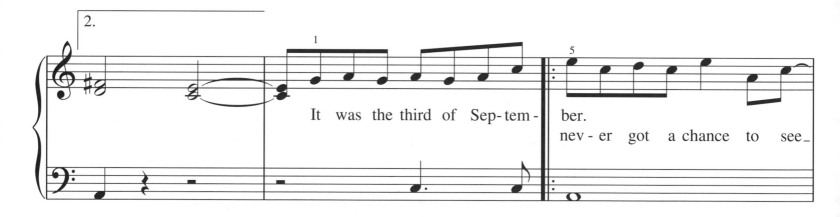

It was the third of Sep-tem - ber.

nev - er got a chance to see_

That day I'll al-ways re-mem - ber, yes, I will,__ 'cause
____ him. Nev - er heard noth-in' but bad things a-bout him.

that was the day— that my dad-dy died.—
Ma-ma, I'm de-pend-ing on you to tell me the truth.—

——————— I — (Spoken:) Mama just hung her head and said, "Son,

Pa-pa was a roll-in' stone."— Wher-ev-er he laid his hat

was his home.— And when he died,— all— he— left— us was a-

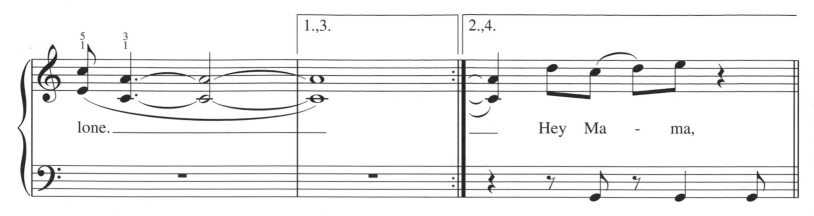

lone. _____ Hey Ma - ma,

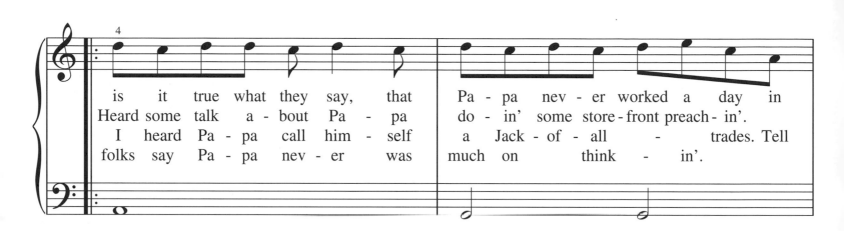

is it true what they say, that Pa - pa nev - er worked a day in
Heard some talk a - bout Pa - pa do - in' some store - front preach - in'.
I heard Pa - pa call him - self a Jack - of - all - trades. Tell
folks say Pa - pa nev - er was much on think - in'.

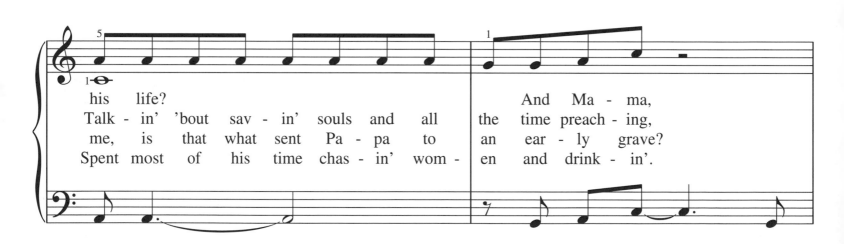

his life? And Ma - ma,
Talk - in' 'bout sav - in' souls and all the time preach - ing,
me, is that what sent Pa - pa to an ear - ly grave?
Spent most of his time chas - in' wom - en and drink - in'.

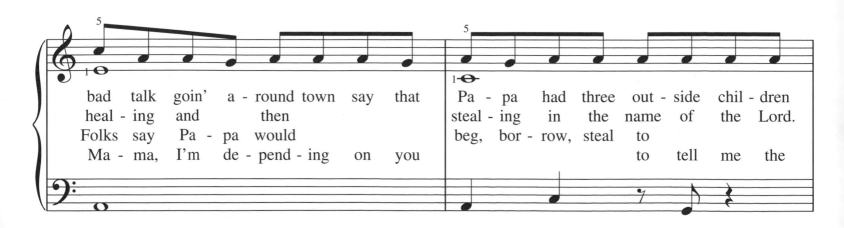

bad talk goin' a - round town say that Pa - pa had three out - side chil - dren
heal - ing and then steal - ing in the name of the Lord.
Folks say Pa - pa would beg, bor - row, steal to
Ma - ma, I'm de - pend - ing on you to tell me the

and an-oth - er wife._
pay his bills._
truth.

1.,3. And that ain't right.
Hey, Ma - ma,

2. *(Spoken:)*
Mama just hung her head and said,

D.S.

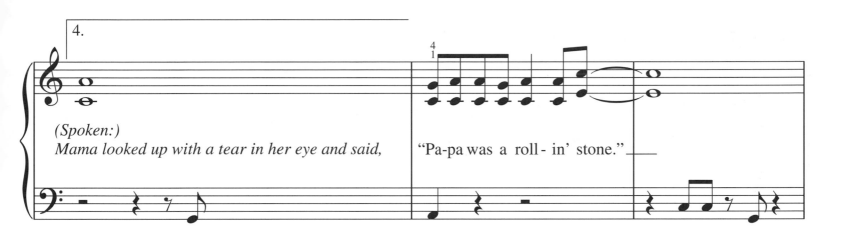

4. *(Spoken:)*
Mama looked up with a tear in her eye and said,

"Pa-pa was a roll - in' stone."__

Wher - ev - er he laid his hat was his home._ And when he died,_ all_

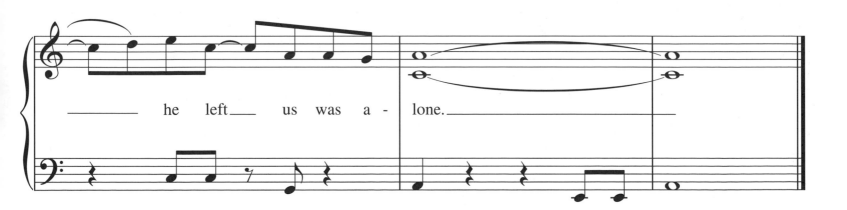

____ he left__ us was a - lone.__

PROUD MARY

Words and Music by
J.C. FOGERTY

Left a good job   in the   cit - y,
Cleaned a lot of plates   in   Mem - phis,
If you come down   to the   riv - er,

work - in' for the man   ev - 'ry   night and   day.
pumped a lot of 'pane   down in   New Or - leans.
bet you gon - na find   some   peo - ple who live.

269

And I nev-er lost____ one min-ute of sleep____ in',
But I nev-er saw____ the good side of the cit - y
You don't have to wor - ry 'cause you have no mon - ey.

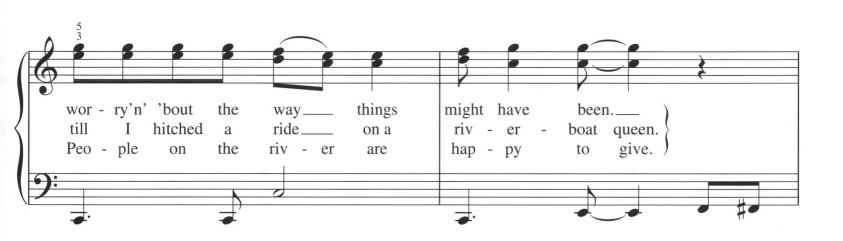

wor - ry'n' 'bout the way____ things might have been.____
till I hitched a ride____ on a riv - er - boat queen.
Peo - ple on the riv - er are hap - py to give.

G   **Am**

Big wheel____ keep on turn - in',____ proud Mar - y keep on

F   **C**   **To Coda** ⊕

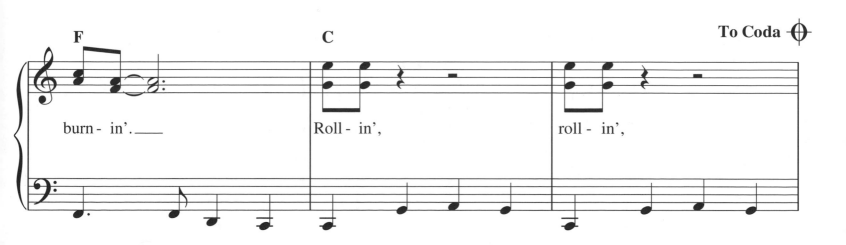

burn - in'.____ Roll - in', roll - in',

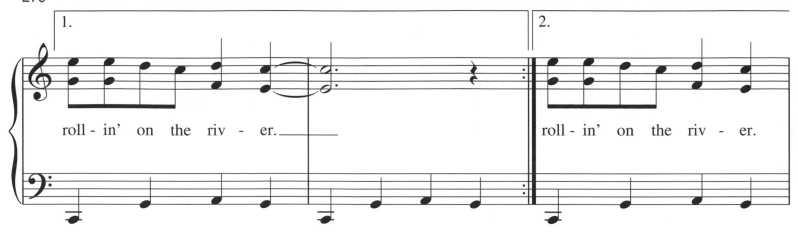

roll - in' on the riv - er.___   roll - in' on the riv - er.

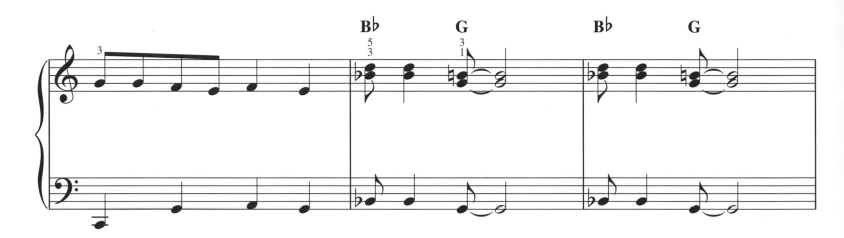

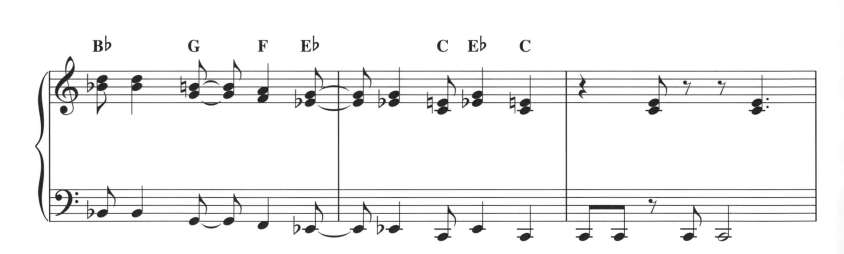

D.S. al Coda

CODA

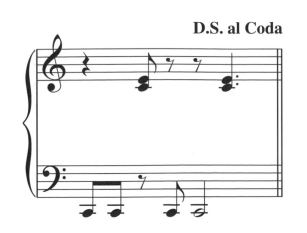

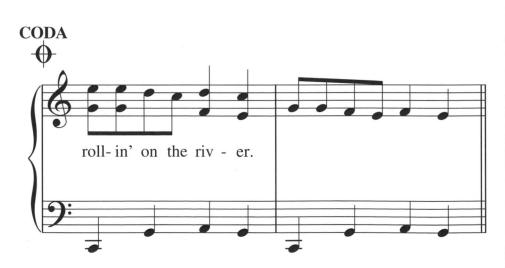

roll - in' on the riv - er.

PURPLE HAZE

Words and Music by
JIMI HENDRIX

'scuse me___ while I kiss the sky.

Pur - ple haze_____ all a - round,

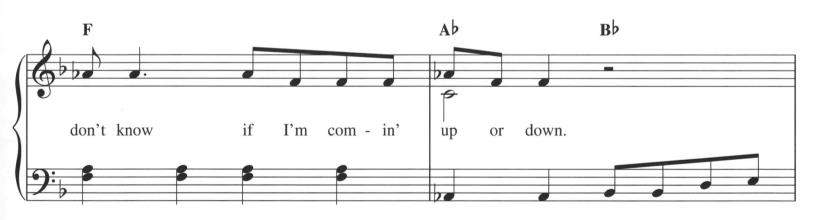

don't know if I'm com - in' up or down.

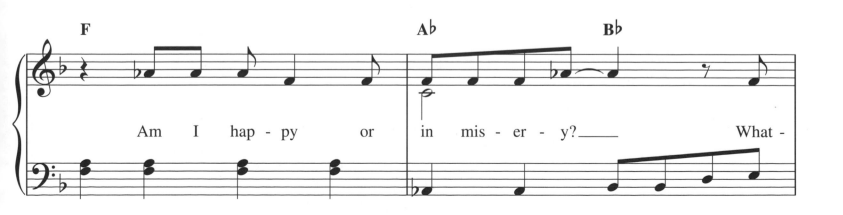

Am I hap - py or in mis - er - y?___ What-

ev-er it is, that girl put a spell on me.

(Spoken:) Help me, help me ah oh no no.

Pur-ple haze___ was in my eyes, don't know if it's

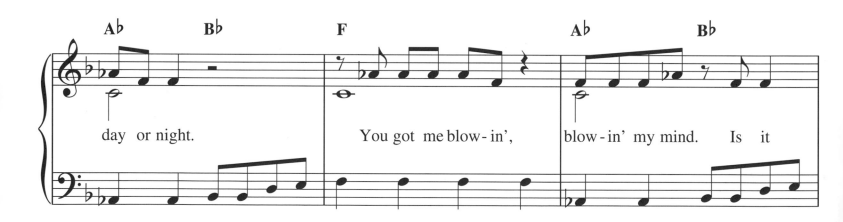

day or night. You got me blow-in', blow-in' my mind. Is it

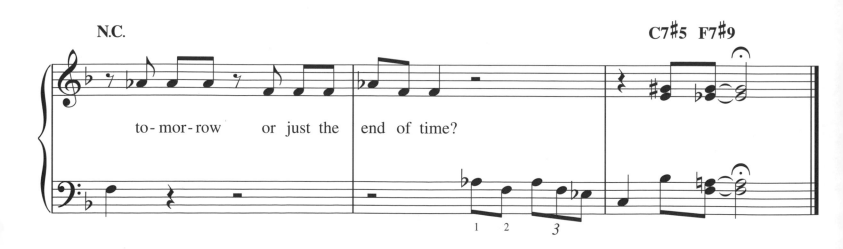

to-mor-row or just the end of time?

RESPECT

Words and Music by
OTIS REDDING

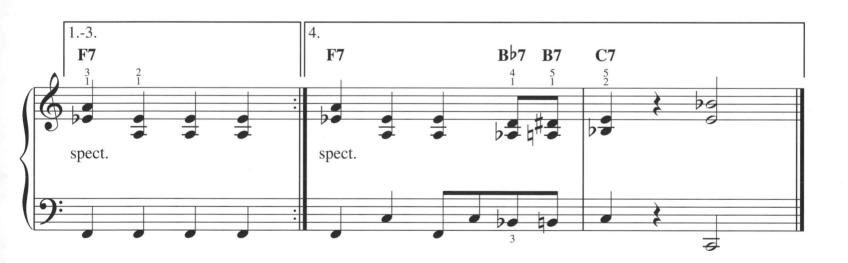

Additional Lyrics

2. I ain't gonna do you wrong while you gone.
   I ain't gonna do you wrong 'cause I don't wanna.
   All I'm askin' is for a little respect, when you come home.
   Baby, when you come home, respect.

4. Ooh, your kisses, sweeter than honey,
   And guess what so here's my money,
   All I want you to do for me is give it to me when you get home.
   Yeah, baby, when you get home.

ROCK AROUND THE CLOCK

Words and Music by MAX C. FREEDMAN
and JIMMY DeKNIGHT

One, two, three o'- clock

four o'- clock rock, five, six, sev - en o'- clock, eight o'- clock rock,

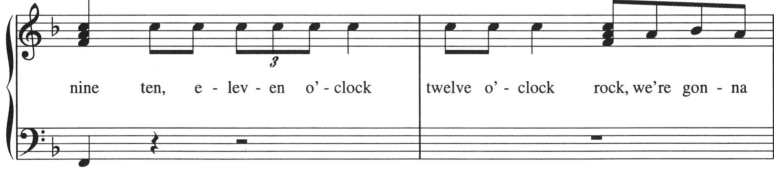

nine ten, e - lev - en o'- clock twelve o'- clock rock, we're gon - na

rock a - round the clock to - night. Put your

glad rags on and join me, Hon, __ we'll have some fun when the
clock strikes two, and three and four. __ If the band slows down we'll

clock strikes one, __ we're gon - na rock a - round the
yell for more, __ we're gon - na rock a - round the

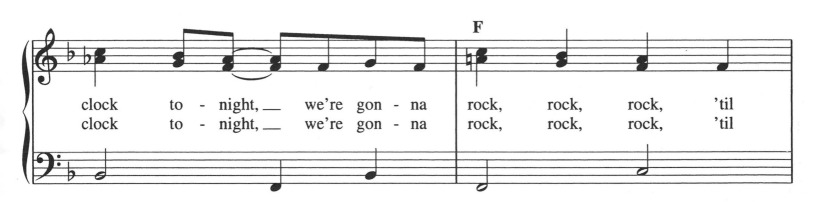

clock to - night, __ we're gon - na rock, rock, rock, 'til
clock to - night, __ we're gon - na rock, rock, rock, 'til

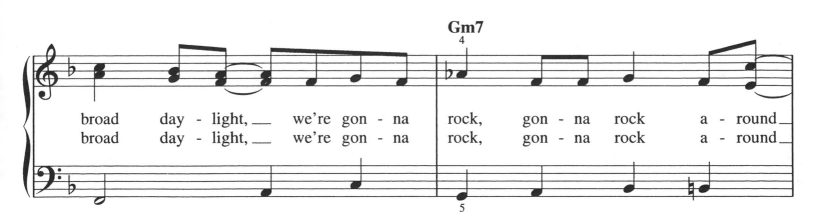

broad day - light, __ we're gon - na rock, gon - na rock a - round __
broad day - light, __ we're gon - na rock, gon - na rock a - round __

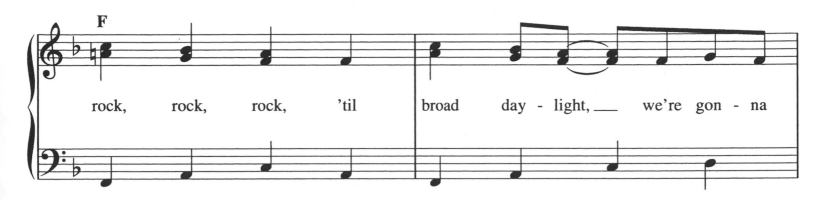

rock,   rock,   rock,   'til   broad   day - light, ___   we're gon - na

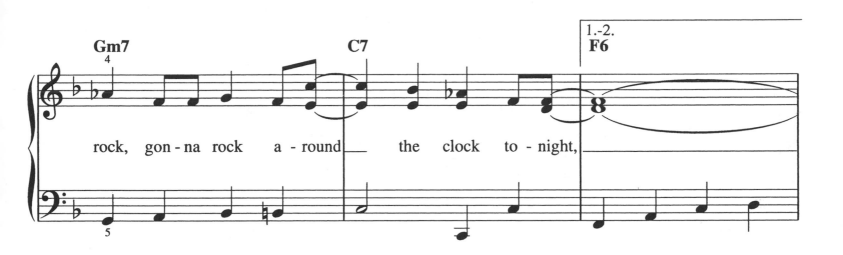

rock, gon - na rock   a - round ___   the   clock   to - night, ___

When it's ___
When the

Additional Lyrics

3. When the clock strikes twelve, we'll cool off, then,
    Start a rockin'·'round the clock again,
    We're gonna rock around the clock tonight,
    We're gonna rock, rock, rock, 'til broad daylight,
    We're gonna rock, gonna rock around the clock tonight.

ROXANNE

Music and Lyrics by
STING

Moderately fast

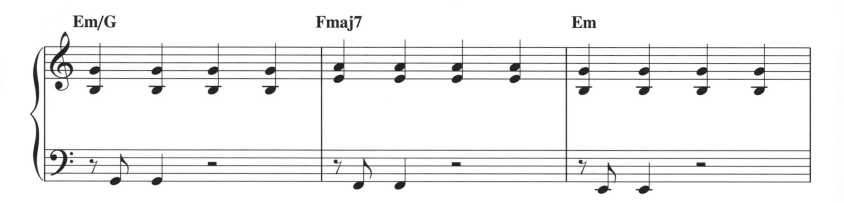

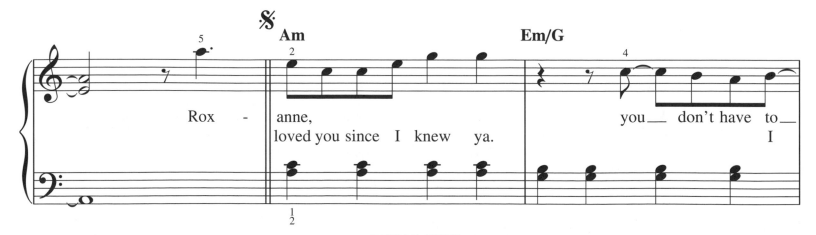

Rox - anne,
loved you since I knew ya.
you___ don't have to___
I

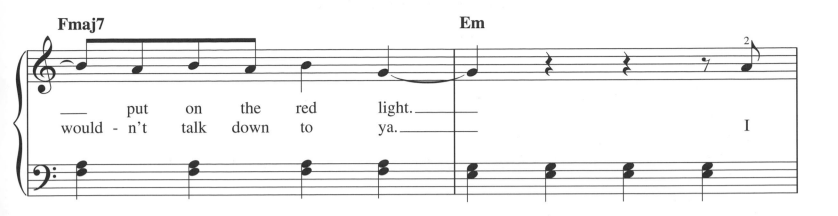

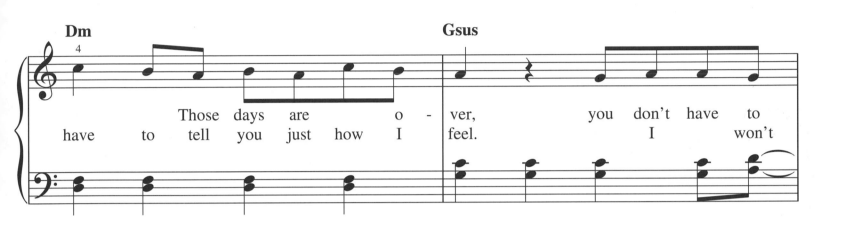

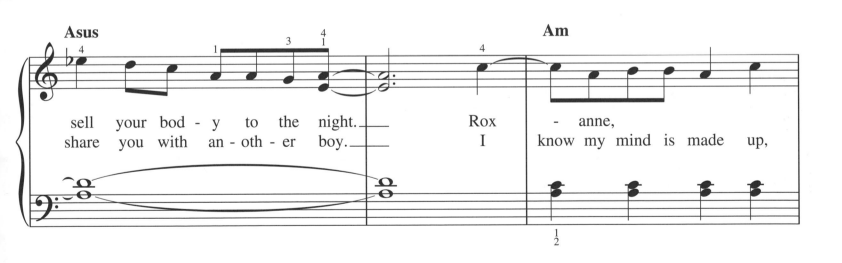

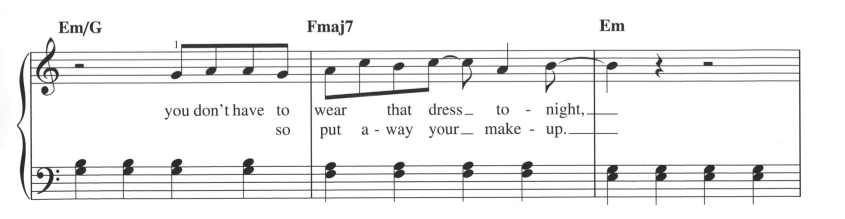

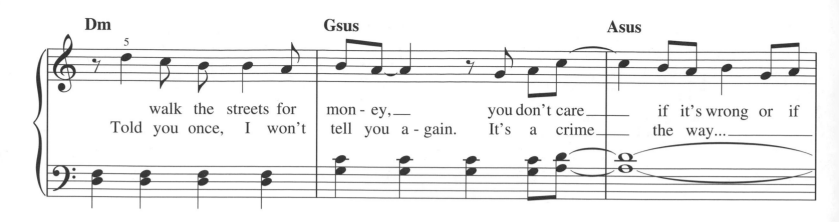

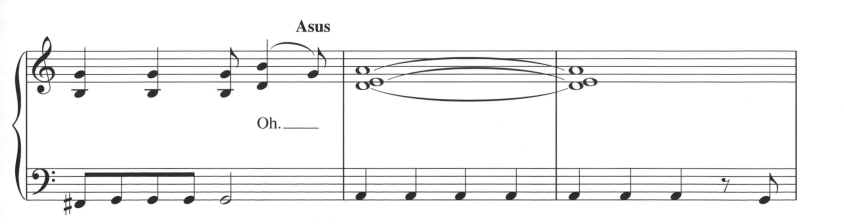

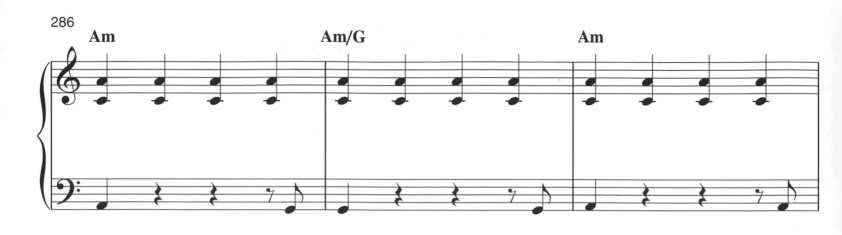

SEXUAL HEALING

Words and Music by MARVIN GAYE,
ODELL BROWN and DAVID RITZ

288

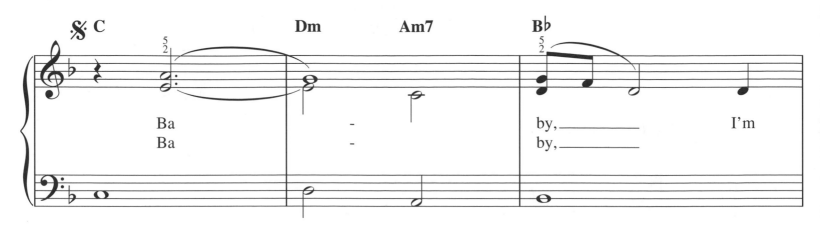

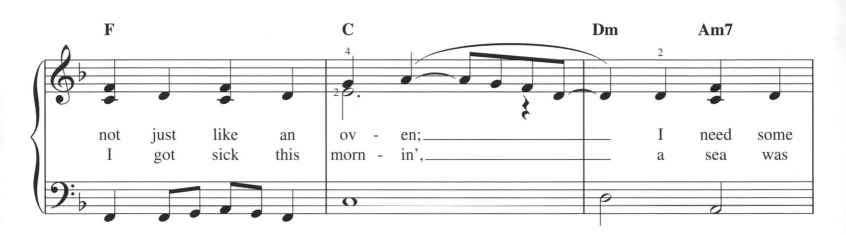

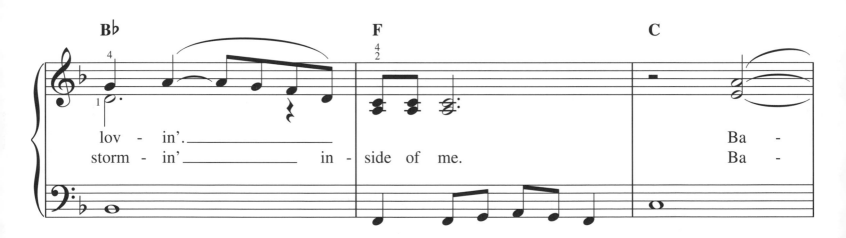

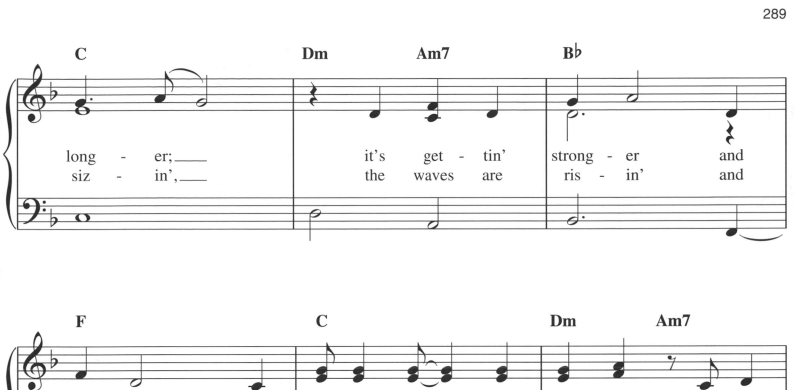

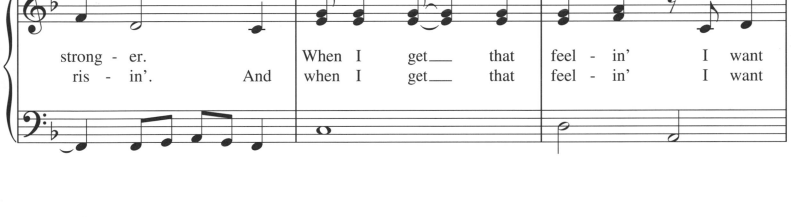

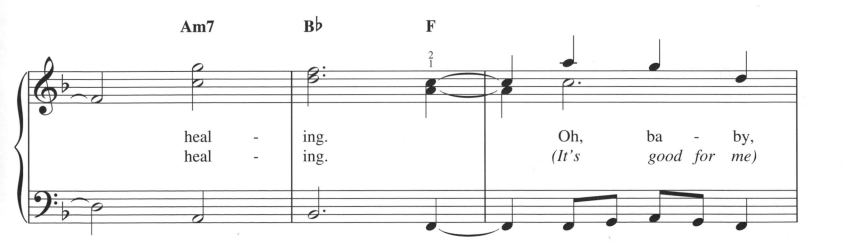

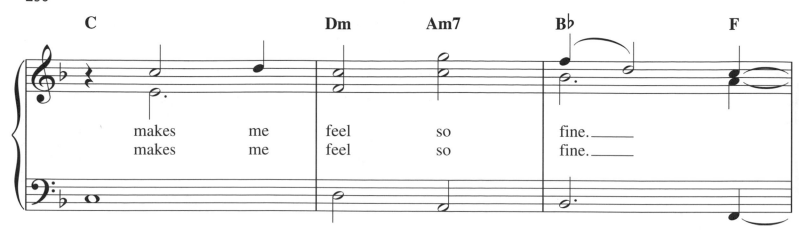

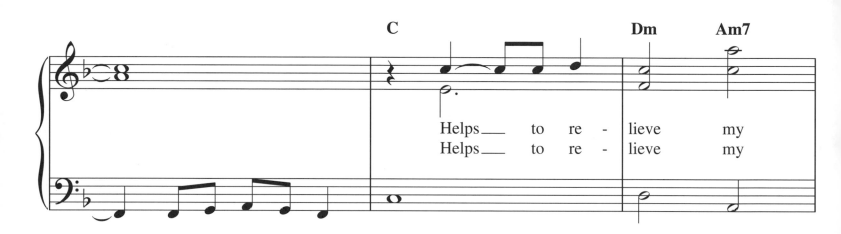

291

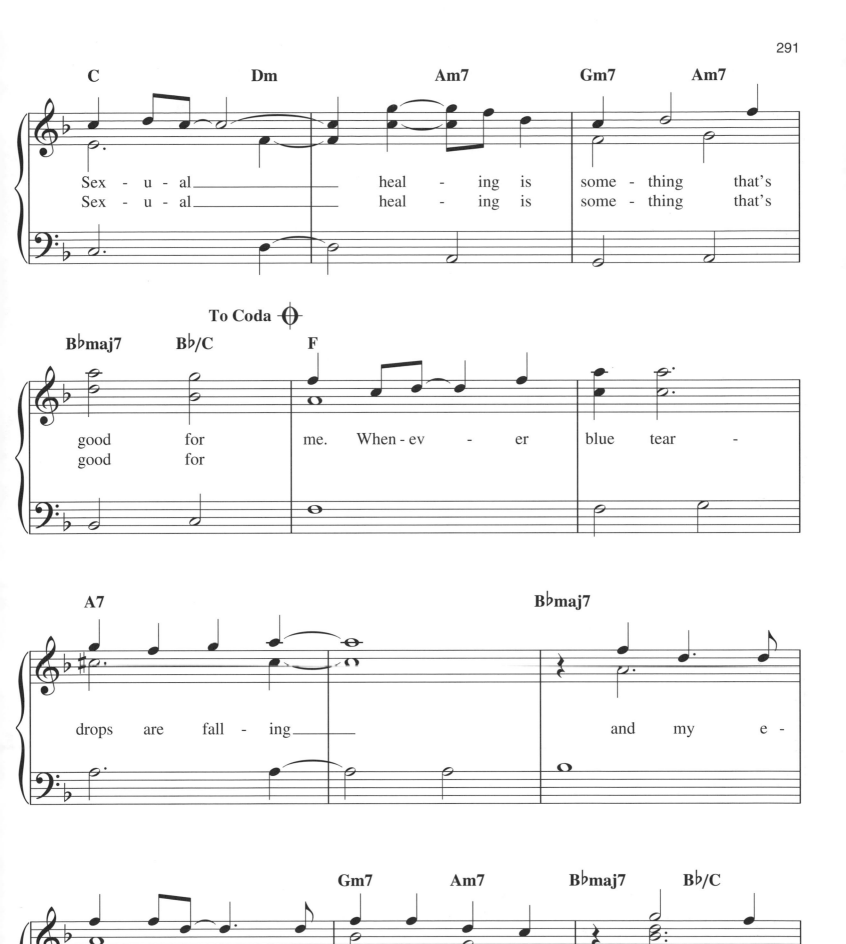

me____ there is some - thing I can do:

I can get on the tel - e - phone and call____

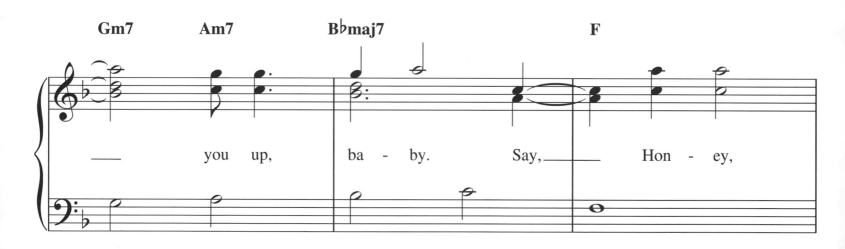

____ you up, ba - by. Say,____ Hon - ey,

I know you'll be there to re - lieve____ me 'cause the

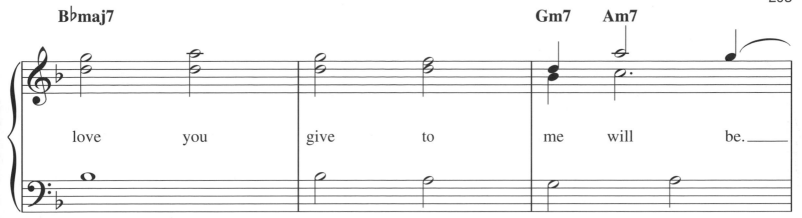

love you   you   give   to   me   will   be.____

____   If   you   don't   know   the   thing   you're

deal - ing,   I   can   tell____   you

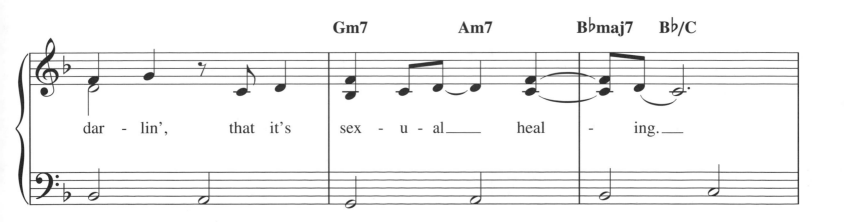

dar - lin',   that   it's   sex - u - al____   heal - ing.____

294

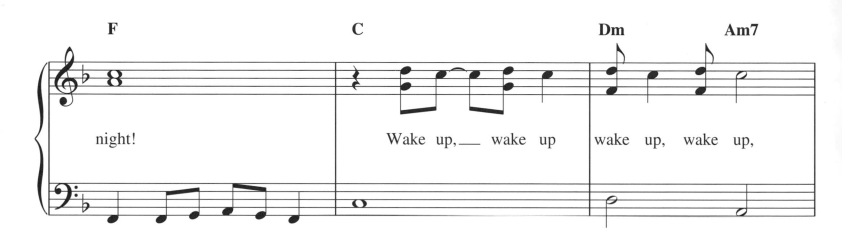

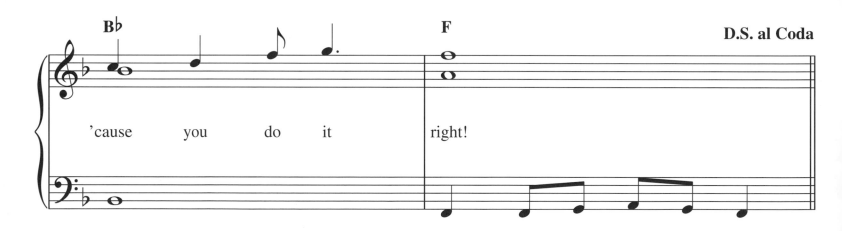

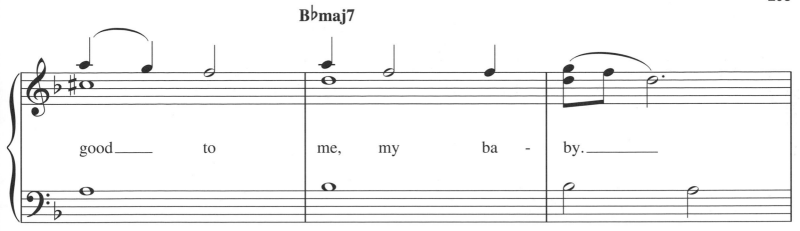

good_____ to me, my ba - by._____

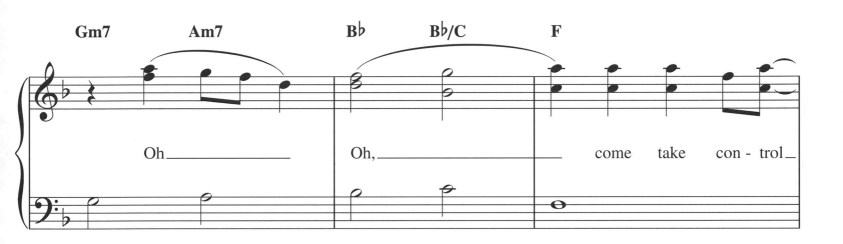

Oh_____ Oh,_____ come take con - trol_____

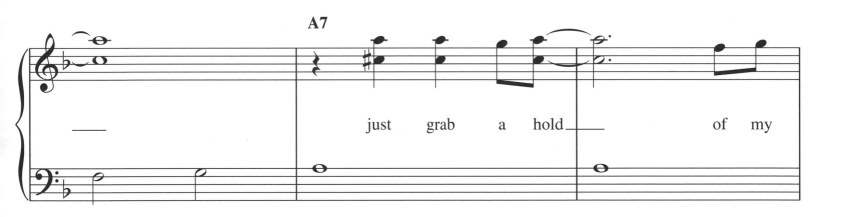

_____ just grab a hold_____ of my

bod - y and mind;_____ soon___ we'll be mak - in' it, hon - ey.

Bbmaj7   Bb/C   F

Oh, we'll be do - in' fine. You're my med - i - cine,

A7   Bbmaj7

o - pen up and let me in.___ Dar - lin',

Gm7   Am7   Bb   Bb/C

you're so pret - ty, I can't wait for you to op - er - ate.___

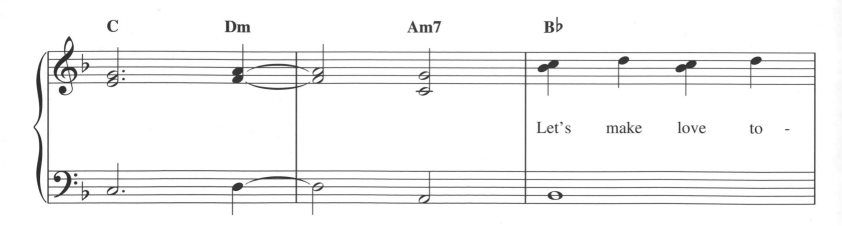

C   Dm   Am7   Bb

Let's make love to -

night!

Wake up, ___ wake up,

wake up wake up, 'cause you do it right!

SHE LOVES YOU

Words and Music by JOHN LENNON
and PAUL McCARTNEY

She loves you yeah, yeah, yeah, She loves you, yeah,

yeah, yeah, She loves you, yeah, yeah, yeah, yeah.

You think you've lost your love? Well, I saw her yester-

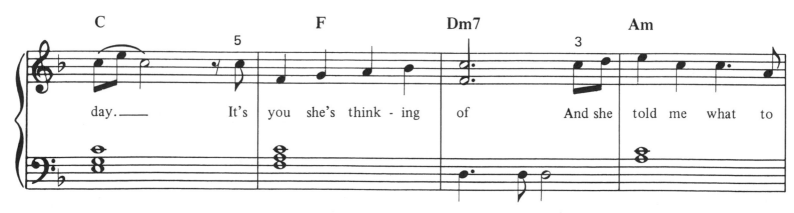

day. It's you she's think-ing of And she told me what to

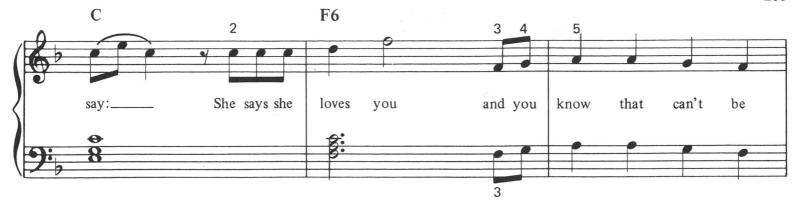

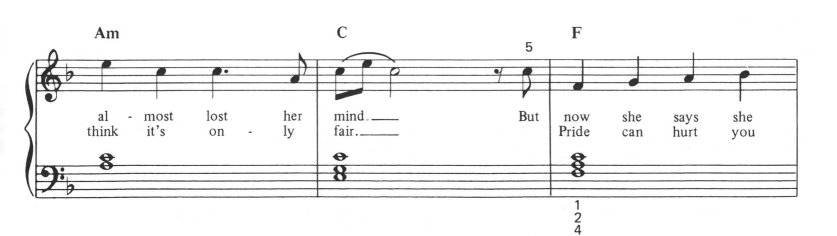

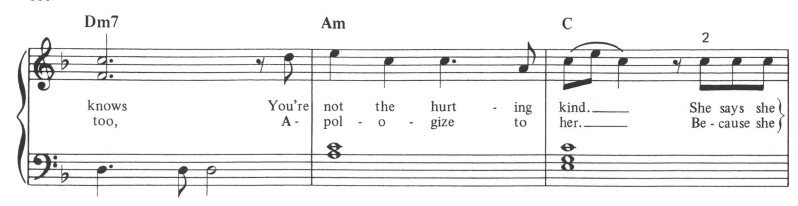

knows   You're | not the hurt - ing | kind.___ She says she
too,   A- | pol - o - gize to | her.___ Be - cause she

loves you   and you | know that can't be | bad. | Yes, she

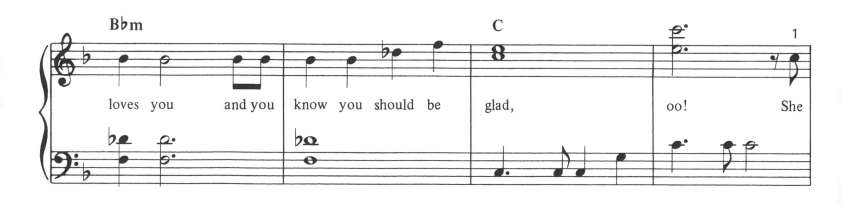

loves you   and you | know you should be | glad, | oo! She

loves you, yeah, | yeah, yeah, She | loves you, yeah,

yeah,   yeah. And with a   love   like   that   you   know   you   should   be

glad._____   You   glad,_____   With a

love   like   that   you   know   you   should   be   glad.   Yeah,   yeah,   yeah,
slowing   *much slower*

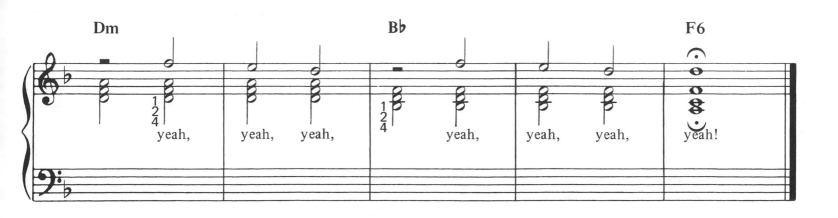

yeah,   yeah,   yeah,   yeah,   yeah,   yeah,   yeah!

SMELLS LIKE TEEN SPIRIT

Words and Music by KURT COBAIN,
KRIST NOVOSELIC and DAVE GROHL

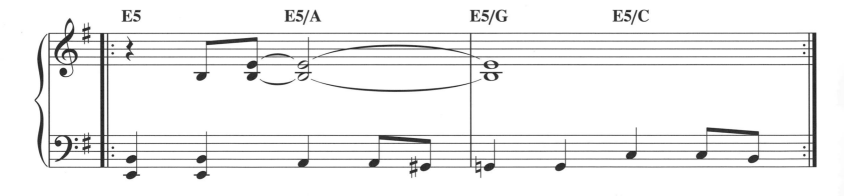

Load up on guns, bring your
I'm worse at what I do
And I for - get just why I

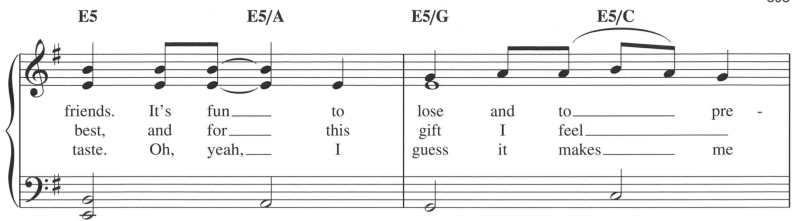

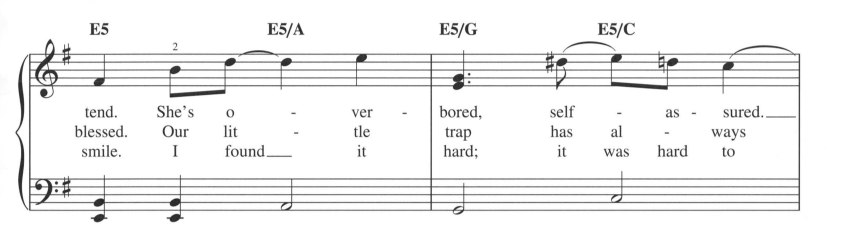

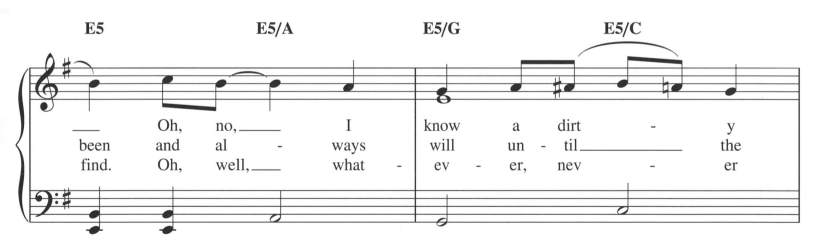

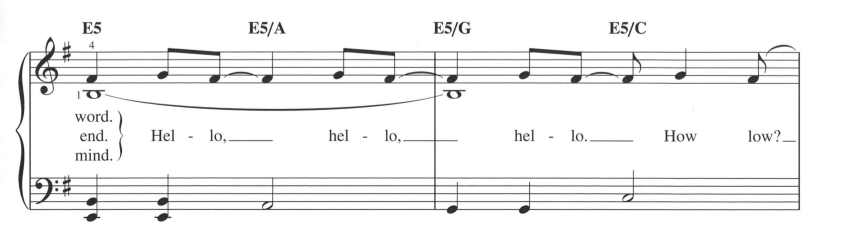

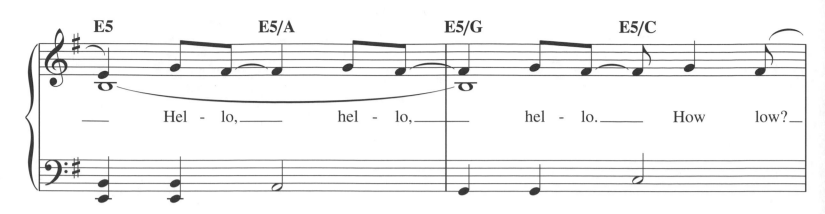

Hel - lo,_____ hel - lo,_____ hel - lo._____ How low?_

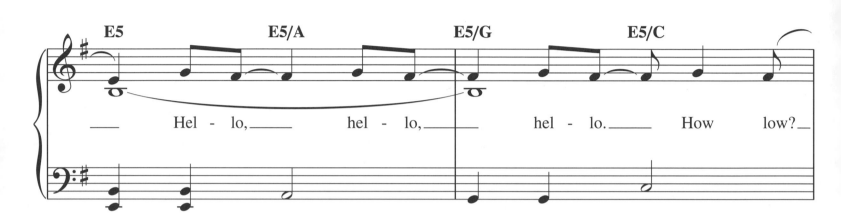

Hel - lo,_____ hel - lo,_____ hel - lo._____ How low?_

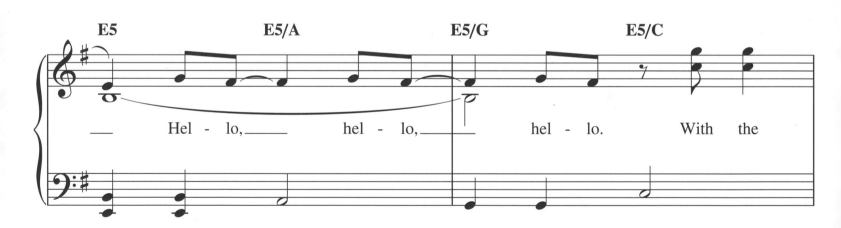

Hel - lo,_____ hel - lo,_____ hel - lo._ With the

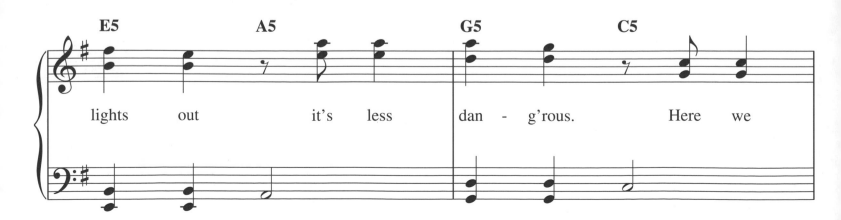

lights out it's less dan - g'rous. Here we

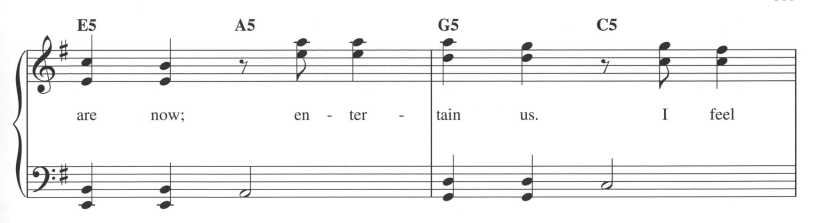

are now; en - ter - tain us. I feel

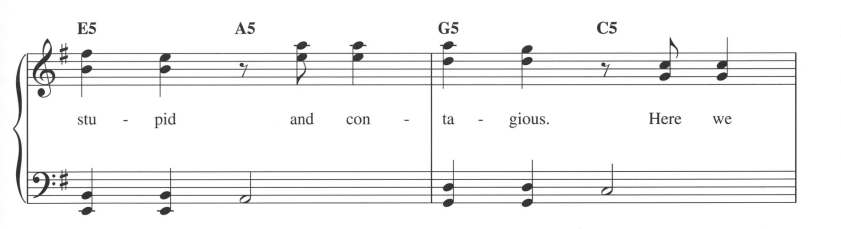

stu - pid and con - ta - gious. Here we

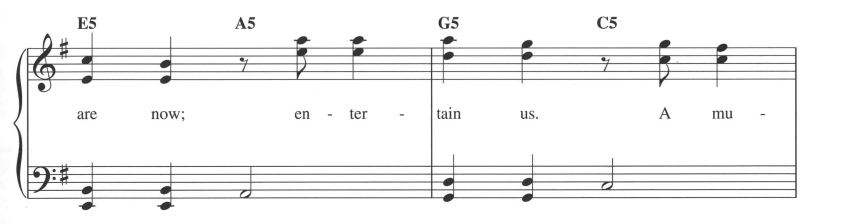

are now; en - ter - tain us. A mu -

To Coda ⊕

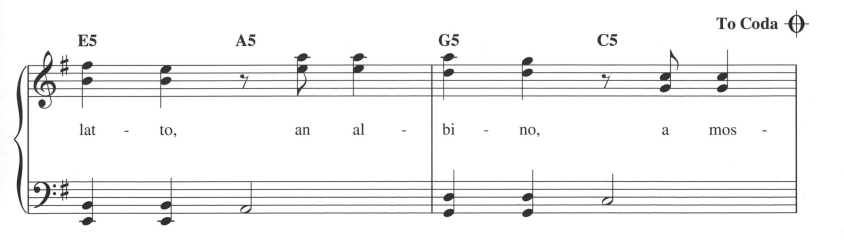

lat - to, an al - bi - no, a mos -

306

qui - to,   my li - bi - do.   Yeah!

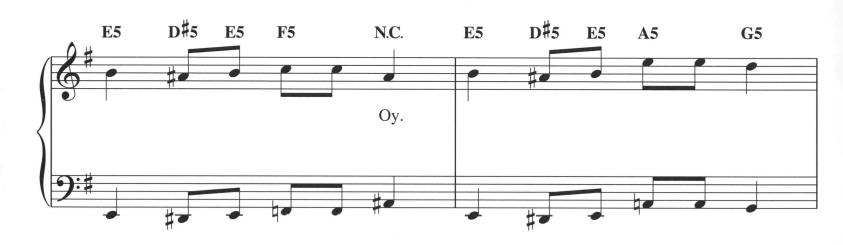

Oy.

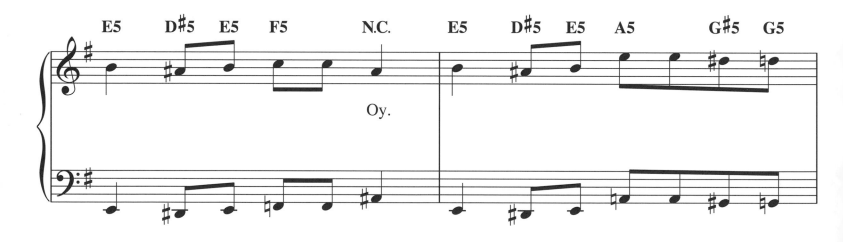

Oy.

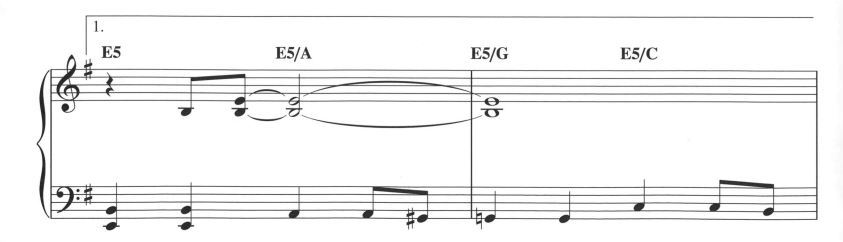

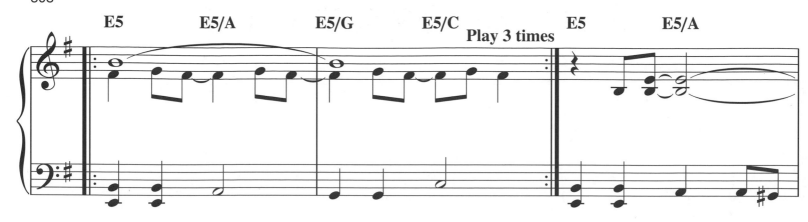

E5   E5/A   E5/G   E5/C   **Play 3 times**   E5   E5/A

D.S. al Coda

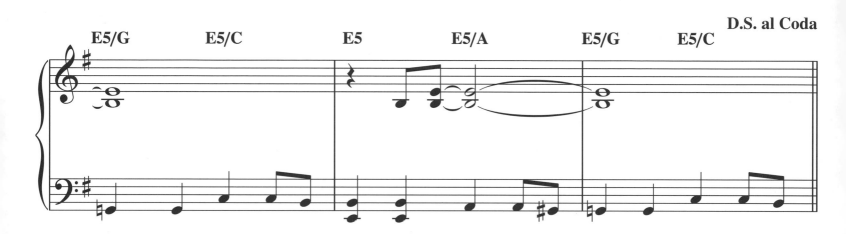

E5/G   E5/C   E5   E5/A   E5/G   E5/C

CODA

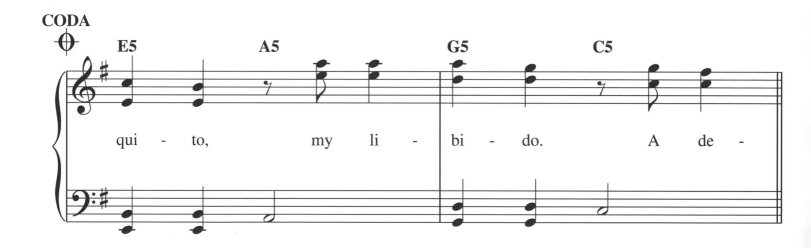

E5   A5   G5   C5

qui - to,   my li - bi - do.   A de -

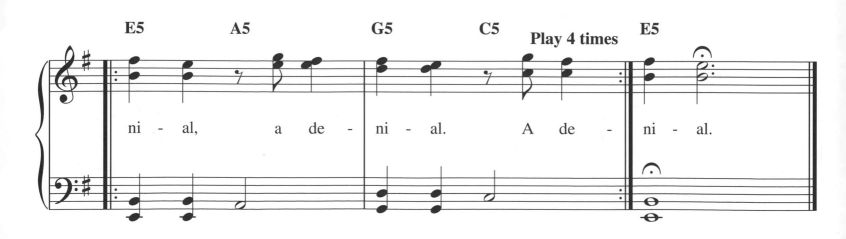

E5   A5   G5   C5   **Play 4 times**   E5

ni - al,   a de - ni - al.   A de - ni - al.

SOMEBODY TO LOVE

Words and Music by
DARBY SLICK

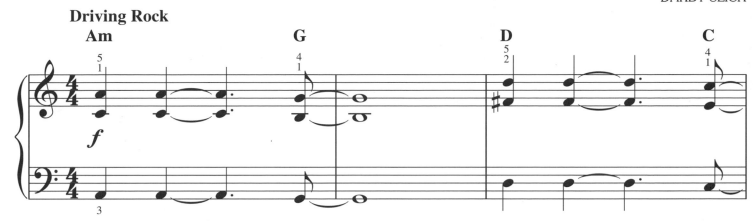

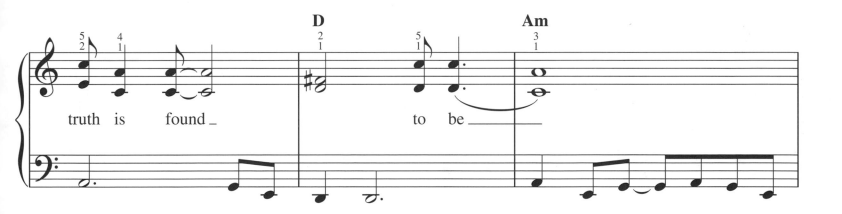

Am

When the

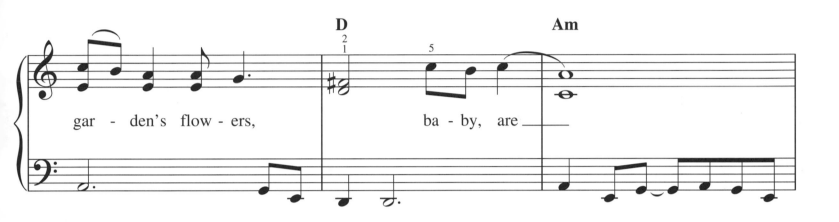

D   **Am**

gar - den's flow - ers,   ba - by, are ____

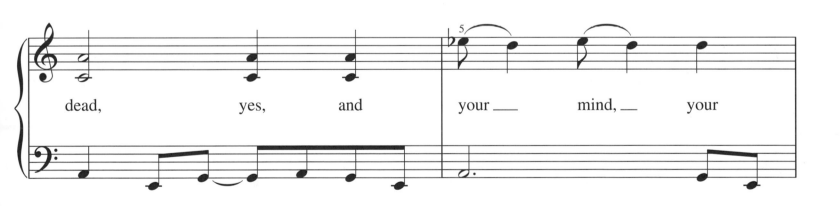

dead,   yes,   and   your ___ mind, ___ your

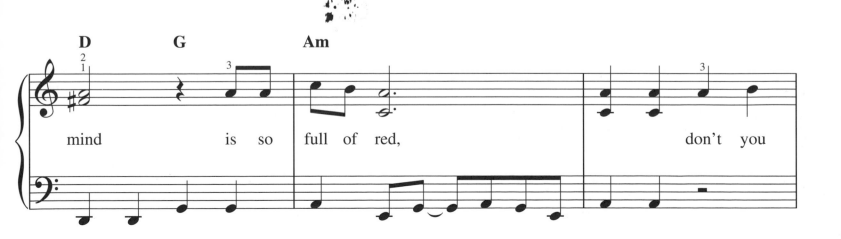

D **G**   **Am**

mind   is   so   full of red,   don't you

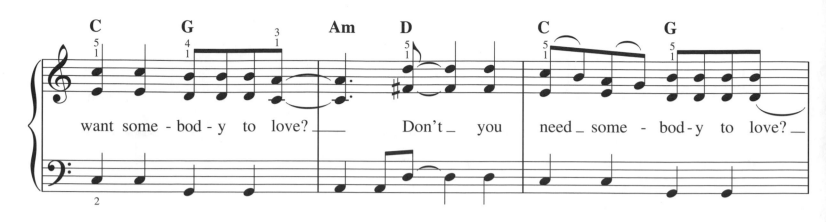

want some - bod - y to love? ___ Don't ___ you need ___ some - bod - y to love? ___

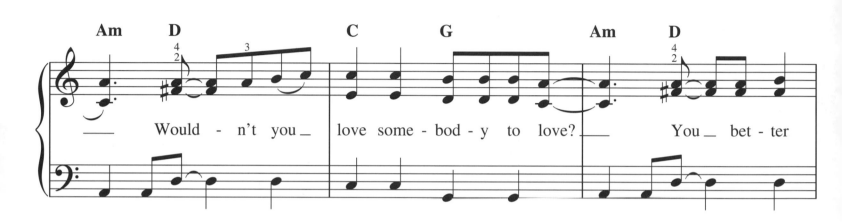

___ Would - n't you ___ love some - bod - y to love? ___ You ___ bet - ter

find some - bod - y to love. ___ Your eyes, ___ I say your eyes ___

___ may look like his. ___ Yeah, but

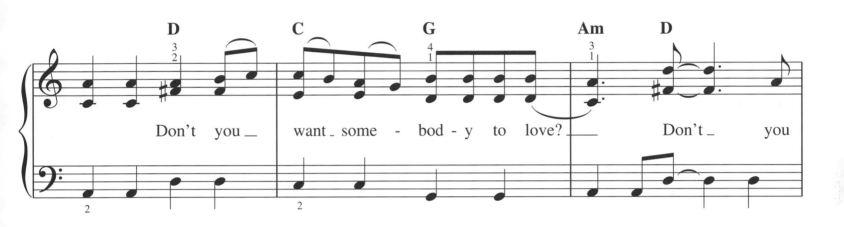

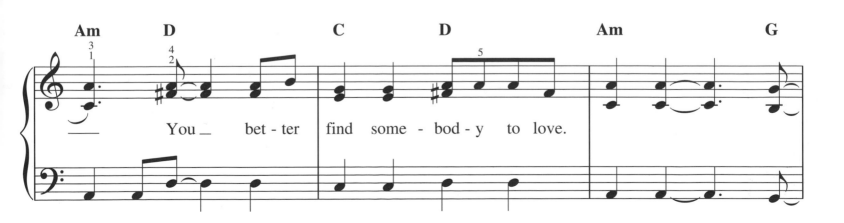

Tears _ are run - ning, _

they're all   run - ning down your breast,   and

your friends,   ba - by,   they treat you   like _ a guest. _

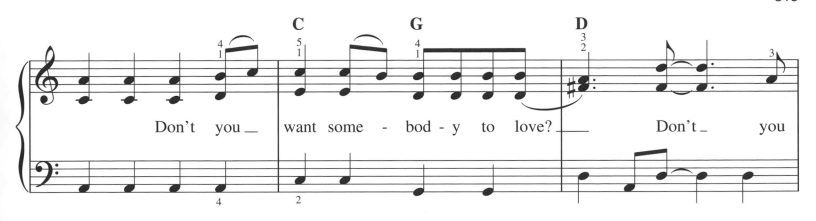

Don't you ___ want some - bod - y to love? ___ Don't ___ you

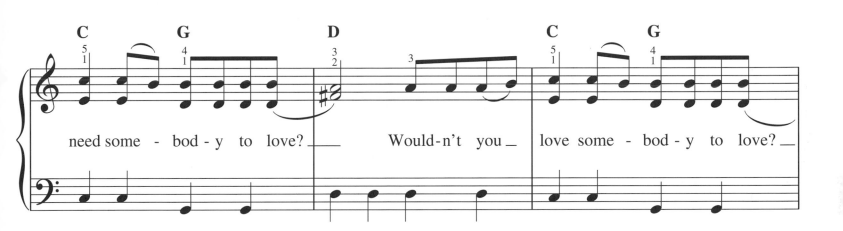

need some - bod - y to love? ___ Would - n't you ___ love some - bod - y to love? ___

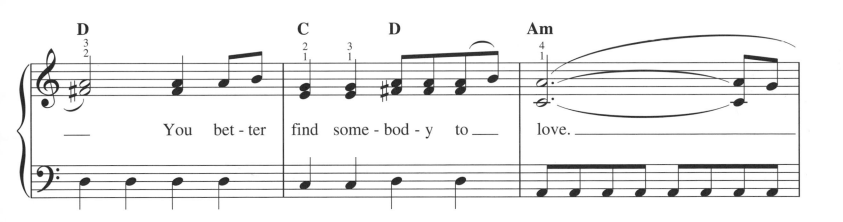

You bet - ter find some - bod - y to ___ love. _____

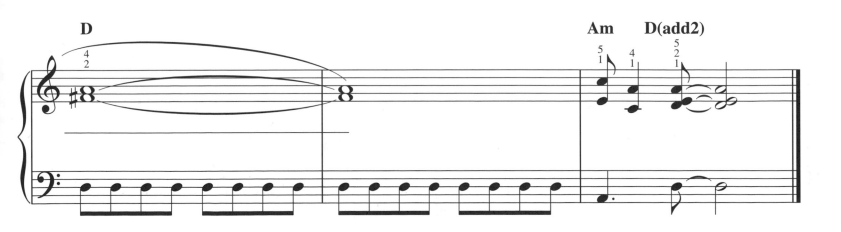

SPACE ODDITY

Words and Music by
DAVID BOWIE

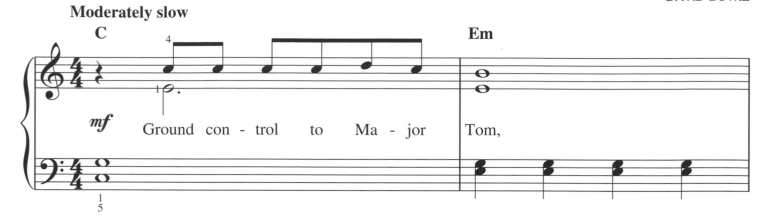

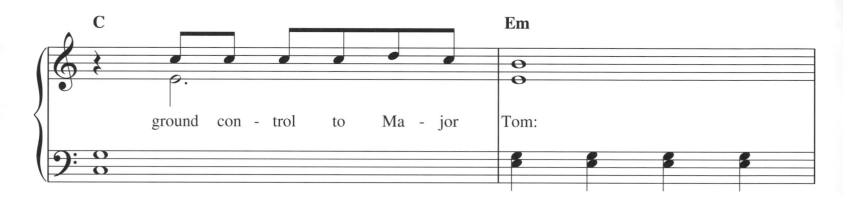

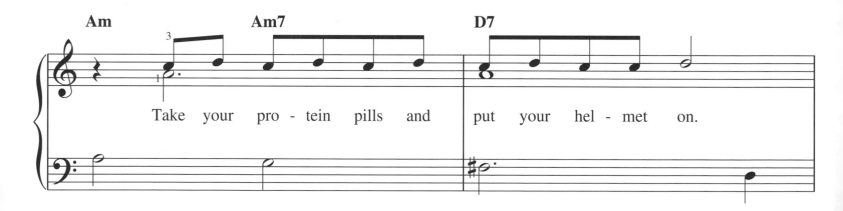

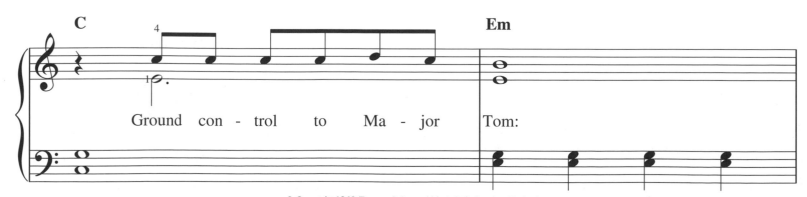

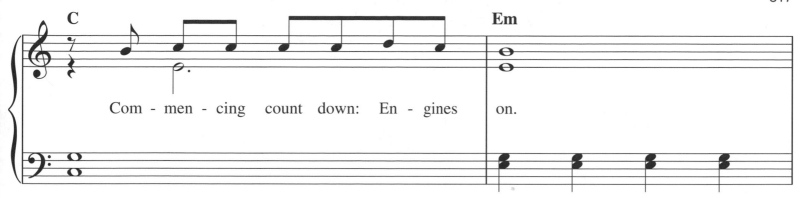

C ... **Em**

Com - men - cing count down: En - gines on.

Am ... **Am7** ... **D7**

Check ig - ni - tion and may God's love be with you.

C9♯11

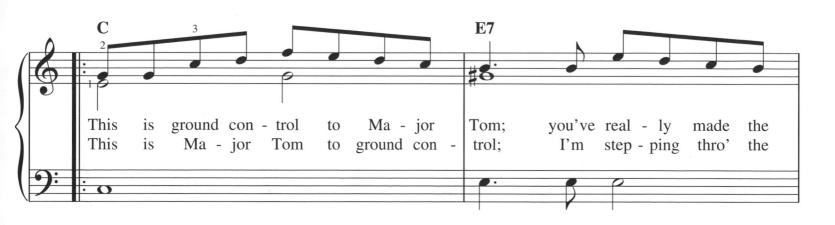

C ... **E7**

This is ground con - trol to Ma - jor Tom; you've real - ly made the
This is Ma - jor Tom to ground con - trol; I'm step - ping thro' the

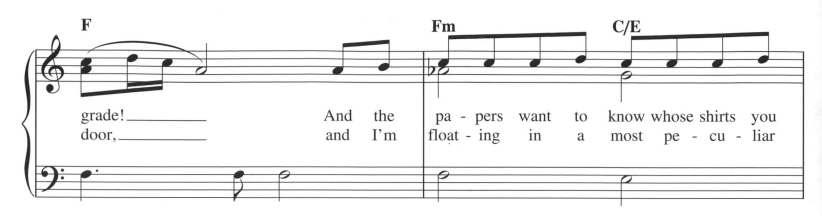

grade!_____ And the pa - pers want to know whose shirts you
door,_____ and I'm float - ing in a most pe - cu - liar

wear.____ Now it's time to leave the cap - sule if you
way.____ And the stars look ver - y dif - fer - ent to -

1.
dare._____

2.
day._____ For

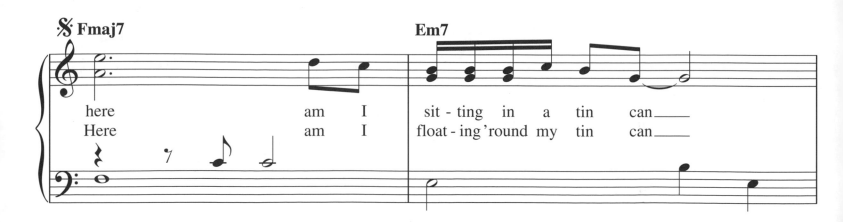

here am I sit - ting in a tin can____
Here am I float - ing 'round my tin can____

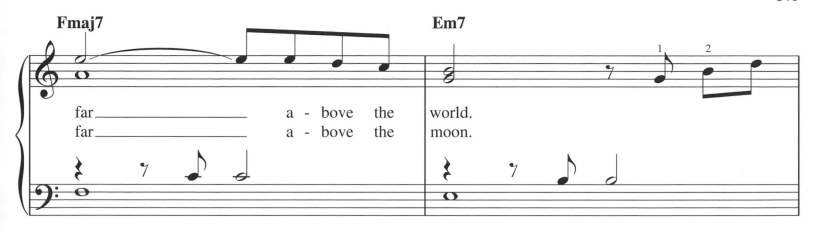

Fmaj7   **Em7**

far_____ a - bove the world.
far_____ a - bove the moon.

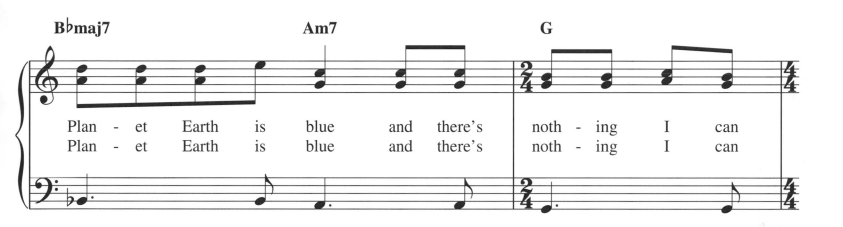

B♭maj7   **Am7**   **G**

Plan - et Earth is blue and there's noth - ing I can
Plan - et Earth is blue and there's noth - ing I can

F   **C** **F**   **G**   **A**   **C** **F**   **G**   **A**

do.
do.

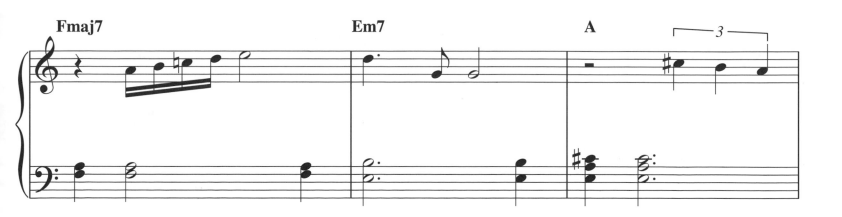

Fmaj7   **Em7**   **A**

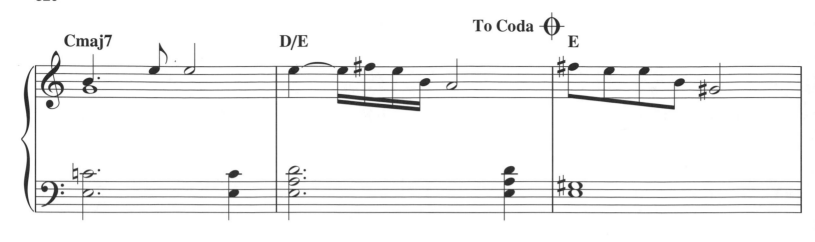

To Coda ⊕

Though I'm past one hun-dred thou-sand miles_____ I'm feel-ing ver - y

still_____ and I think my space-ship knows which way to

go.___ Tell my wife I love her ver - y much.__ "She

F   G   E7

knows." _____   "Ground con - trol   to   Ma - jor   Tom: Your

Am   Am7   D7/F#

cir - cuit's dead. There's some-thing wrong. Can you   hear   me   Ma - jor   Tom?   Can you

C/G   G   **D.S. al Coda**

hear   me   Ma - jor   Tom?   Can you   hear   me   Ma - jor   Tom?   Can you?"

CODA

E   D/E   C(add9)

rit.

STAND BY ME

Words and Music by BEN E. KING,
JERRY LEIBER and MIKE STOLLER

When the night has come and the

land_____ is dark, and the moon_____ is the

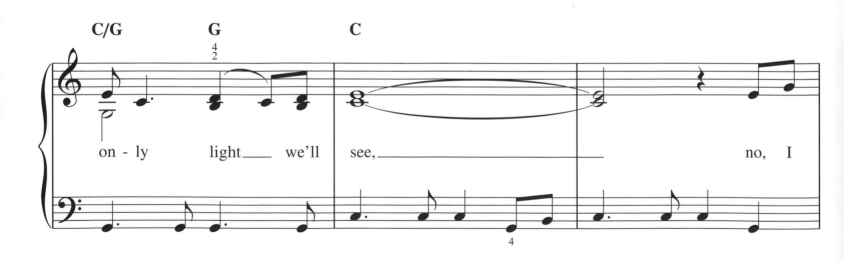

on - ly light____ we'll see,_____ no, I

324

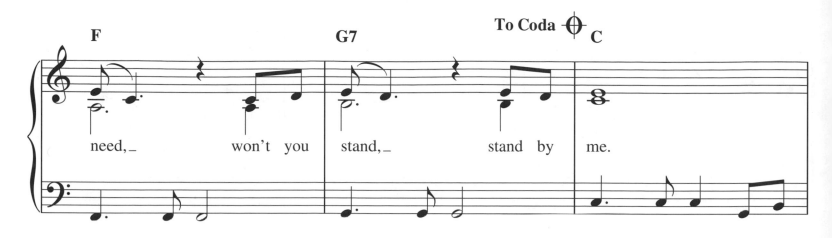

need,— won't you stand,— stand by me.

And if the sky that we look up -

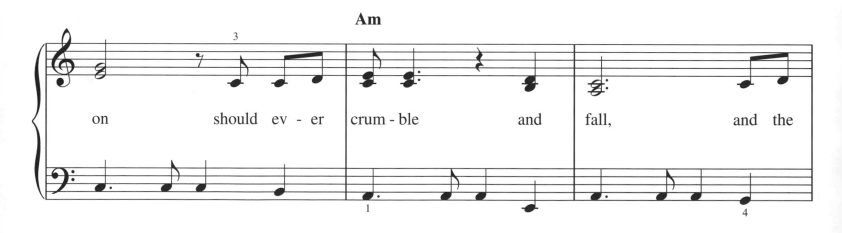

on should ev - er crum - ble and fall, and the

moun - tains_____ should fall_____ to the sea,_____

325

no, I   won't_   be a - fraid,_   no,   I

won't_____   shed a tear,   just as   long_   as you

stand,_   stand by   me.   Dar - ling,

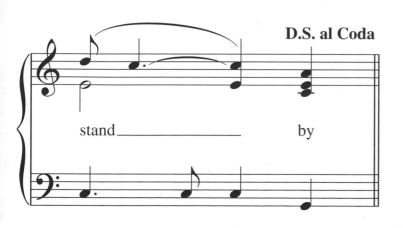

stand_____ by

me.

START ME UP

Words and Music by MICK JAGGER
and KEITH RICHARDS

327

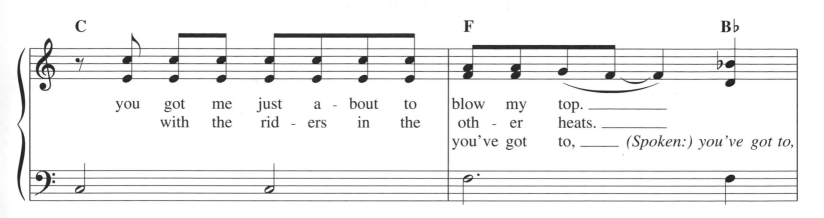

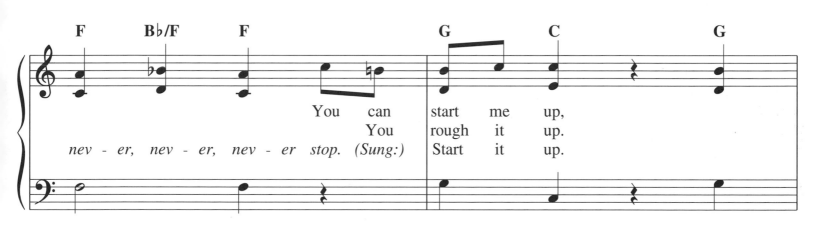

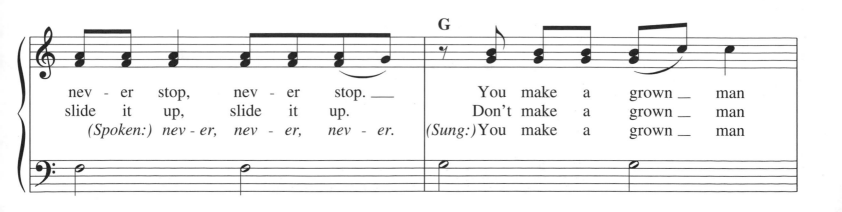

cry, _____ you make a grown _ man cry, _____
cry, _____ don't make a grown _ man cry, _____
cry, _____ you make a grown _ man cry, _____

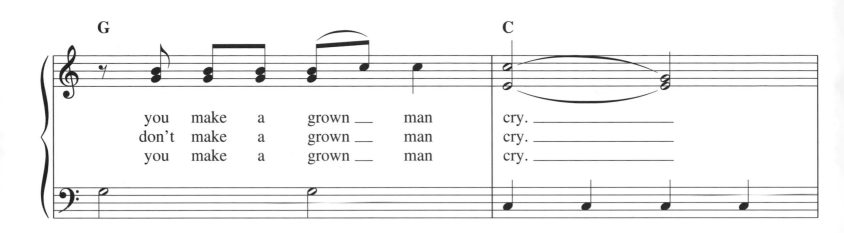

you make a grown _ man cry. _____
don't make a grown _ man cry. _____
you make a grown _ man cry. _____

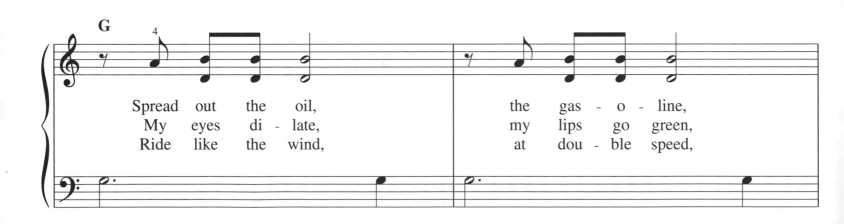

Spread out the oil, the gas - o - line,
My eyes di - late, my lips go green,
Ride like the wind, at dou - ble speed,

F/G   **To Coda** ⊕

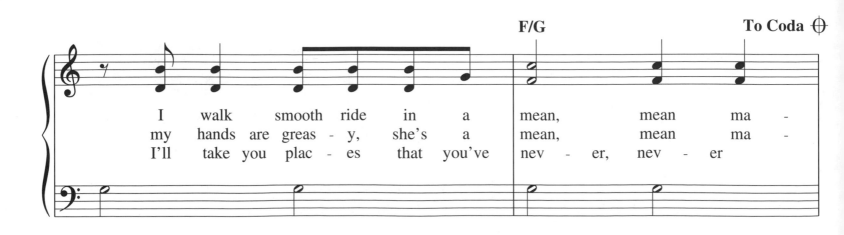

I walk smooth ride in a mean, mean ma -
my hands are greas - y, she's a mean, mean ma -
I'll take you plac - es that you've nev - er, nev - er

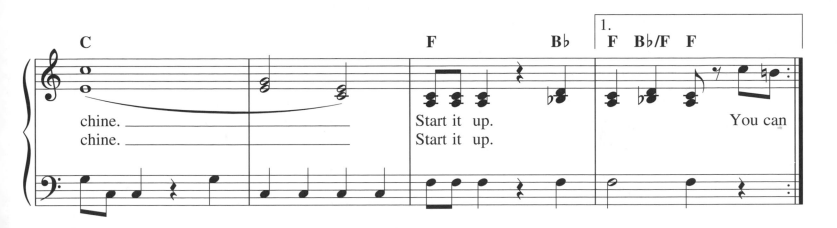

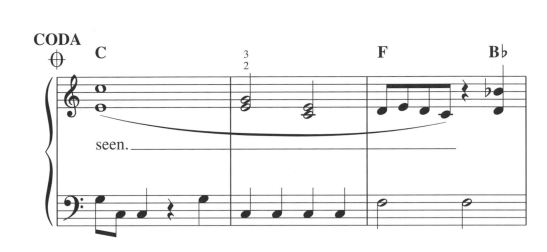

STAYIN' ALIVE

Words and Music by ROBIN GIBB,
MAURICE GIBB and BARRY GIBB

331

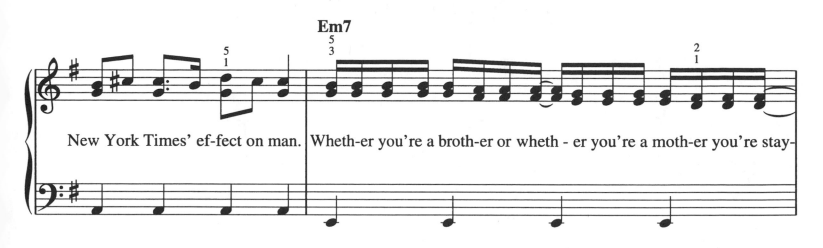

New York Times' ef-fect on man. Wheth-er you're a broth-er or wheth - er you're a moth-er you're stay-

- in' a -live,__ stay-in'a-live.__ Feel the cit-y break-in' and ev-'ry bod-y shak-in', and we're

stay-in' a - live,__ stay-in' a - live.__ Ah, ha, ha, ha,

stay-in' a - live,__ stay-in' a - live.__ Ah, ha, ha, ha,

Some-bod - y help me.____   Some-bod - y help__ me yeah.__

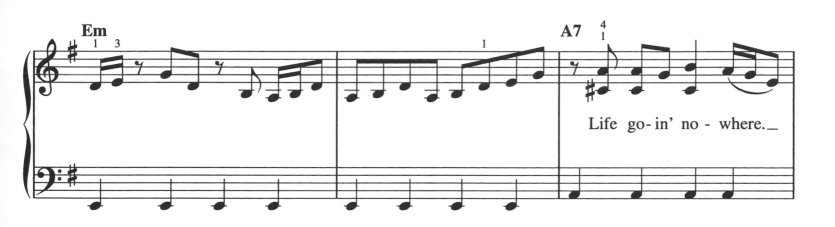

Em

A7

Life go-in' no - where.__

Some-bod - y help__ me yeah.__   Stay-in' a-live.

Em

STRAWBERRY FIELDS FOREVER

Words and Music by JOHN LENNON
and PAUL McCARTNEY

Slowly, but not dragging

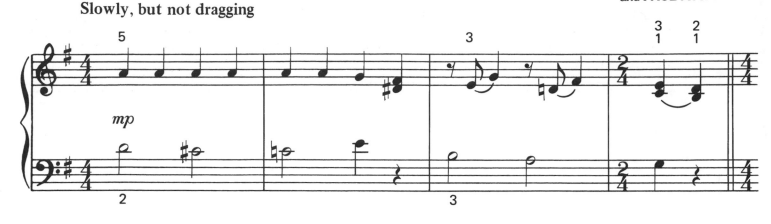

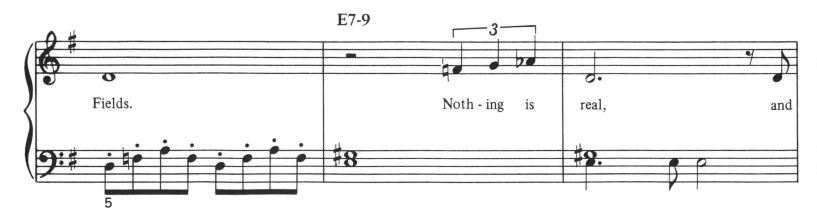

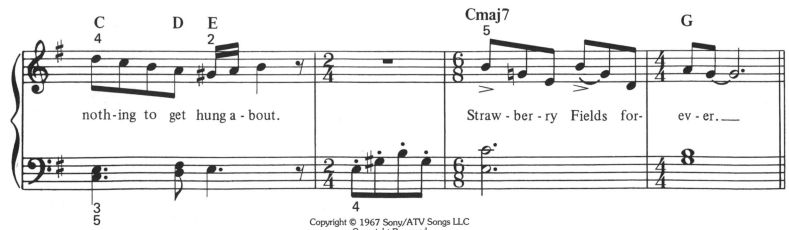

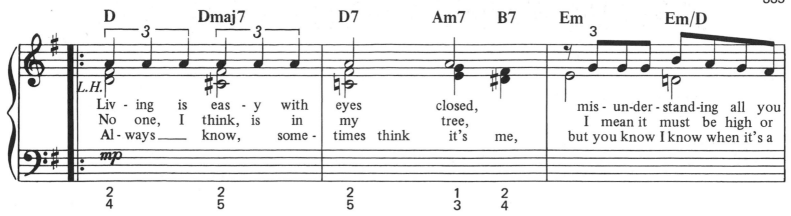

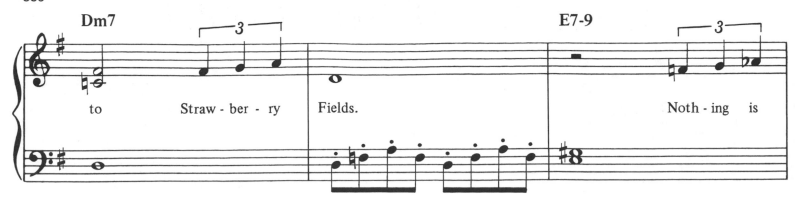

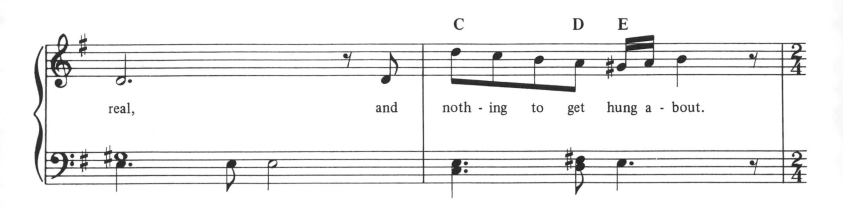

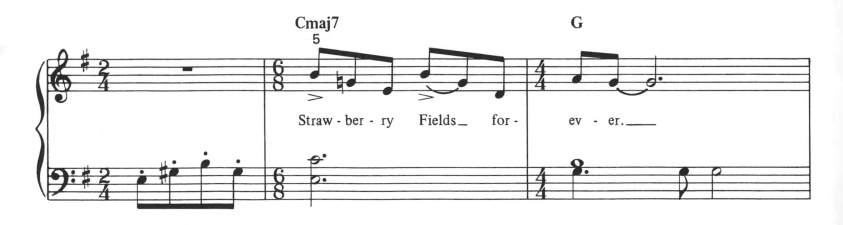

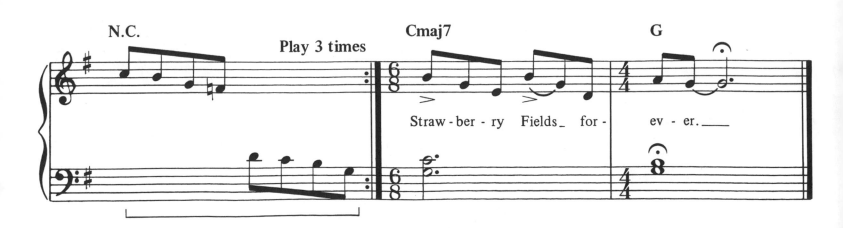

SUNSHINE OF YOUR LOVE

Words and Music by JACK BRUCE,
PETE BROWN and ERIC CLAPTON

It's get-ting near dawn;
with you, my love;

when the

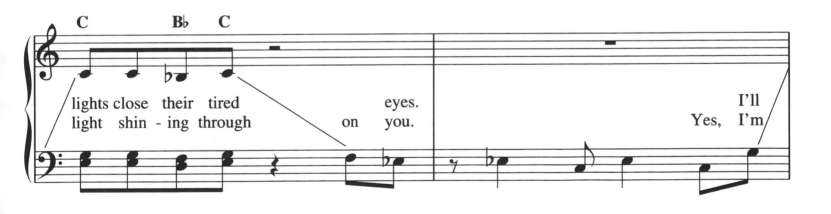

lights close their tired
light shin-ing through

eyes.
on you.

I'll
Yes, I'm

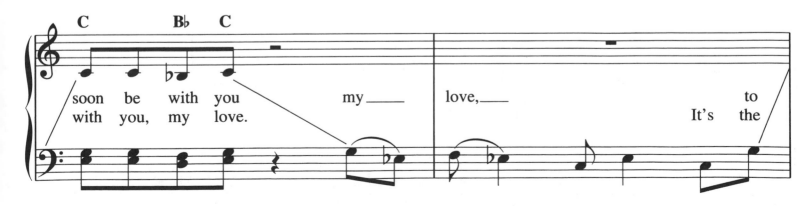

soon be with you
with you, my love.

my ___ love, ___

to
It's the

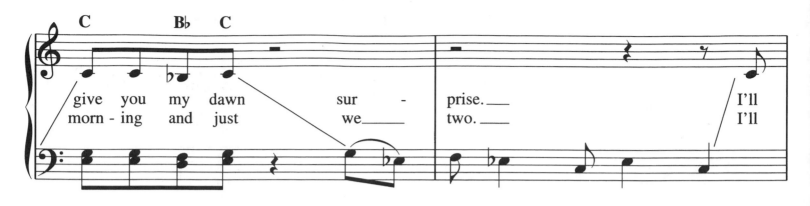

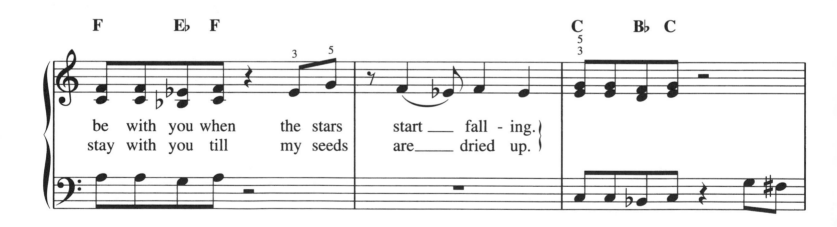

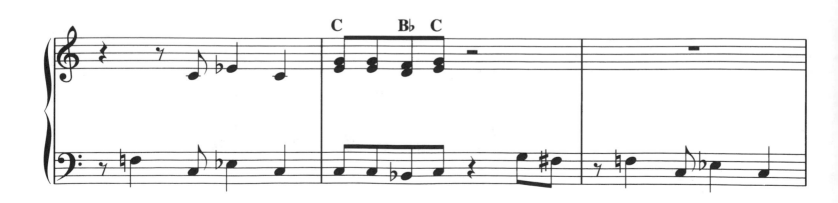

339

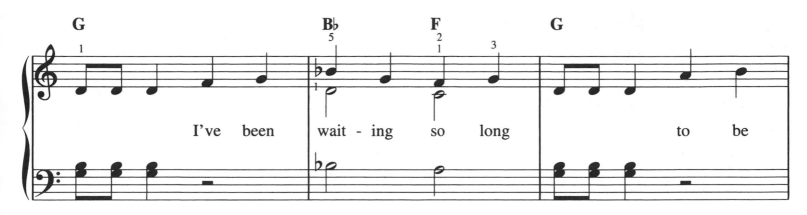

I've been   wait - ing   so   long   to be

where   I'm   go - ing   in the   sun - shine of your

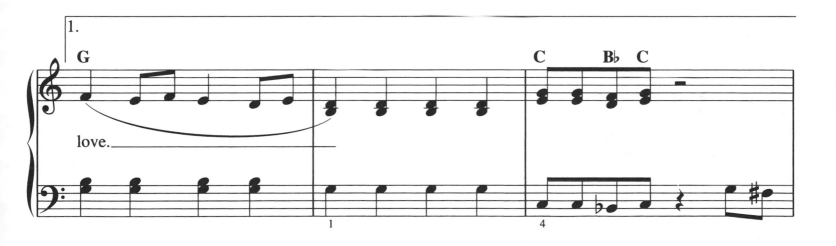

1.

love.

2.

I'm / love.

SUITE: JUDY BLUE EYES

Words and Music by
STEPHEN STILLS

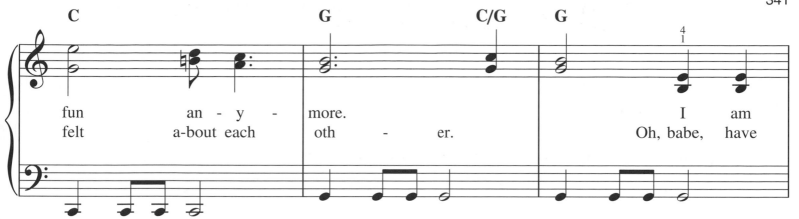

fun — an - y - more.
felt — a-bout each — oth - er. — Oh, babe, — have

sor - — ry.
mer - — cy. — Some - times — it
Don't — let — the

hurts — so — bad - ly — I — must — cry___ out
past — re - mind — us — of — what — we — are — not

loud.
now. — I — am — lone - — ly.___
I — am — not — dream - — ing.___

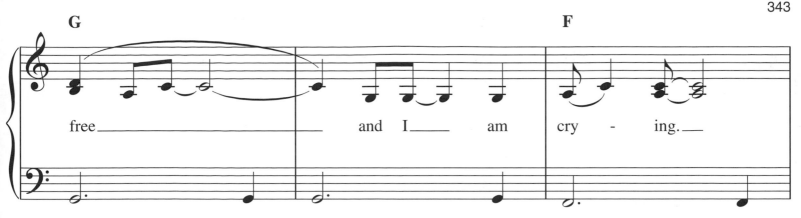

free_____ and I____ am cry - ing.____

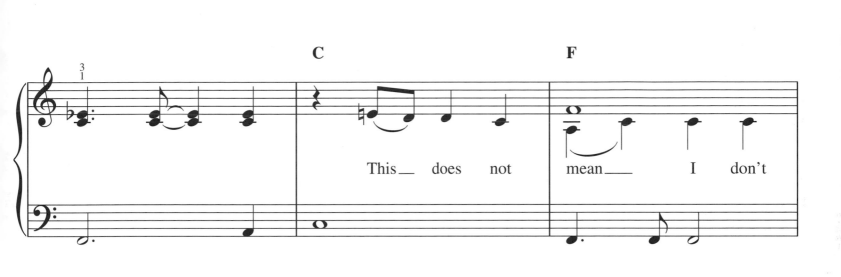

This__ does not mean____ I don't

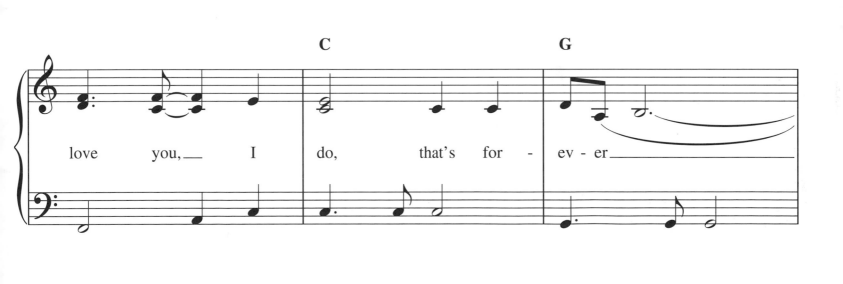

love you,__ I do, that's for - ev - er_____

____ yes, and__ for al - ways._____ I am

yours,   you are   mine,   you are   what you are.

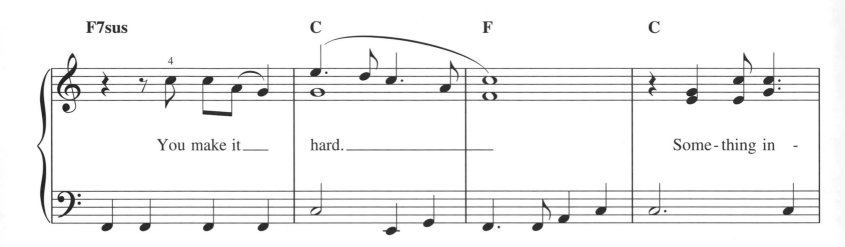

You make it___ hard._____   Some-thing in -

side   is   tell - ing me___ that   I've got___ your

se - cret.   Are you still   lis - t'ning?

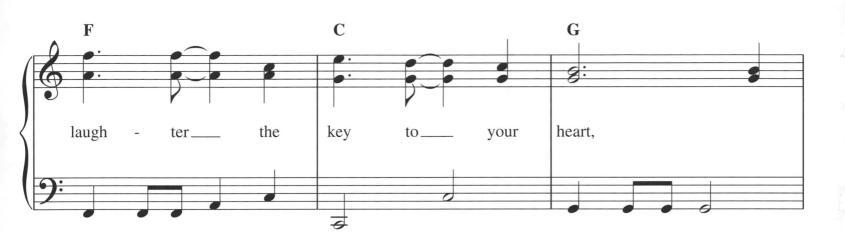

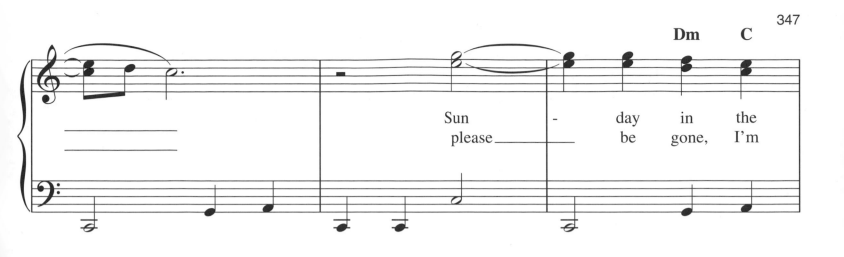

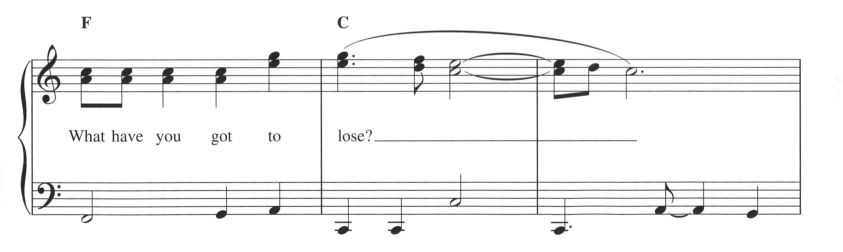

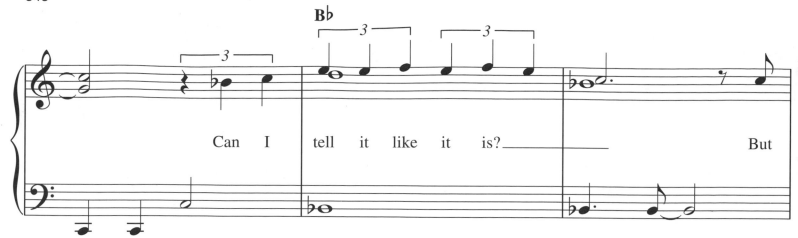

Can I tell it like it is?____ But

lis - ten to me, ba - by.____ It's my heart___

___ that's a - suf - f'rin'. It's a - dy - in'. And that's what I_____ have to

lose.____

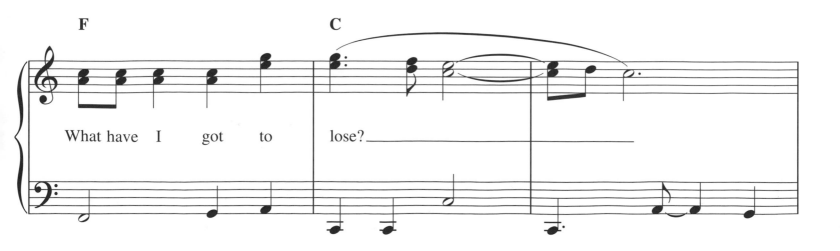

1. **2.**

Bb/C **C**

Chest - nut brown___ ca - nar - y,_____
Voic - es of___ the an - gels,_____
Lac - y, lilt - ing lyr - ic,_____

F/C **C7**

ru - by throat - ed spar - row,
ring a - round___ the moon - light,
los - ing love,___ la - ment - ing,

Bb/C

sing a song,___ don't be long,___
ask - ing me, said she so free,___
change my life,___ make it right,___

SUMMERTIME BLUES

Words and Music by EDDIE COCHRAN
and JERRY CAPEHART

I'm a - gon-na raise a fuss, I'm a - gon-na raise a hol - ler,

a - bout a - work-in' all sum-mer just to

try to earn a dol - lar. Ev -'ry

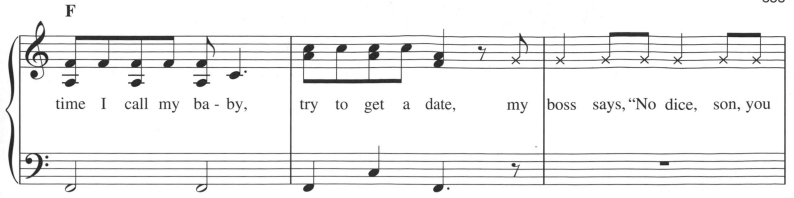

time I call my ba - by,   try to get a date,   my boss says, "No dice, son, you

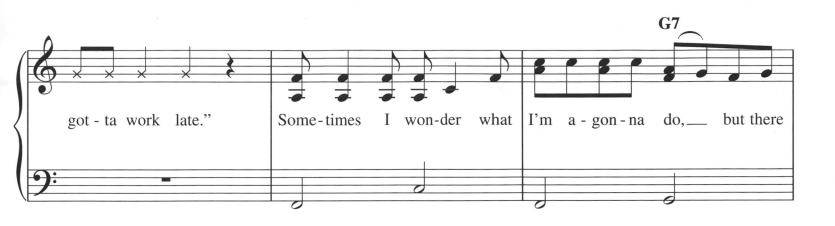

got - ta work late."   Some - times I won - der what   I'm a - gon - na do,__ but there

ain't no cure for the   sum - mer - time__ blues.

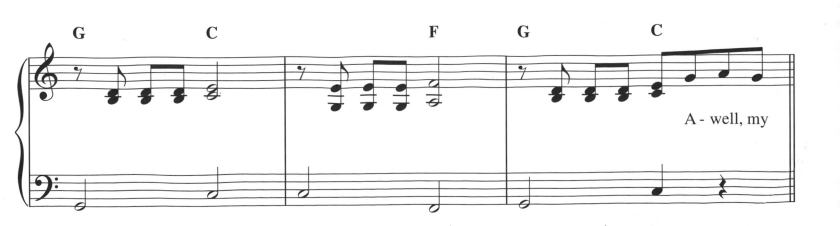

A - well, my

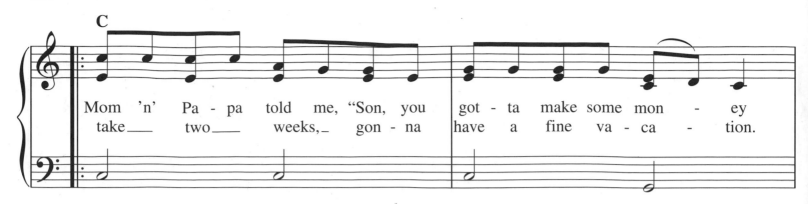

Mom 'n' Pa - pa told me, "Son, you got - ta make some mon - ey
take___ two___ weeks,___ gon - na have a fine va - ca - tion.

if you wan-na use the car to go a -
I'm gon-na take__ my__ prob-lem to the

rid - in' next Sun - day."   Well, I
U - nit-ed Na - tions!   Well, I

did - n't go to work, told the boss I was sick,___ "Now you
called__ my__ Con-gress-man and he__ said quote,___ "I'd___

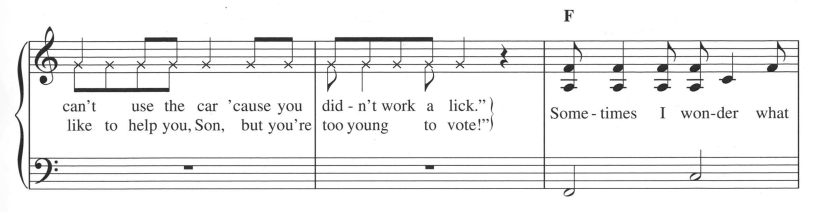

can't use the car 'cause you did-n't work a lick."
like to help you, Son, but you're too young to vote!"

Some-times I won-der what

I'm a-gon-na do,__ but there ain't no cure for the sum-mer-time__ blues.

I'm gon-na

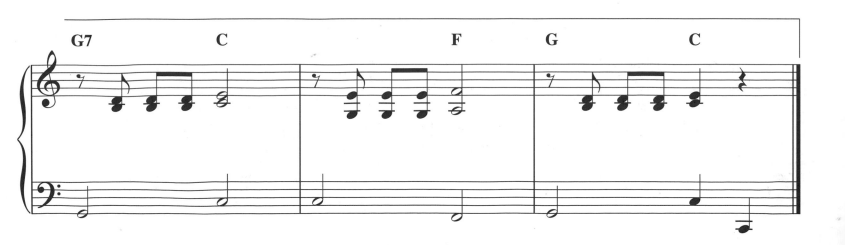

SUPERSTITION

Words and Music by
STEVIE WONDER

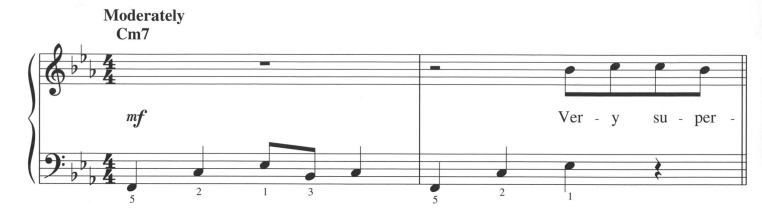

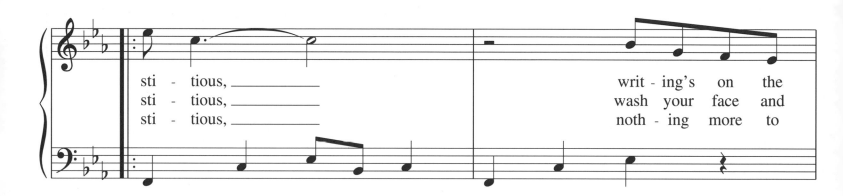

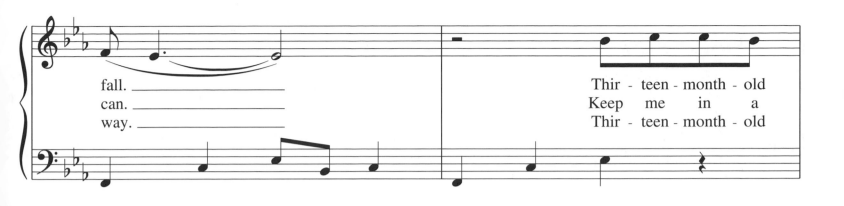

fall. _____
can. _____
way. _____

Thir - teen - month - old
Keep me in a
Thir - teen - month - old

ba - by _____
day - dream, _____
ba - by _____

broke the look - in'
keep me go - in'
broke the look - in'

glass. _____
strong. _____
glass. _____

Sev - en years of
You don't wan - na
Sev - en years of

bad luck, _____
save me, _____
bad luck, _____

the good things in your
sad ____ is my
the good things in your

past. _____
song. _____
past. _____

G   **Ab**

When you be-lieve ____ in things   that you don't

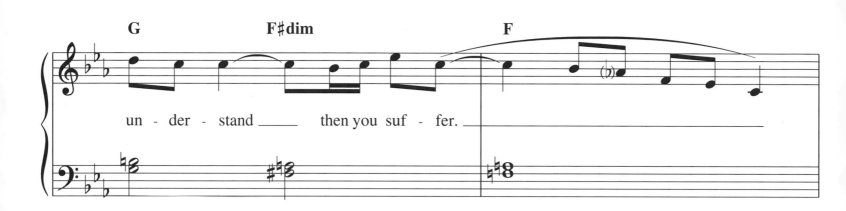

G   **F#dim**   **F**

un - der - stand ____ then you suf - fer. _____

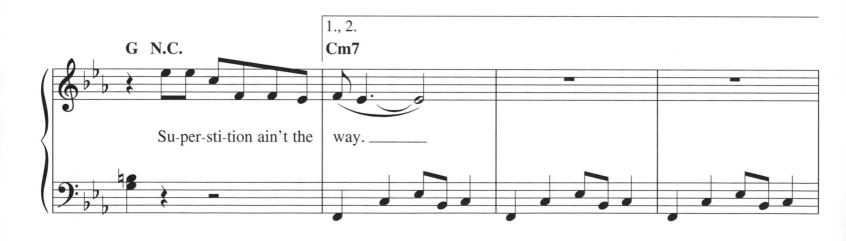

G **N.C.**   1., 2. **Cm7**

Su-per-sti-tion ain't the | way. _____

3. **Cm7**   **C7#9**

Ver-y su-per- | way. ___
Ver-y su-per-

rit.

TANGLED UP IN BLUE

Words and Music by
BOB DYLAN

knows I've paid some dues ___ get - tin' through.
meet a - gain some - day ___ on the av - e - nue.
nev - er 'scaped my mind ___ and I just grew ___

1.-7.

Tan - gled up in blue. ___
tan - gled up in blue. ___

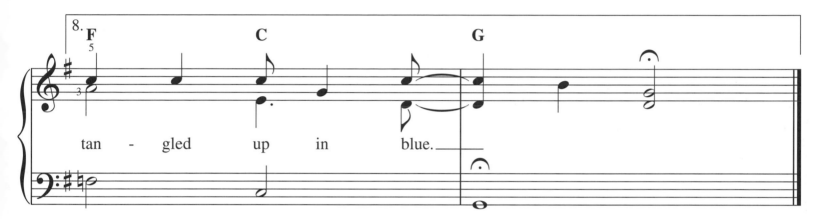

tan - gled up in blue.

Additional Lyrics

4. She was working in topless place
   And I stopped in for a beer.
   I just kept looking at the side of her face
   In the spotlight so clear.
   And later on when the crowd thinned out
   I was just about to do the same.
   She was standing there in back of my chair,
   Said to me, "Don't I know your name?"
   I muttered something underneath my breath.
   She studied the lines on my face.
   I must admit I felt a little uneasy
   When she bent down to tie the laces of my shoe,
   Tangled up in blue.

5. She lit a burner on the stove
   And offered me a pipe.
   "I thought you'd never say hello," she said.
   "You look like the silent type."
   Then she opened up a book of poems
   And handed it to me,
   Written by an Italian poet
   From the thirteenth century.
   And every one of them words rang true
   And glowed like burning coal,
   Pourin' off of every page
   Like it was written in my soul,
   From me to you,
   Tangled up in blue.

6. I lived with them on Montague Street
   In a basement down the stairs.
   There was music in the cafes at night
   And revolution in the air.
   Then he started in the dealing in slaves
   And something inside of him died.
   She had to sell everything she owned
   And froze up inside.
   And when finally the bottom finally fell out
   I became withdrawn.
   The only thing I knew how to do
   Was to keep on keeping on,
   Like a bird that flew
   Tangled up in blue.

7. So now I'm going back again.
   I got to get to her somehow.
   All the people we used to know,
   They're an illusion to me now.
   Some are mathematicians,
   Some are carpenter's wives.
   Don't know how it all got started,
   I don't know what they do with their lives.
   But me, I'm still on the road
   Headin' for another joint.
   We always did feel the same,
   We just saw it from a different point of view,
   Tangled up in blue.

THAT'LL BE THE DAY

Words and Music by JERRY ALLISON,
NORMAN PETTY and BUDDY HOLLY

366

that-'ll be the day _____ when I die.__ Well, when Cu - pid shot his dart,

he shot it at your heart, so if we ev - er part and I leave you,

you say you told me an' you, told me bold - ly that some day, well,

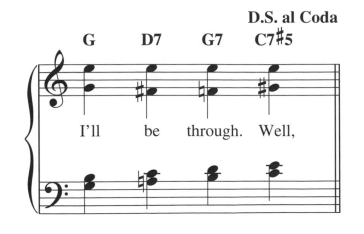

I'll be through. Well,

___ when I die.__

THUNDER ROAD

Words and Music by
BRUCE SPRINGSTEEN

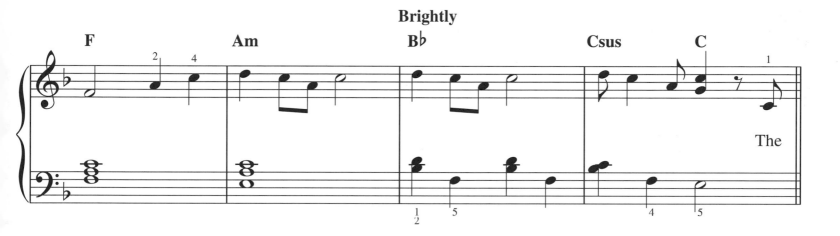

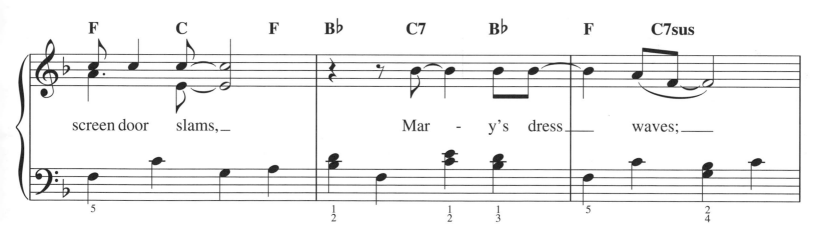

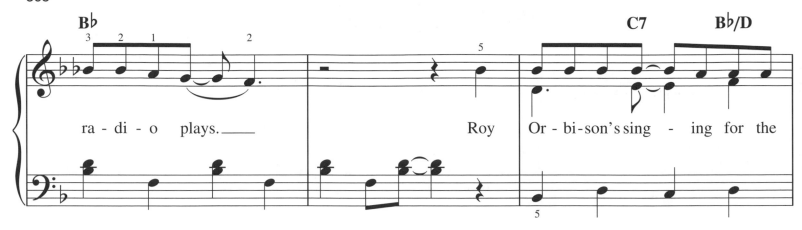

ra - di - o plays.____ Roy Or - bi-son's sing - ing for the

lone - ly. Hey, that's me, and I want you on - ly. Don't turn me

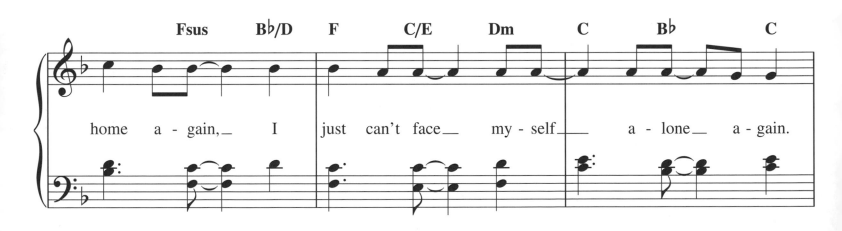

home a - gain,___ I just can't face___ my - self___ a - lone___ a - gain.

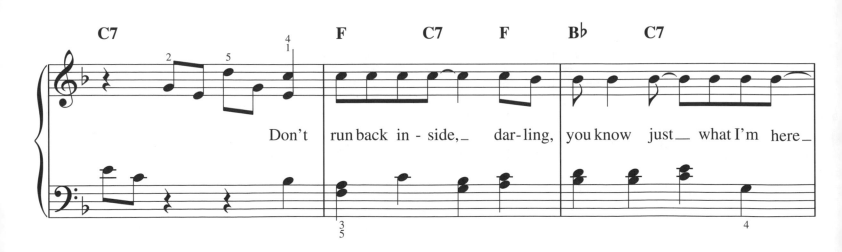

Don't run back in - side,___ dar - ling, you know just___ what I'm here___

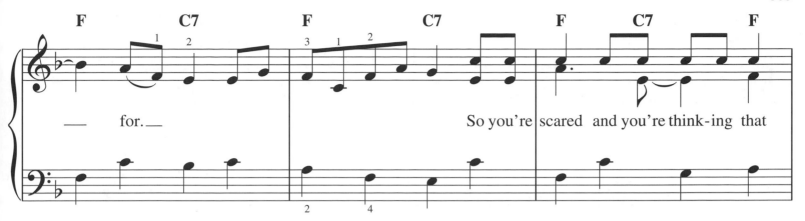

for. __ So you're scared and you're think-ing that

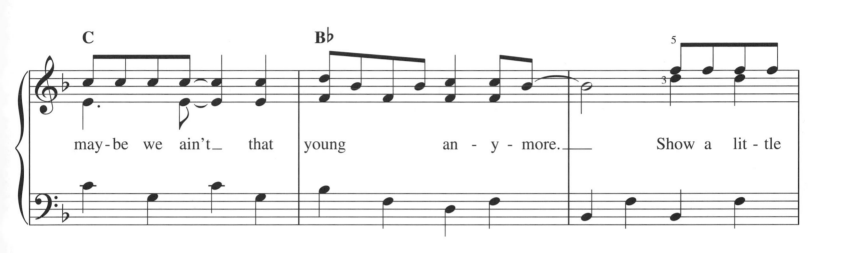

may-be we ain't__ that young an - y - more.__ Show a lit - tle

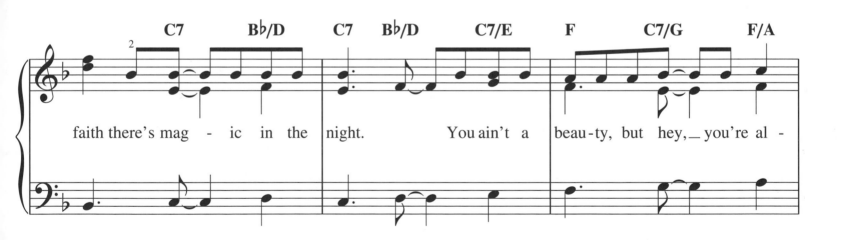

faith there's mag - ic in the night. You ain't a beau-ty, but hey,__ you're al -

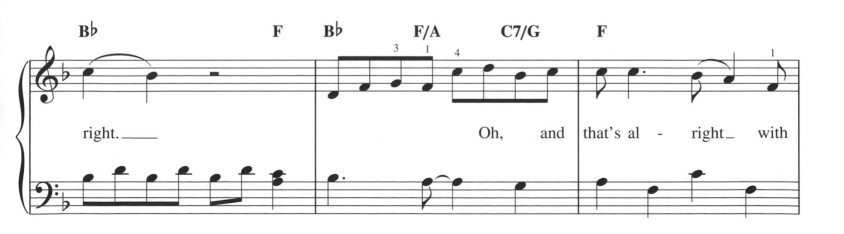

right.____ Oh, and that's al - right__ with

370

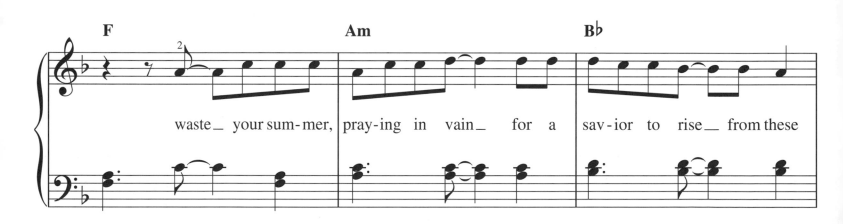

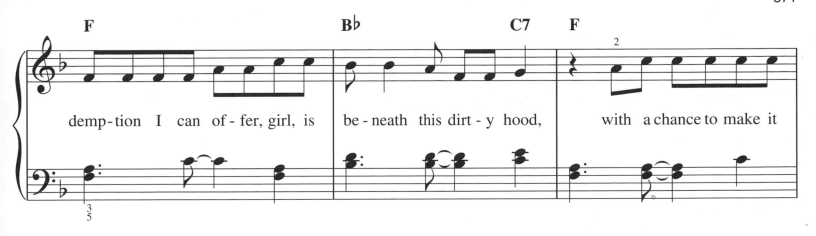

demp-tion I can of-fer, girl, is   be-neath this dirt-y hood,   with a chance to make it

good some - how.__ Hey,   what else can we do   now,   ex - cept

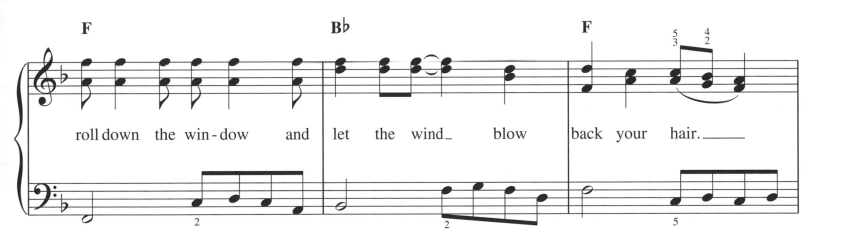

roll down the win-dow   and   let the wind__ blow   back your hair.____

Well, the   night's bust-ing o-pen, these   two lanes will take   us

an - y - where. We got one last chance __ to make it

real. __ To trade in these wings on some wheels.

Climb in __ back, heav - en's wait-ing down on __ the tracks. __

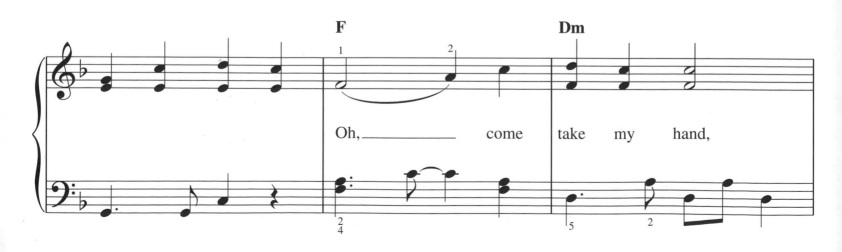

Oh, __ come take my hand,

373

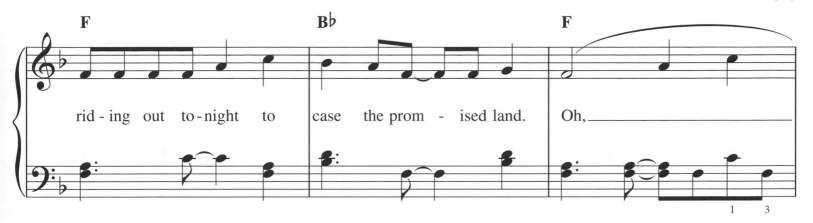

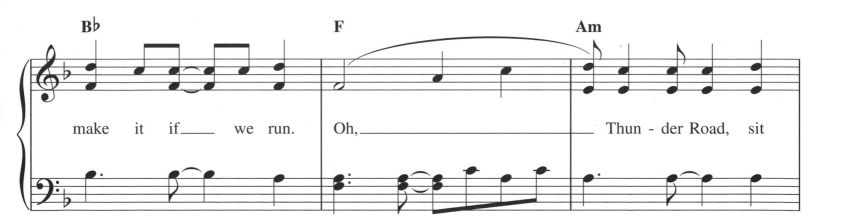

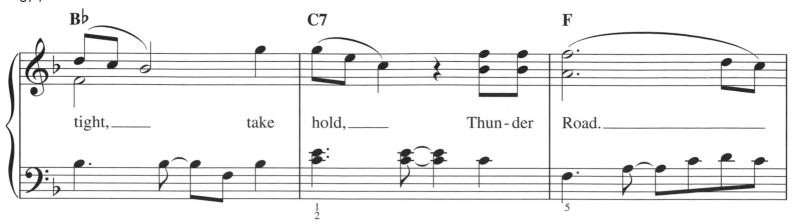

tight,_____ take hold,_____ Thun-der Road._____

Well, I got__ this gui-tar, and I learned how to make it talk.

_____ And my car's out back, if you're

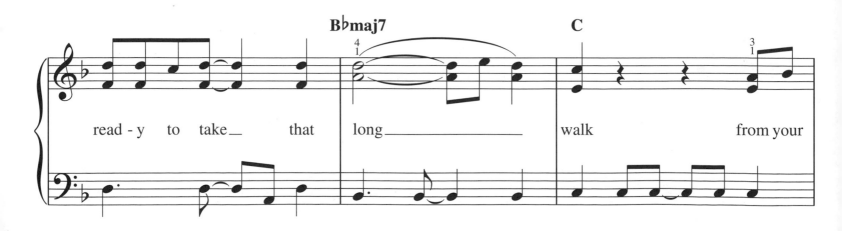

read-y to take__ that long_____ walk from your

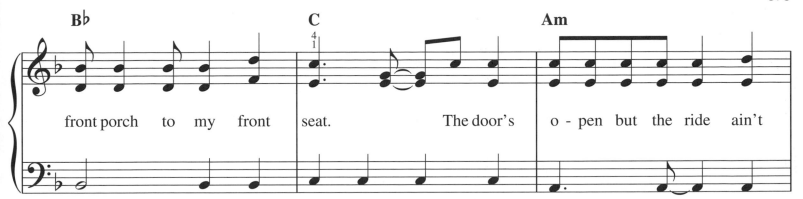

front porch to my front seat. The door's o-pen but the ride ain't

free,___ and I know you're lone-ly for words that I ain't spo - ken, but to-

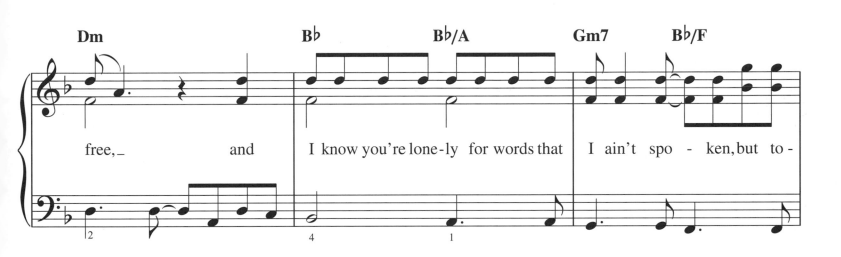

night we'll be free.___ All the prom-is - es 'll be bro - ken. There were

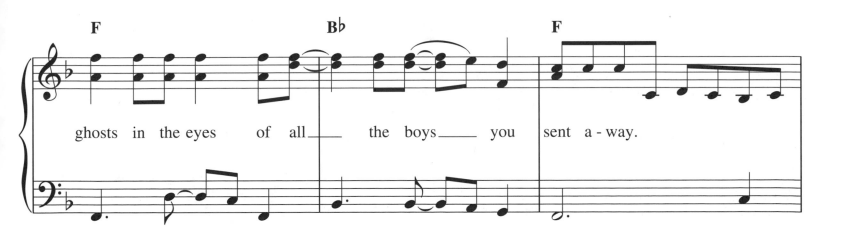

ghosts in the eyes of all___ the boys___ you sent a - way.

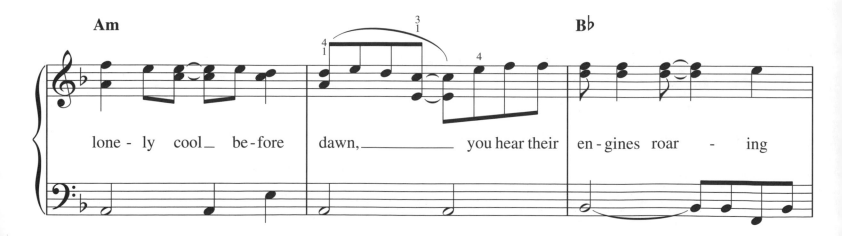

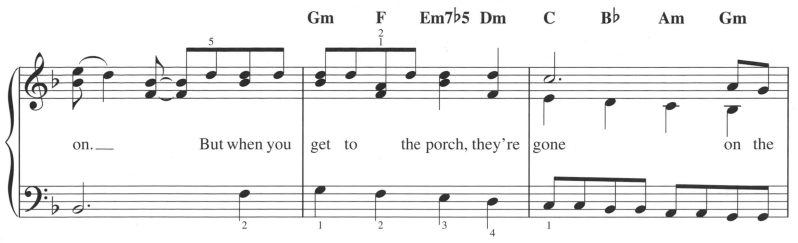

on.___ But when you get to the porch, they're gone ___ on the

wind.___ So, Mar - y climb in.___

It's a town full of los - ers,___ I'm pull-ing out of here to win.___

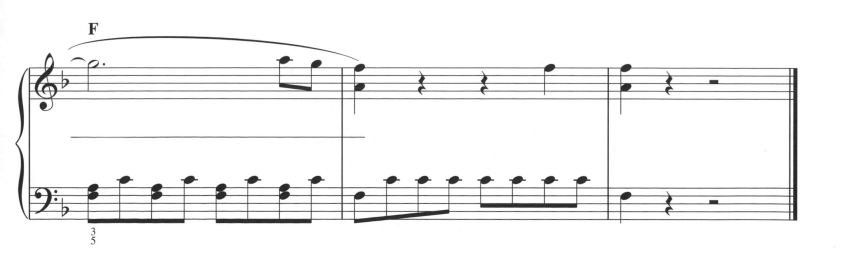

THE TWIST

Words and Music by
HANK BALLARD

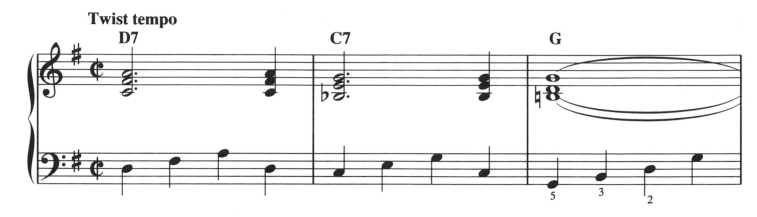

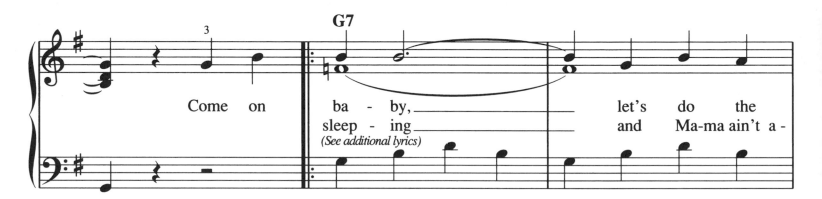

Come on ba - by,_____ let's do the
sleep - ing_____ and Ma-ma ain't a-
(See additional lyrics)

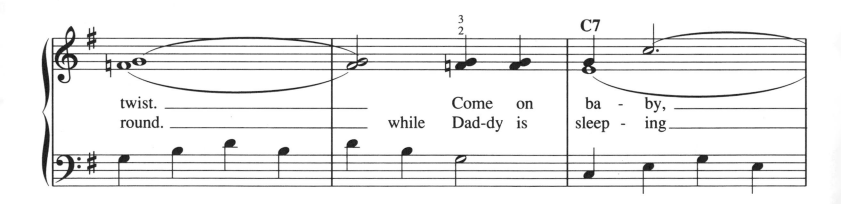

twist._____
round._____ while Come on Dad-dy ba - by,_____
is sleep - ing_____

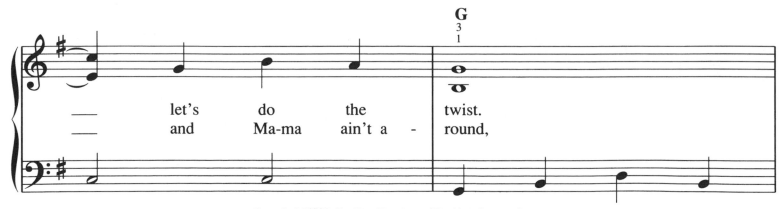

_____ let's do the twist.
_____ and Ma-ma ain't a - round,

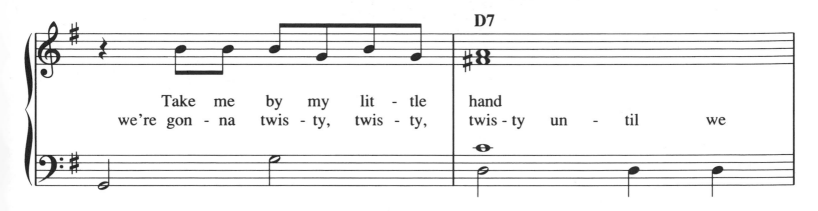

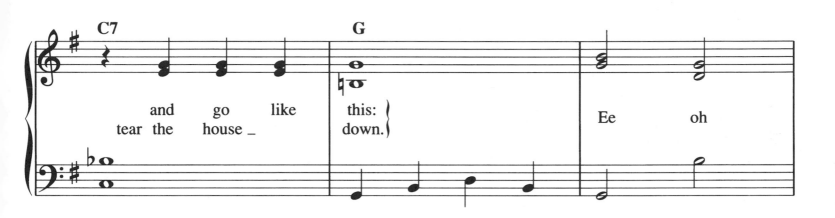

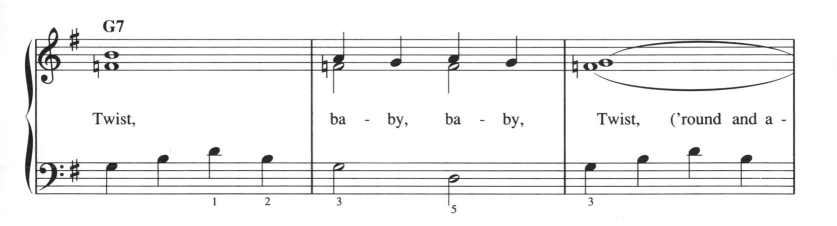

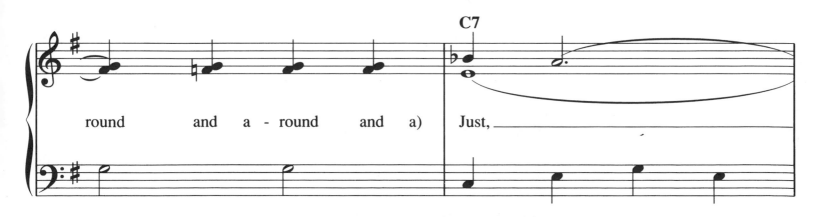

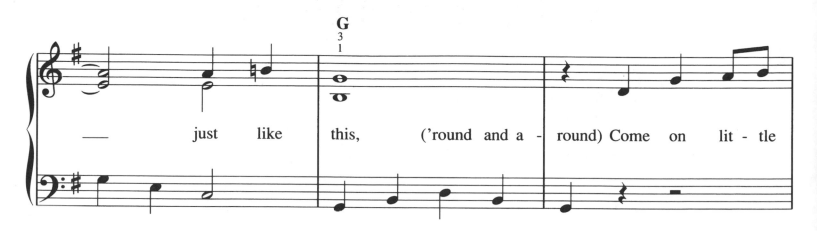

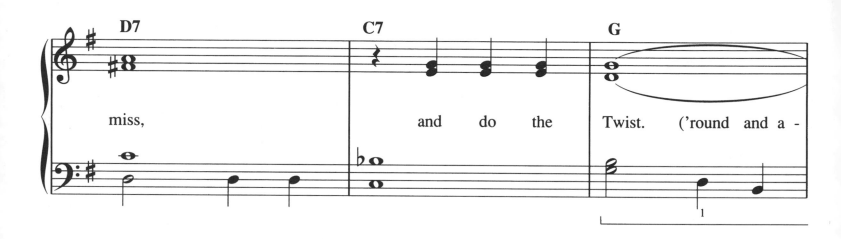

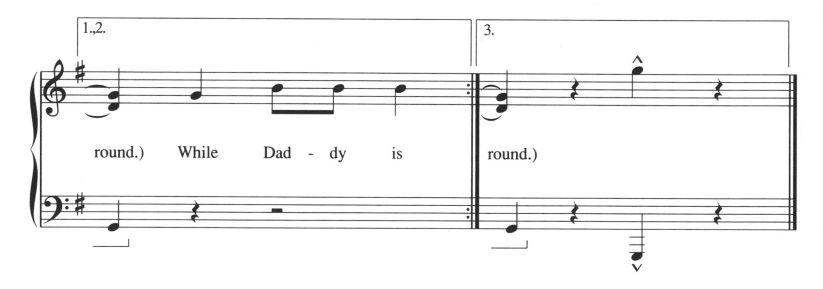

Additional Lyrics

3. You should see my little sis.
    You should see my little sis.
    She knows how to rock and she knows how to Twist.

WHAT'S GOING ON

Words and Music by MARVIN GAYE,
AL CLEVELAND and RENALDO BENSON

Moderately

Moth - er, moth - er, / there's too man - y
Fa - ther, fa - ther, / we don't need to
Moth - er, moth - er, / ev - 'ry - bod - y

of you cry - ing. / You see
es - ca - late.___ / Ah, but
thinks we're wrong.__

Cmaj7

Broth - er, broth - er, broth - er,   there's far too man - y
war is not the an - swer,   for on - ly love can
who are they to judge us   sim - ply 'cause our

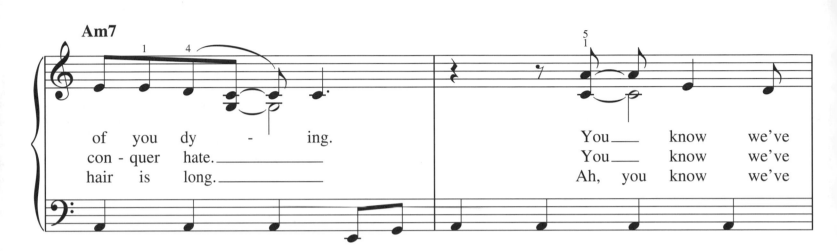

Am7

of you dy - ing.   You___ know we've
con - quer hate.___   You___ know we've
hair is long.___   Ah, you know we've

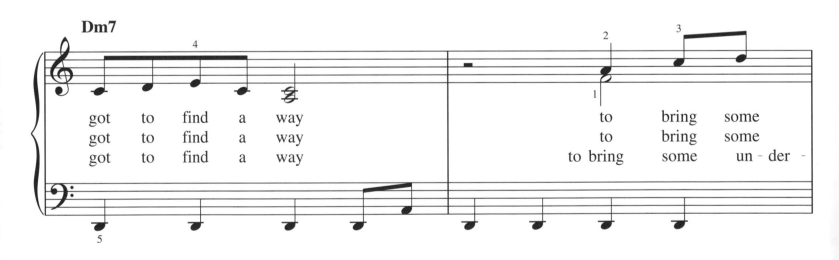

Dm7

got to find a way   to bring some
got to find a way   to bring some
got to find a way   to bring some un - der -

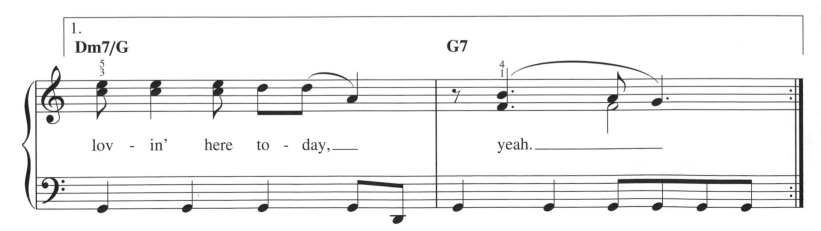

1.
Dm7/G   **G7**

lov - in' here to - day,___   yeah.___

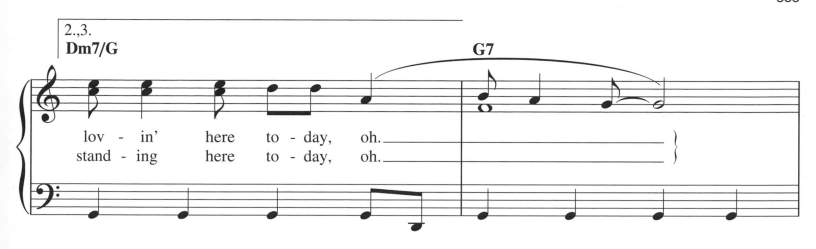

2.,3.

Dm7/G **G7**

lov - in' here to - day, oh._____
stand - ing here to - day, oh._____

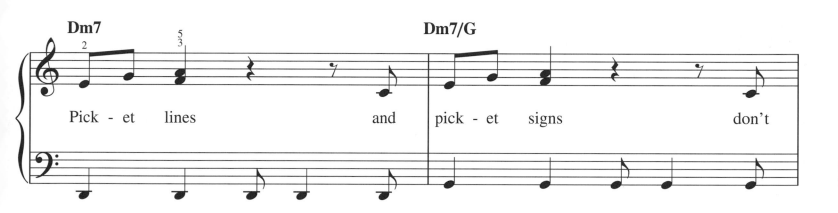

Dm7 **Dm7/G**

Pick - et lines and pick - et signs don't

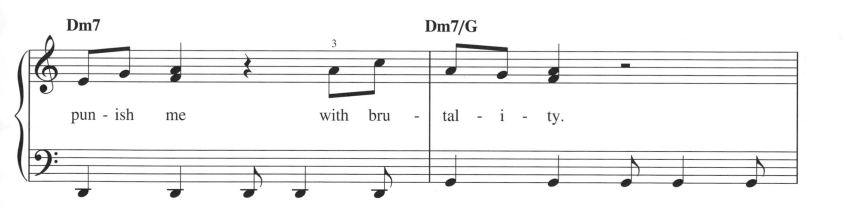

Dm7 **Dm7/G**

pun - ish me with bru - tal - i - ty.

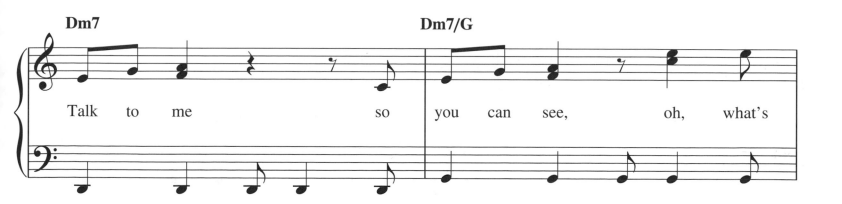

Dm7 **Dm7/G**

Talk to me so you can see, oh, what's

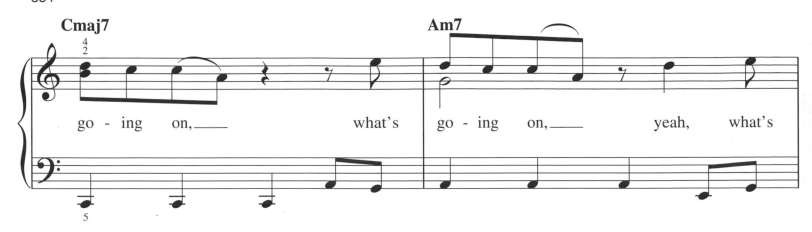

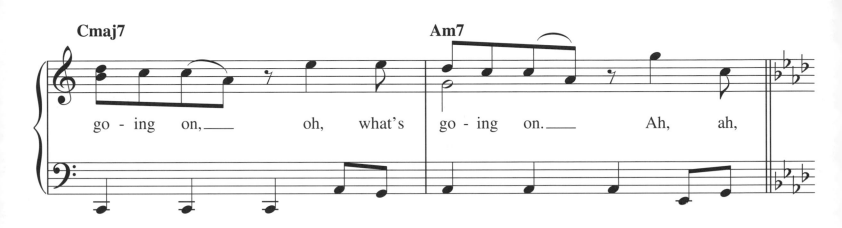

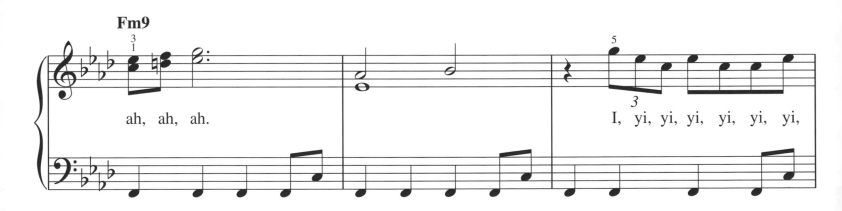

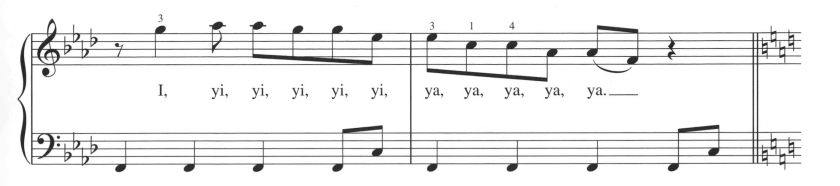

I, yi, yi, yi, yi, yi, ya, ya, ya, ya, ya.____

F/G

Be, doot, de doot; Be, be, be, doot; Be be, be, doot;

To Coda ⊕   **D.S. al Coda**
(take 2nd ending)

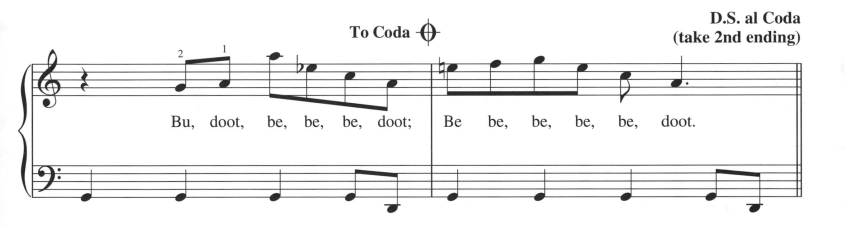

Bu, doot, be, be, be, doot; Be be, be, be, be, doot.

CODA
⊕

Cmaj7

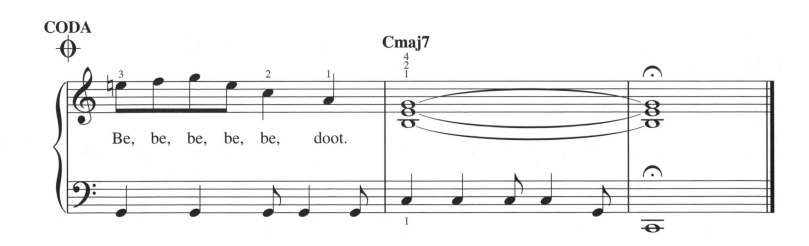

Be, be, be, be, be, doot.

TWIST AND SHOUT

Words and Music by BERT RUSSELL
and PHIL MEDLEY

Moderate Rock and Roll beat

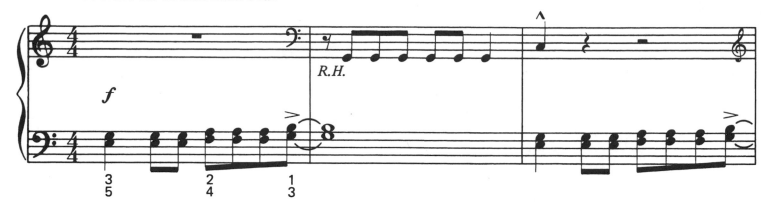

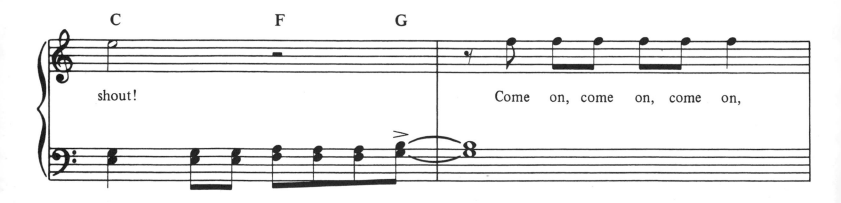

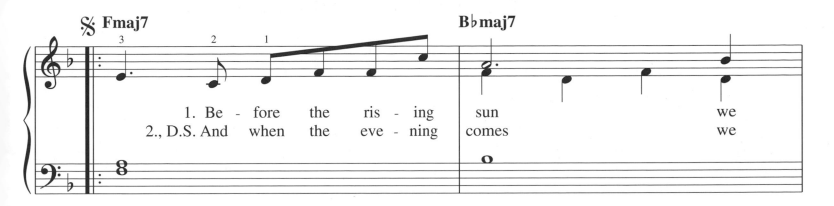

% **Fmaj7**   **B♭maj7**

1. Be - fore the ris - ing sun   we
2., D.S. And when the eve - ning comes   we

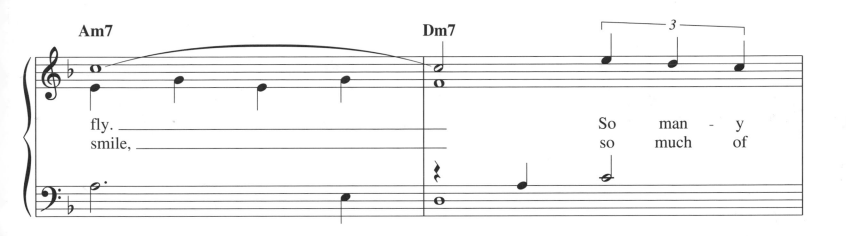

Am7   **Dm7**

fly. _____   So man - y
smile, _____   so much of

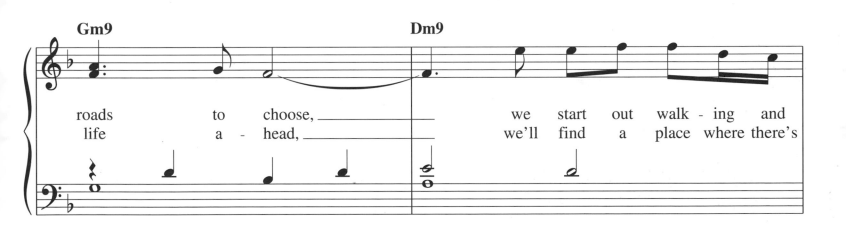

Gm9   **Dm9**

roads   to choose, _____   we start out walk - ing and
life   a - head, _____   we'll find a place where there's

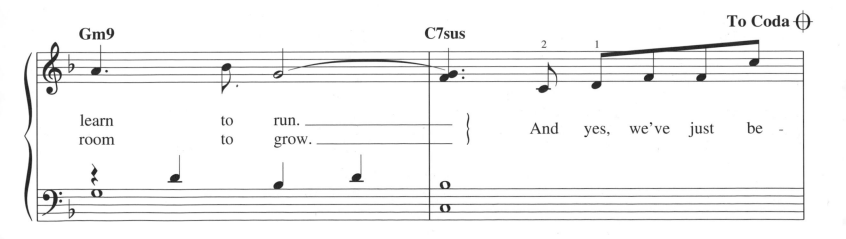

Gm9   **C7sus**   **To Coda** ⊕

learn   to run. _____   And yes, we've just be -
room   to grow. _____

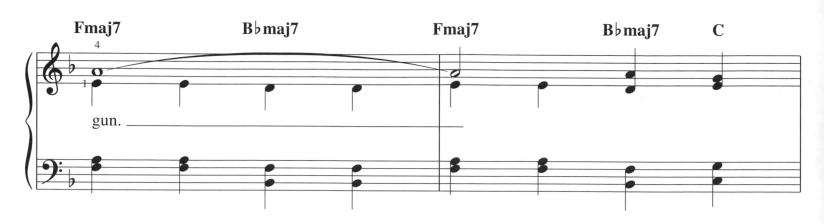

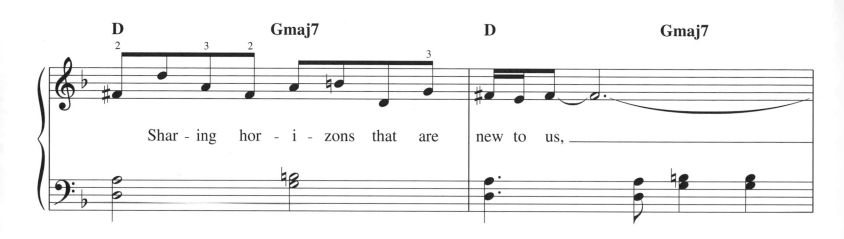

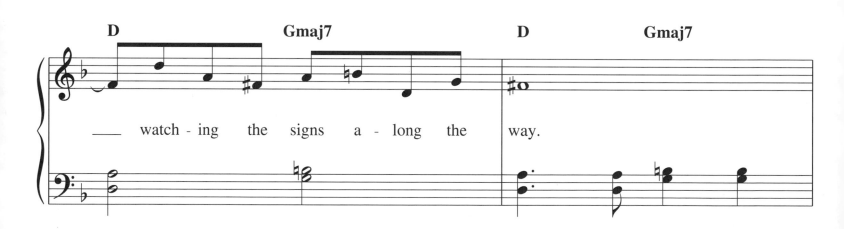

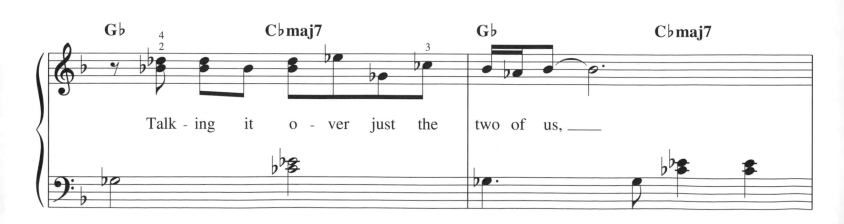

403

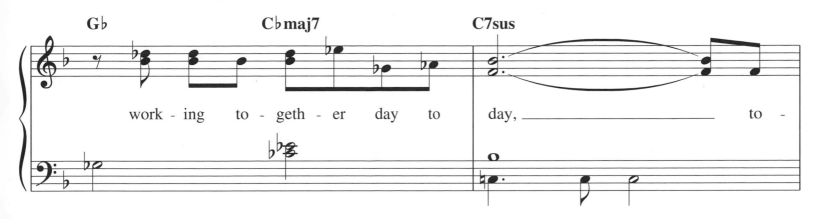

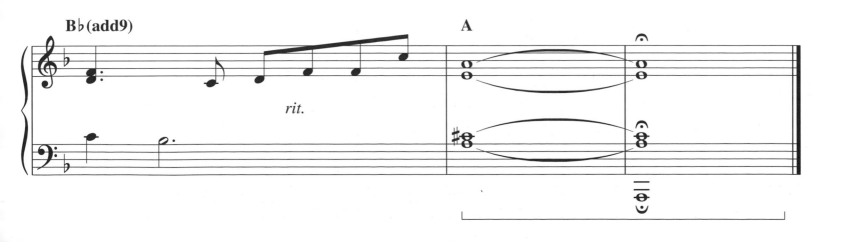

WHAT'D I SAY

Words and Music by
RAY CHARLES

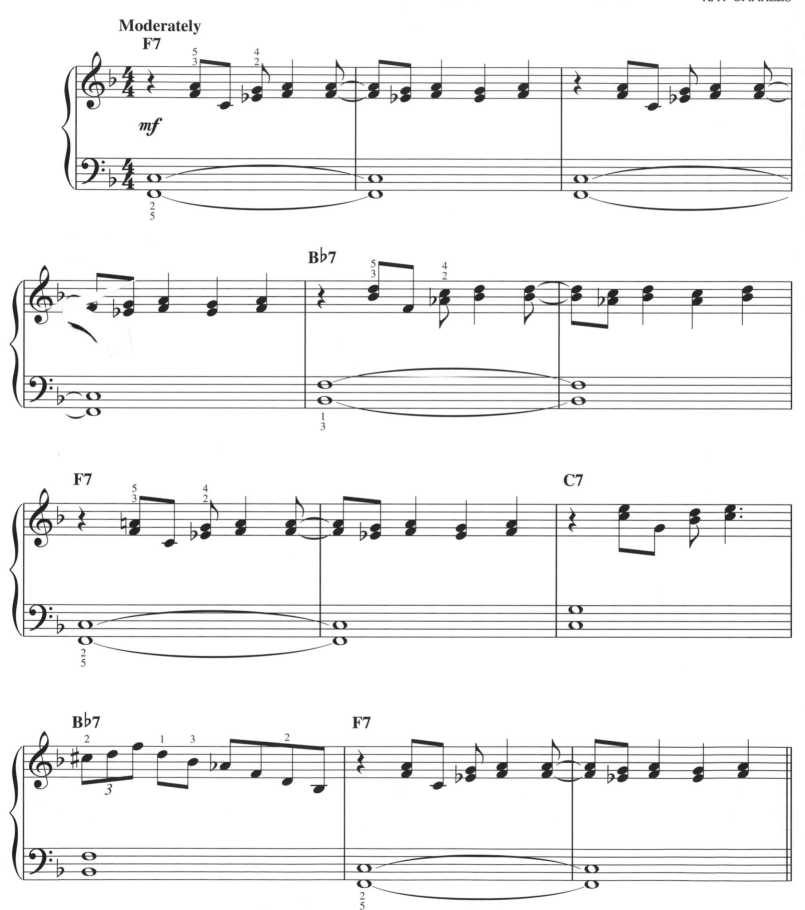

405

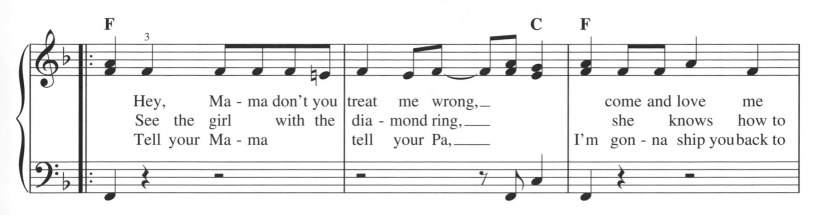

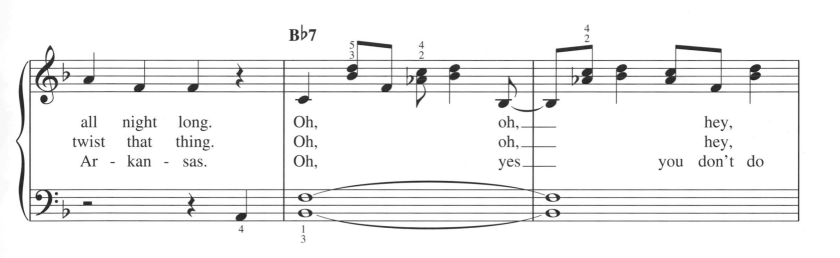

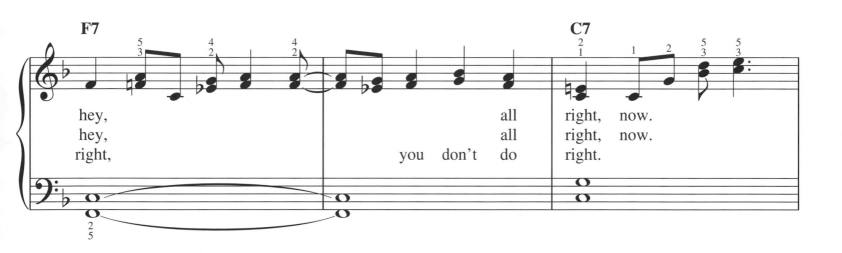

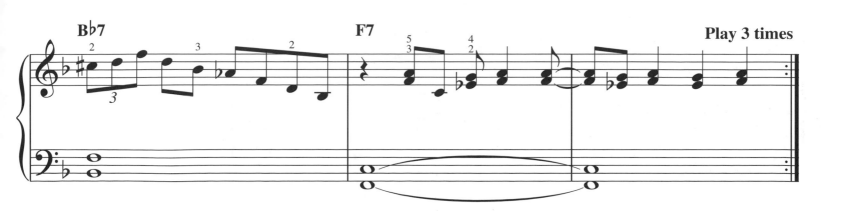

Tell me what I'd | say? / know. | Tell me what I'd / I wan - na

say right now? / know. | Tell me what'd I / Ba - by, I wan - na | say?___ / know right now.

Tell me what'd I / Yes, I wan - na | say? / know. | Tell me what I'd / Hon - ey, I wan - na

say?___ / know.___ | Tell me what'd I / Yes, I wan - na | say? / know.

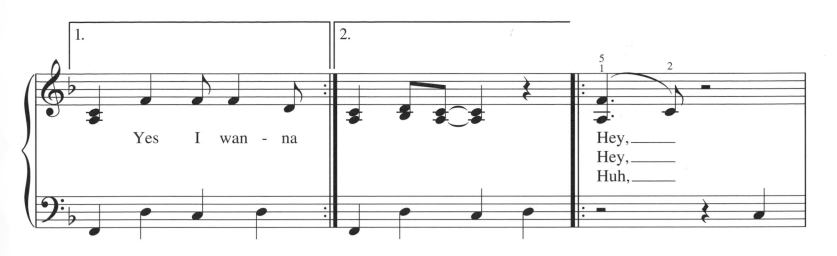

1.   2.

Yes   I   wan - na

Hey, _____
Hey, _____
Huh, _____

(hey) _____   ho, _____   (ho) _____
(hey) _____   ho, _____   (ho) _____
(huh) _____   ho, _____   (ho) _____

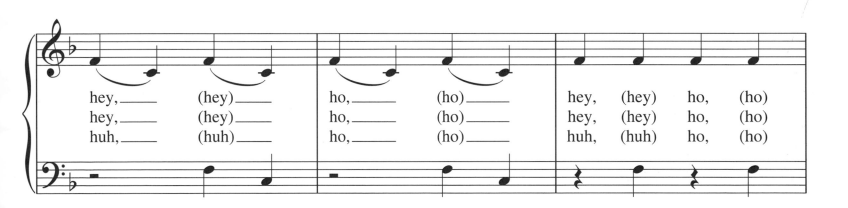

hey, _____   (hey) _____   ho, _____   (ho) _____   hey,   (hey)   ho,   (ho)
hey, _____   (hey) _____   ho, _____   (ho) _____   hey,   (hey)   ho,   (ho)
huh, _____   (huh) _____   ho, _____   (ho) _____   huh,   (huh)   ho,   (ho)

hey. Sing   me   one   more   time.   Sing   me   one   more
hey. Make   me   feel   so   good.   Make   me   feel   so
huh. Ba - by,   it's   all   right.   Ba - by,   it's   all

B♭7

time.
good.
right, right now.

Sing me one more
Make me feel so
Ba - by, it's all

time.___
good right now.
right.___

F

Sing me one more
Make me feel so
Ba - by, it's all

time.
good.
right.

Sing me one more
Make me feel so
Ba - by, it's all

C7   **B♭7**   **F**

time.___
good.___
right.___

Sing me one more
Make me feel so
Ba - by, it's all

time.
good.
right.

1., 2.   3.

Come on twist that thing.
right.

Come on, twist that
Well, I feel all

thing.
right.

Keep a twist-in' that
Well, I feel all

B♭7

thing.
right.

Keep a twist-in' that
Well, I feel all

F

thing.
right.

Keep a twist-in' that
Well, I feel all

C7

thing.
right.

B♭7

Keep a twist-in' that
Well, I feel all

F

thing.
right.

1.

Make me feel all

2.

F9

WHEN DOVES CRY

Composed by PRINCE

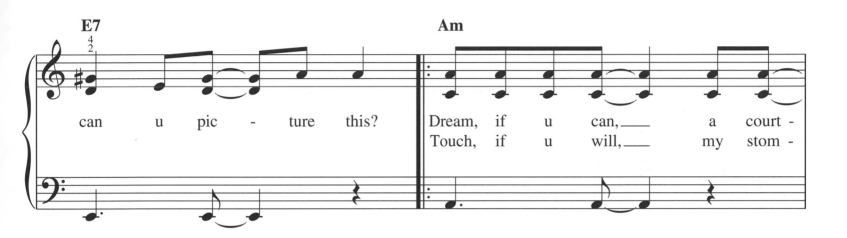

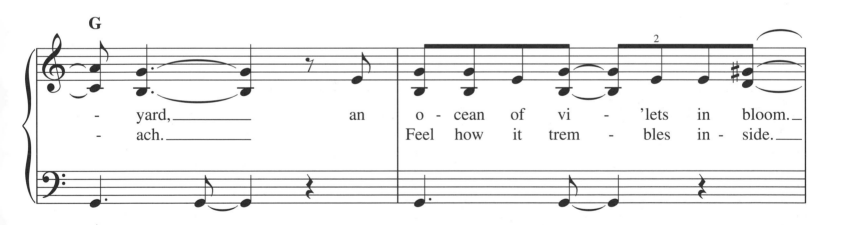

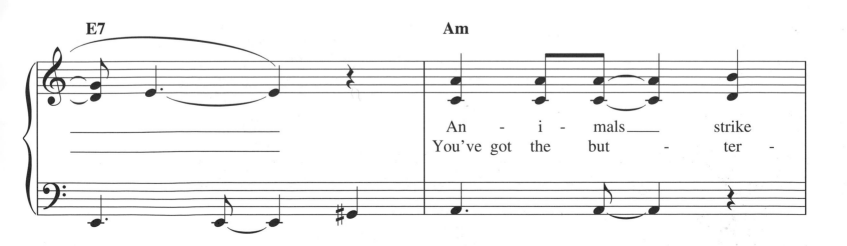

412

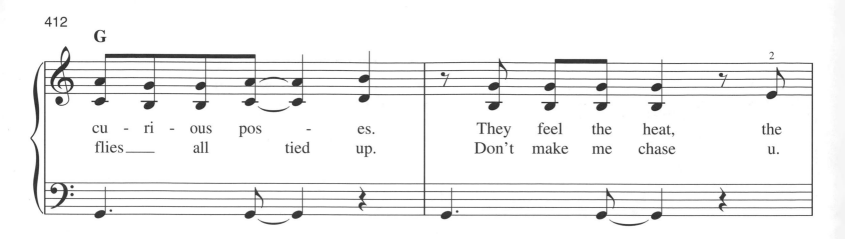

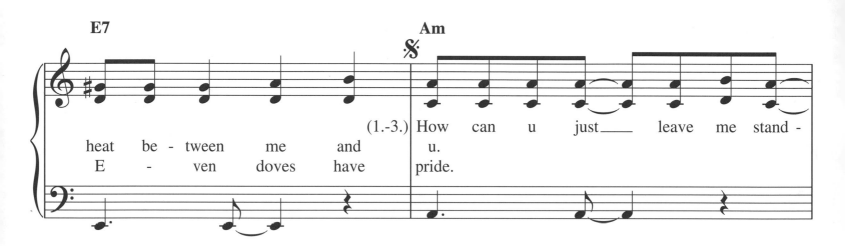

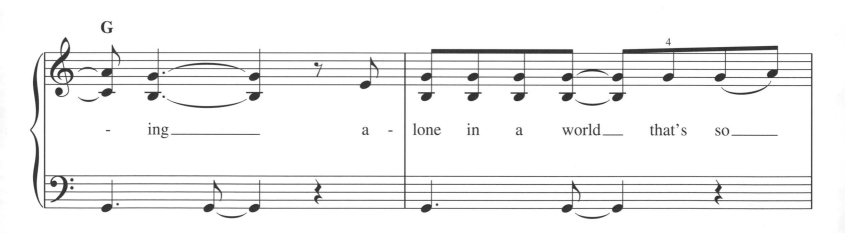

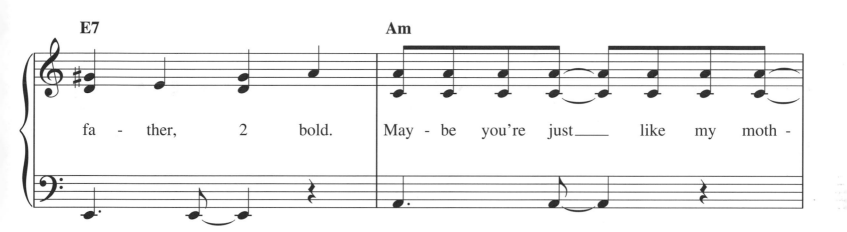

414

WILD THING

Words and Music by
CHIP TAYLOR

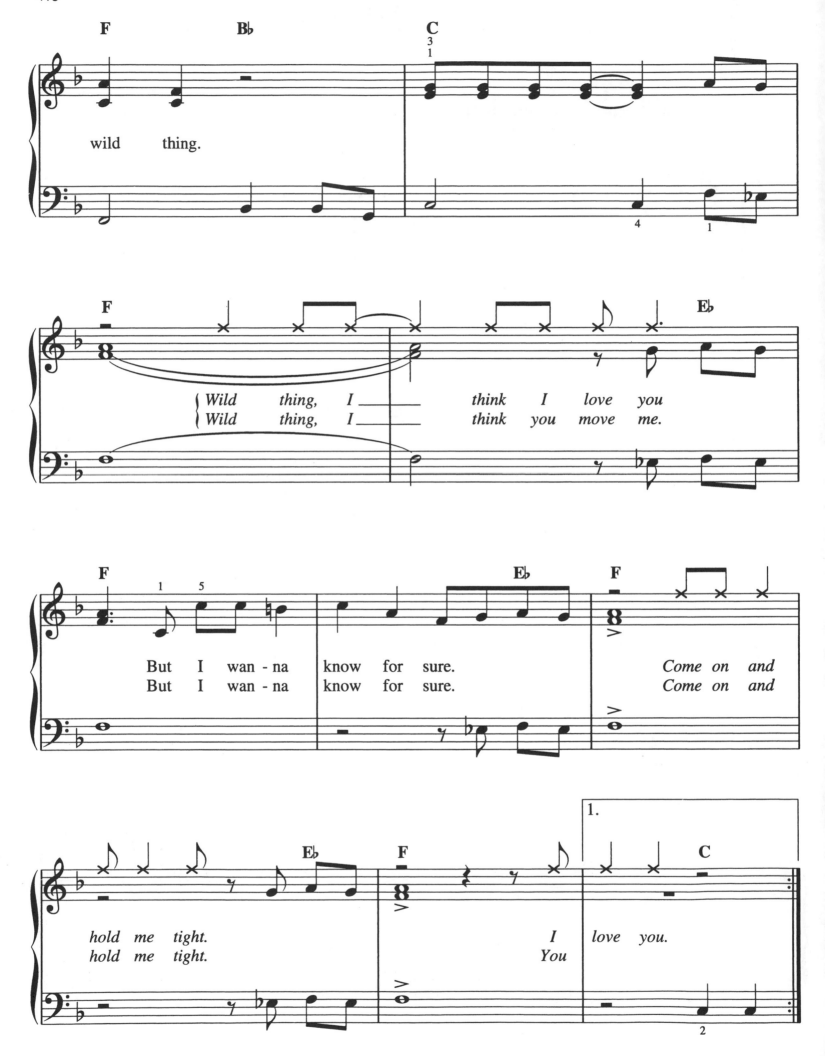

move me. Wild thing, you make my

heart sing. You make

ev - 'ry - thing groov - y,

Repeat and Fade

wild thing.

Yesterday

Words and Music by JOHN LENNON
and PAUL McCARTNEY

Moderately, with expression

Yes - ter - day,   all my trou - bles seemed so
Sud - den - ly   I'm not half the man I

far a - way,   Now it looks as though they're
used to be,   There's a sha - dow hang - ing

here to stay,_ Oh   I be - lieve_ in   yes - ter - day._
o - ver me,_ Oh   yes - ter - day_ came   sud - den - ly._

Why she had to go I don't know, she would - n't say.

I said some-thing wrong, now I long for yes - ter - day.

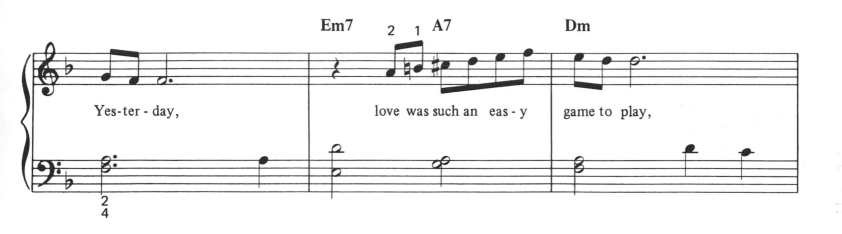

Yes-ter - day, love was such an eas - y game to play,

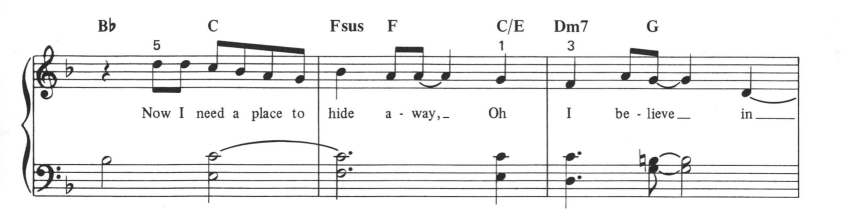

Now I need a place to hide a - way,_ Oh I be - lieve_ in_

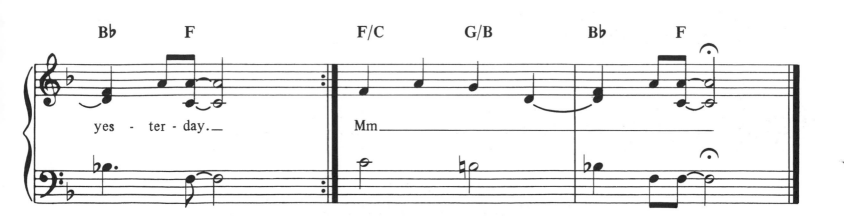

yes - ter - day._ Mm _

YOU SHOOK ME ALL NIGHT LONG

Words and Music by ANGUS YOUNG,
MALCOLM YOUNG and BRIAN JOHNSON

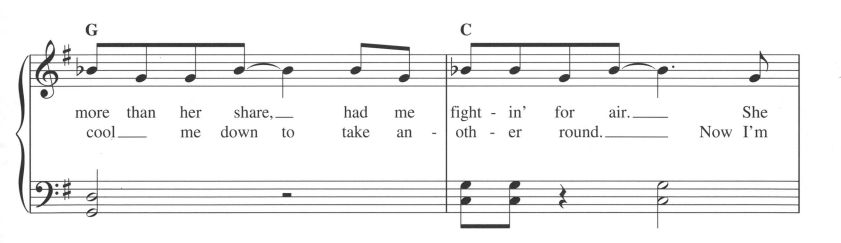

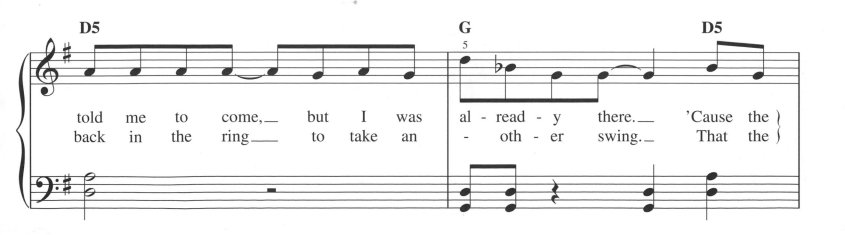

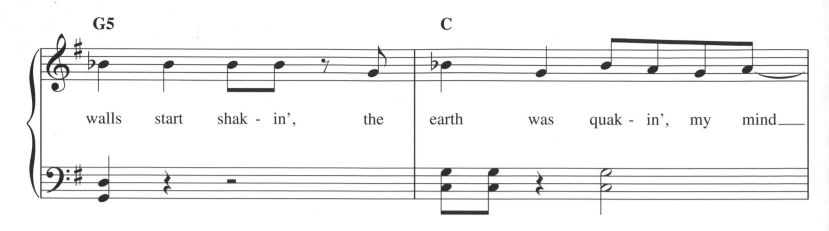

walls start shak-in', the earth was quak-in', my mind

___ was ach - in' and we were mak - in' it. And

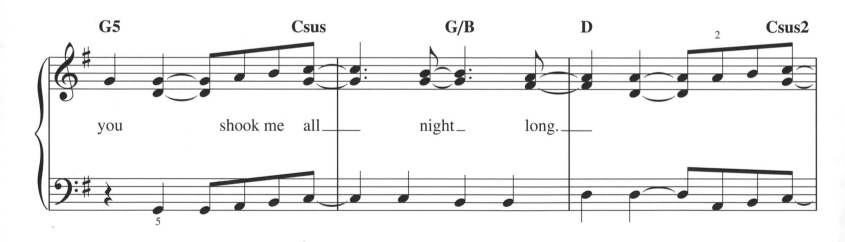

you shook me all___ night__ long.___

Yeah, you_____ shook me all___ night__ long.__

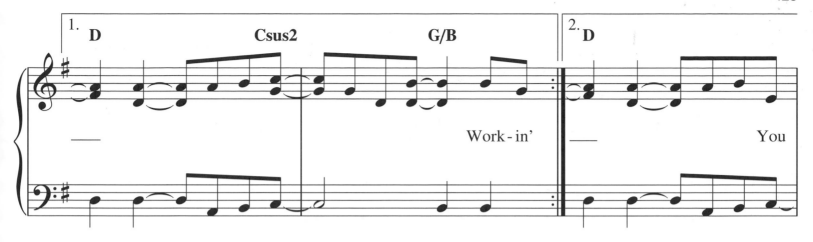

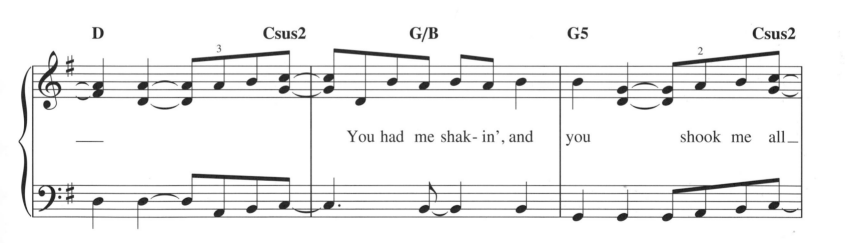

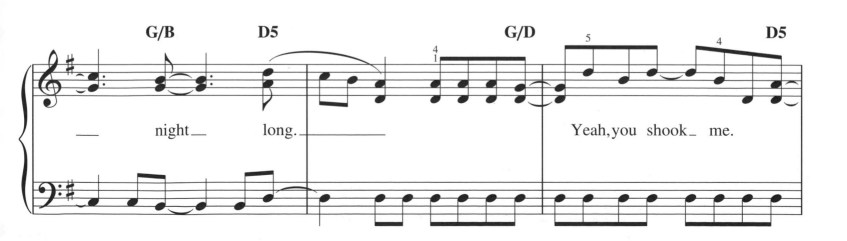

424

night_____ long._____ You real - ly got me and

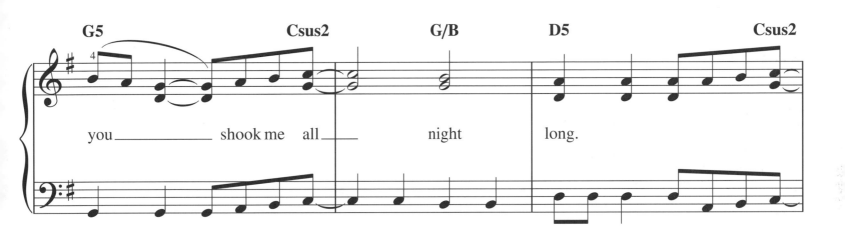

you_____ shook me all____ night long.

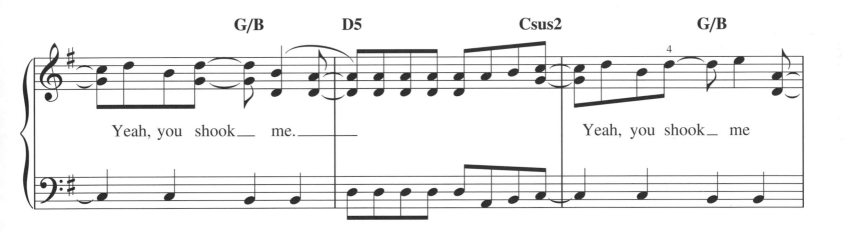

Yeah, you shook___ me._____ Yeah, you shook___ me

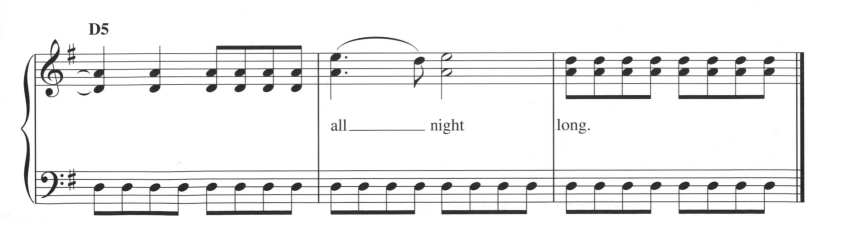

all_____ night long.

YOUR SONG

Words and Music by ELTON JOHN
and BERNIE TAUPIN

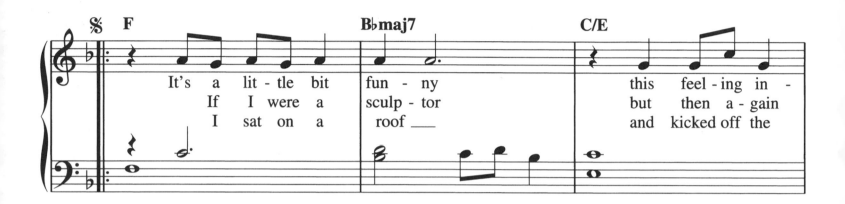

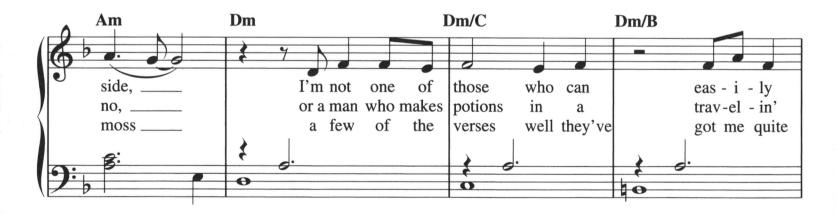

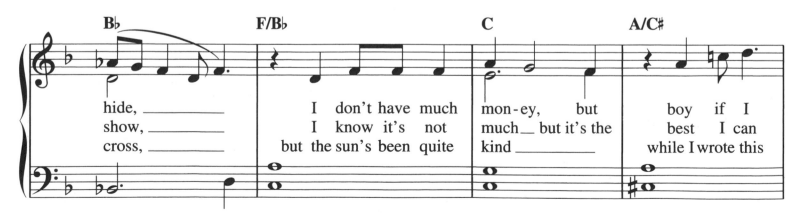

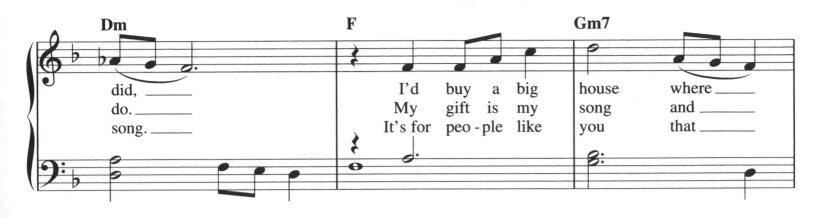

Dm did, _____ / do. _____ / song. _____ **F** I'd buy a big / My gift is my / It's for peo-ple like **Gm7** house where _____ / song and _____ / you that _____

1. B♭ we both _ could **C Csus C** live. _____ **2., 3. B♭** this one's _ for / keep it _____ turned

F B♭ you. / on. **F** cresc. **C/E** *mf* And you can tell

Dm ev - 'ry-bod - y **Gm7** this is your **B♭** song. _____

It may be quite____ sim-ple, but now that it's

done,____ **To Coda** I hope you don't mind, I hope you don't mind
cresc.

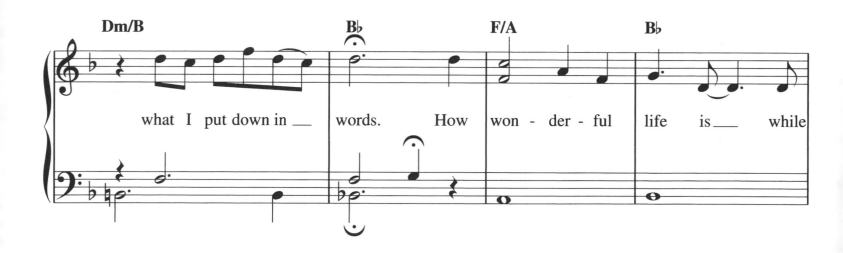

what I put down in __ words. How won-der-ful life is __ while

D.S. al Coda
(with repeats)

you're__ in the world. _____
dim.

CODA

Dm   **Dm/C**

cresc.

I hope you don't mind,   I hope you don't mind

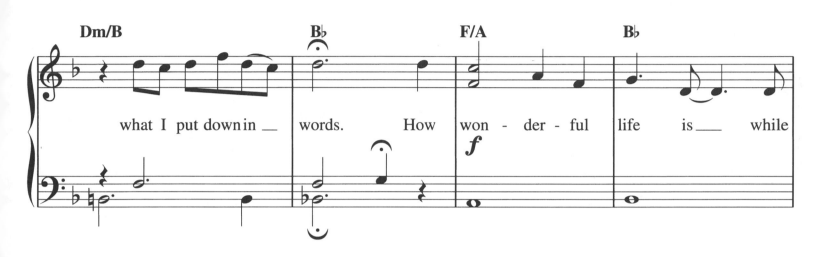

Dm/B   **B♭**   **F/A**   **B♭**

what I put down in __ words. How won - der - ful life is __ while

f

F   **B♭**   **F**

you're_ in the world.

dim.   *p*

B♭/F   **C/F**   **B♭/F**   **F**

rit.

YOU REALLY GOT ME

Words and Music by
RAY DAVIES

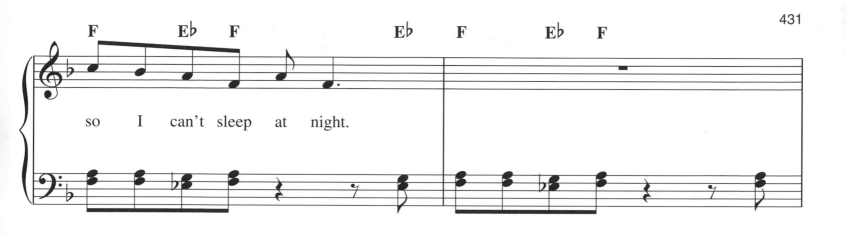

so I can't sleep at night.

Yeah, you real-ly got me now, you got me

so I don't know what I'm do-ing. Oh

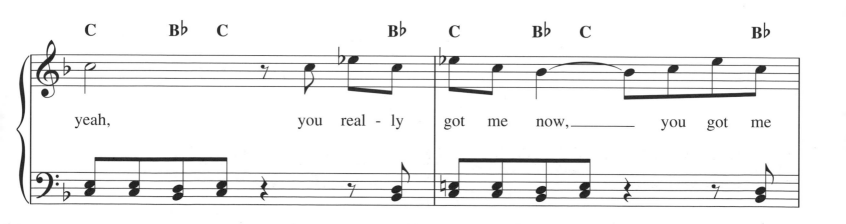

yeah, you real-ly got me now,_____ you got me

432

so I can't sleep at night, you real - ly got me,_____ you

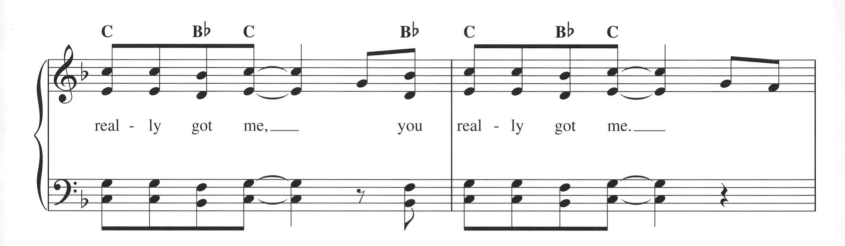

real - ly got me,_____ you real - ly got me._____

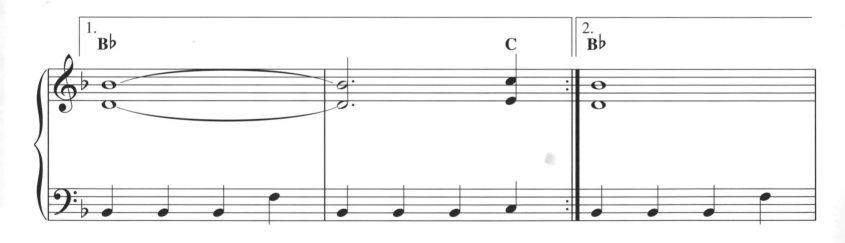